LOCAL DEMOCRACY AND GOOD GOVERNANCE

Five Decades of Panchayati Raj

LOCAL DEMOCRACY AND GOOD GOVERNANCE

Five Decades of Panchayati Raj

Editors

RANBIR SINGH

and

SURAT SINGH

DEEP & DEEP PUBLICATIONS PVT. LTD.

F-159, Rajouri Garden, New Delhi - 110 027

LOCAL DEMOCRACY AND GOOD GOVERNANCE
Five Decades of Panchayati Raj

ISBN 978-81-8450-319-7

Typeset by PRINT INDIA, A-38/2, Phase I, Mayapuri, New Delhi-110064.

Printed in India at ELEGANT PRINTERS, A-38/2, Phase I, Mayapuri, New Delhi-110064.

Published by DEEP & DEEP PUBLICATIONS PVT. LTD.,
F-159, Rajouri Garden, New Delhi-110027. Phones: 25435369, 25440916.
E-mail: deep98@del3.vsnl.net.in
Sales Showroom: 2/13, Ansari Road, Daryaganj, New Delhi-110002
Phone/Fax: 23245122

Contents

ART IV

EXPERIENCES OF DEMOCRATIC DECENTRALISATION IN STATES

PART V

DEMOCRATIC DECENTRALISATION AND WOMEN EMPOWERMENT

Preface

As the apex training and research institute of the State, the Haryana Institute of Rural Development, Nilokheri (Karnal) annually organises National Seminars on the themes of conceptual and operational utility in the fields of Rural Development and Panchayati Raj and also publishes their proceedings in the form of edited volumes. The Panchayati Raj completed five decades on October 2, 2009. Its Golden Jubilee Celebration are being held at Nagaur (Rajasthan). Meanwhile, the Institute also decided to organize a National Seminar on 'Democratic Decentralisation and Good Governance' and to publish the papers presented at it.

It may be recalled here that the Panchayati Raj was set-up as a system of local democracy in 1959 by implementing the scheme of democratic decentralisation recommended by the Balvantray Mehta Study Team (1957) which aimed at streamlining the Community Development Programme and strengthening decentralised rural governance.

According to the High Powered Committee on Panchayati Raj, popularly known as the Asoka Mehta Committee (1978), Panchayati Raj underwent three phases—the phase of 'ascendency' (1959-64); the 'phase of stagnation' (1965-69), the phase of 'decline' (1969-77). However, it entered the phase of revitalisation in the post-1977 period which culminated in the enactment of the 73rd Constitutional Amendment Act (1992).

This Act not only accorded a constitutional status to local democracy but also broadened its base by making provision for one-third reservation for women and also reservation for the Scheduled Castes/Scheduled Tribes in proportion to their population. Besides, it empowered the states to give reservation to the Other Backward Classes as well. Further, the Act transformed the role of Panchayati Raj Institutions by mandating them to make and implement plans for economic development and social justice on the functions devolved by the state legislatures on them out of the 29 subjects listed in the 11th schedule of the Indian Constitution.

Almost all the states of the Indian Union implemented the Act by enacting conformity legislation in 1994. The Act was also extended to the Scheduled areas in 1996. As many as three Panchayat Elections have so far been conducted. As a result, a large cadre of local leaders has emerged at the district, block and village levels. Interestingly, more than one-third of them are women, and one-fifth, the Scheduled Castes and the Scheduled Tribes. Now, the Government of India has mooted a proposal to extend reservation for women from 33 to 50 percent. Some states like Uttarakhand have already done so.

The 74th Constitutional Amendment has made provision for decentralised planning through the Panchayati Raj Institutions and the Urban Local Bodies and has duly stipulated for the creation of the District Planning Committees (DPCs) for consolidating their plans. By now, almost all the states have constituted these. The Planning Commission has made it mandatory for the State Governments to prepare their Annual Plans under the 11th Five Year Plan on the basis of the District Plans prepared by the DPCs.

Thus, the 73rd and the 74th Constitutional Amendments aimed at revitalizing the local democracy. Simultaneously, these have also introduced the dimension of Good Governance to it, by creating a mechanism for social audit making it more transparent and accountable. The enactment of the Right to Information Act (2005) too is an attempt in that direction. The Panchayati Raj Institutions are covered by the term 'public authorities' which are supposed to give information to the information-seekers.

This edited volume is a compilation of the select papers presented at the above mentioned National Seminar. It also includes certain articles invited from distinguished scholars for filling up the gaps.

We express our profound thanks to the contributors, who enabled us to bring out this volume. Prof. K. Gopal Iyer and Dr. D.R. Mishra, HES (Rtd.) must be thanked for their valuable help in bringing out this volume. Mr. Sunil Kumar, Data Entry Operator deserves our special appreciation for his skill in the word processing of this manuscript. We also thank Deep & Deep Publications for bringing out this elegant volume in a record time on the occasion of Golden Jubilee Year of Panchayati Raj. Further, we express our profound gratitude to Ms. Urvashi Gulati, IAS, Financial Commissioner and Principal Secretary to Government of Haryana, Department of Development and Panchayats and Chairperson of the Institute, for her help and guidance in this respect.

We earnestly hope that this volume will be of immense use to the policy-makers and implementers, social scientists, researchers, trainers, students and all others who have a stake in the success of local democracy which is needed for cementing the foundation of our largest democracy of the world whose survival has been an enigma to the foreign political observers.

RANBIR SINGH
SURAT SINGH

List of Contributors

Dr. A.S. Malik, Professor and Chairman, Department of Public Administration, Kurukshetra University, Kurukshetra.

Dr. Anupama Arya, Associate Professor in Political Science, P.G. Arya College for Girls, Ambala Cantt (Haryana).

Prof. Aswini K. Ray, Former Dean, School of Social Sciences, Jawaharlal Nehru University, New Delhi.

Dr. B.K. Kaushik, Associate Professor in Political Science, DAV College, Karnal (Haryana).

Dr. Chaitali Pal, Research Officer, Indian Institute of Manpower, Delhi.

Dr. D. Sundar Ram, Editor, *Journal of Grassroots Governance*, Tirupati (Andhra Pradesh).

Dr. George Mathew, Director, Institute of Social Sciences, New Delhi.

Dr. Jagroop Kaur, Professor, Department of Political Science, Punjabi University, Patiala.

Prof. K. Gopal Iyer, Consultant, Haryana Institute of Rural Development, Nilokheri (Haryana).

Mr. K.B. Saxena, IAS (Rtd.), Professor, Council for Social Development, New Delhi.

Dr. Kesar Singh, Associate Research Co-oridinator, CRRID, Chandigarh.

Dr. M. Padalia, Professor of Political Sciences, Kamaun University, Nainital.

Dr. Mohinder Singh, Professor of Public Administration, Kurukshetra University, Kurukshetra.

Dr. Mridula Sharda, Senior Lecturer, Rajiv Gandhi College, Shimla.

Ms. Neha Kirti Prasad, Research Scholar, Department of Political Science, Kamaun University, Nainital.

Dr. O.P. Bohra, Economist, NIPFP, New Delhi.

Prof. P.C. Mathur, Consultant Public Administration, V.M. Open University, Kota (Rajasthan).

Dr. P.P. Balan, Professor & Director, CRRID, Chandigarh.

Dr. Parmod Chand, Guest Lecturer in Political Science, Government College, Narwana (Haryana).

Dr. Paramvir Singh, Research Investigator, CRRID, Chandigarh.

Prof. Partha Nath Mukherji, S.K. Dey Chair, Institute of Social Sciences, New Delhi.

Dr. Prem R. Bhardwaj, Associate Professor in Political Science, Government P.G. College, Nahan (HP).

Dr. Ramashray Roy, Former Director, Centre for the Study of Development Societies, Delhi.

Prof. Ranbir Singh, Consultant, Haryana Institute of Rural Development, Nilokheri (Haryana).

Dr. Rekha Chaudhary, Research Scholar, Department of Law, Kurukshetra University, Kurukshetra.

Dr. S. Bhatnagar, Formerly Professor of Political Science, Directorate of Correspondence Courses, Punjab University, Chandigarh.

Dr. S.K. Singh, Professor, National Institute of Rural Development, Hyderabad.

Mr. Sahib Singh, Research Scholar, Department of Public Administration, Kurukshetra University, Kurukshetra.

Dr. Sahib Singh Bhayana, Professor (Rtd.), Department of Public Administration, Panjab University, Chandigarh.

Ms. Saroj Malik, Lecturer, CRM Jat College, Hisar (Haryana).

Dr. Shamim Qureshi, Research Scholar, Department of Public Administration, University of Rajasthan, Jaipur.

Ms. Sunita Dhaka, Research Scholar, Department of Management, Kurukshetra University, Kurukshetra.

Dr. Surat Singh, Director, Haryana Institute of Rural Development, Nilokheri (Karnal), Haryana.

Dr. Sushma Yadav, Ambedkar Professor, Indian Institute of Public Administration, New Delhi.

Ms. Urvashi Gulati, IAS, Chief Secretary, Government of Haryana, Chandigarh.

Dr. V. Eshwar Anand, Assistant Editor, *The Tribune*, Chandigarh.

Ms. Vimlesh Rathore, Assistant Professor, Haryana Institute of Rural Development, Nilokheri (Karnal), Haryana.

Dr. Vinay Kumar Malhotra, Principal, Markanda National PG College, Shahabad, Kurukshetra (Haryana).

Dr. Yatindra Singh Sisodia, Professor, Madhya Pradesh Institute of Social Sciences, Ujjain (MP).

Ms. Yogmaya, Lecturer in Political Science, Mata Sundri Khalsa College for Girls, Nissing (Karnal), Haryana.

Introduction

Local democracy refers to the local level institutions, and not to those operating at the provincial/state and federal/national/union levels. It assumes the form of a participatory democracy wherein the people are involved directly in the decision-making process.[1] Their participation in it is an effective way to decide as to what is likely to happen to them, to their neighbours and to their community. This is the most effective way to ensure that the public services meet their needs and expectations in a better manner. A *sine-qua-non* of a local democracy is the devolution of powers, funds and responsibilities, from the highest to the lowest level. In other words, local democracy is to make the institutions of local government more democratic, powerful and autonomous. There will always be a need for a positive engagement of citizens to make it really vibrant.[2]

While, in the Indian context, Thomas Isaac[3] has used the term 'local democracy' to denote 'People's Campaign for Decentralised Planning in Kerala'. Girish Kumar has conceptualized it as the decentralisation which, ever since the implementation of the Balvantray Mehta Study Team's recommendations in 1959 assumed the form of Panchayati Raj. We too have used the term 'local democracy' in the same sense as the concept of democratic decentralisation.

It is universally acknowledged that all the democratic political systems are based on local democracy. Nevertheless, the thrust of the Indian Constitution was primarily towards the Parliamentary Democracy at the Centre and State levels and the word *'Panchayat'*, the Indian nomenclature of *Local Democracy*, did not find place in the Draft Constitution of India. Even the strong plea of Dr. Rajendra Prasad, the President of the Constituent Assembly, was ignored by the Chairman of the Drafting Committee, Dr. B.R. Ambedkar. However, the passionate pleas of the Gandhians like Prof. N.G. Ranga and others virtually forced Dr. Ambedkar to accept an Amendment moved by K. Santhanam which later on got incorporated as Article 40 of the Directive Principles of the State Policy in the Constitution of India. It directed the State to set-up Village Panchayats and endow them with authority to function as units of 'Self-Government'.[5]

This did lead to the enactment of Gram Panchayat Acts by various states but they were no more than half-hearted attempts for the creation of rural local government institutions. However, the failure of the Community Development Programme, which had been launched on October 2, 1959 for bringing a silent revolution in rural society by awakening the slumbering masses, led to the appointment of the Balvantray Mehta Study Team which suggested democratic decentralisation (1957) for streamlining it and also for the creation of new system for rural local government. This was the prelude to the inauguration of Panchayati Raj by the then Prime Minister of India, Pt. Jawaharlal Nehru on October 2, 1959 at Nagaur in Rajasthan.[6]

Consequently this stimulated the setting up of local democracy at the district, block and village levels in the form of Gram Panchayats, Panchayat Samitis and Zila Parishads respectively. However, Panchayati Raj proved to be the proverbial 'god that failed' on account of several reasons. The main among these, was the hostile attitude of the political leaders and the bureaucracy. The concept of Panchayati Raj developed during 1959-64, became stagnant during 1964-71 and decayed thereafter.[7] Even the attempt of the Asoka Mehta Committee (1978) failed to revitalise the Panchayati Raj Institutions.[8] However, the states of West Bengal, Karnataka and Andhra Pradesh did take lead in that direction.[9] But the real rejuvenation process started as a result of the enactment of 73rd Constitutional Amendment Act (1992) which led to the establishment of a new system of Panchayati Raj in the states in 1994 through the enactment of conformity legislation.[10]

The papers contributed in this volume are an attempt to understand the process of strengthening the *Local Democracy* in different States in India.

I

The Section on 'Theme Papers' includes the contributions by eminent experts like Ms. Urvashi Gulati, Dr. Ramashray Roy, Prof. Aswini K. Ray, Prof. Partha Nath Mukherji and Dr. George Mathew. Ms. Gulati has discussed the genesis and development of the concepts of democratic decentralisation and good governance in India. She has also analysed their operational dimensions. She has highlighted how good governance through the Panchayati Raj Institutions has really remained an unfinished agenda. She has concluded by emphasizing the need for achieving good governance through the Panchayati Raj Institutions by empowering the citizens through RTI and e-Governance.

Dr. Roy has provided a theoretical perspective of *Democratic Decentralisation*. He has advocated a meaningful participation of the people in the decision-making process for ensuring good governance, and laid stress on going beyond the 73rd and the 74th Constitutional Amendments.

Prof. Ray has suggested the need for a complete economic, administrative and political decentralisation. He has stressed the necessity for demystifying the concept of democracy and lamented that the majority of people are not aware of their basic rights and the options for redressal in case they are violated and transgressed. He has, therefore, pleaded for civil society initiatives against the misuse or atrophy of Panchayati Raj Institutions.

Prof. Mukherji has examined the conceptual and substantive issues of participatory democracy in India in the context of democratic decentralisation and brought into sharp focus the challenges in the way of the successful working of Panchayati Raj. He has stressed that the rural masses will have to play a vital role in meeting these. According to him, "when the major challenges are overcome, the nation can proudly proclaim its contribution to democratic theory and practice that can perhaps be universalized."

Dr. Mathew has highlighted the need for good governance in India in a democratic and decentralised mode. According to him this task has acquired greater urgency on account of reduced agricultural production on the one hand and the crises in Public Distribution System on the other. According to him the herculean task of the implementation of the Right to Food Security cannot be performed in an effective manner without it. He is of the view that this task can be accomplished only by building a knowledge base. Therefore, Mathew has made a passionate appeal to the university and college teachers in the disciplines of Social Sciences to undertake this responsibility through an inter-disciplinary approach.

II

The Section on 'Special Papers' includes the contributions by Professors K.B. Saxena, P.C. Mathur, K. Gopal Iyer, Sahib Singh Bhayana, Sushma Yadav, A.S. Malik (in association with Mr. Sahib Singh) and Mohinder Singh and Doctors V. Eshwar Anand, D. Sundar Ram, Prem R. Bhardwaj and Vinay Kumar Malhotra.

Prof. Saxena has attempted an incisive analysis of the functioning of Panchayati Raj Institutions and has underlined that the root cause of their bad health is deficit of politics. After diagnosing the problem, he has suggested that "a vigorous political mobilisation alone would extricate the PRIs from the culture of dependence on 'top down' concessions by removing their inferiority and subordination to higher political formation."

Prof. Mathur has departed radically from the conventional analyses of the Panchayati Raj Institutions. He has highlighted the conceptual ambiguity of the character of these institutions: Local-Self Government Institutions or Institutions of Self-Government. Besides, he has meticulously analysed the prospects of economic revitalisation of Panchayats in the era of post-1991 LPG India and raised certain pertinent issues in this context.

Dr. Iyer has dealt with the nature of grassroots governance in the tribal area of Chhattisgarh in the backdrop of the Naxalite Movement. He has discussed the violation of the powers of the Gram Sabhas, as prescribed in the PESA Act by the District Administration. He has concluded that the grassroots governance has been seriously affected by the long drawn conflict between the State and the Maoist Naxalite groups.

Prof. Bhayana has highlighted the conceptual parameters of good governance and various issues involved in the empowerment of the Panchayati Raj Institutions, *vis-à-vis* the spirit behind the 73rd Constitutional Amendment, and traced how far it has been operationalised in terms of 3Fs (functions, funds and functionaries). He has also made a strong case for the functional and financial empowerment of the PRIs.

Prof. Yadav has focused on equity and social justice and elaborated the meaning and application of these terms in the context of service delivery. Her contention is that local governance can make the public service delivery affordable and accessible in as much as it can provide appropriate services to all categories of a population in equal measure and with particular concern for the welfare of economically and socially marginalised groups.

Prof. Malik and Mr. Singh have presented the findings of an empirical study of the Gram Panchayats in Haryana and asserted that local bodies have to be evaluated in terms of efficiency, efficacy and resource mobilisation. Besides this the evaluation of the performance of local bodies may also be attempted from the viewpoint of the citizens through their feedback.

In his paper, Dr. Anand contends that the 73rd and the 74th Constitutional Amendment Acts (1992) have given a real fillip to democratic decentralisation and made the PRIs inclusive through the empowerment of women, but much more remains to be done by way of removing the bottlenecks through the financial empowerment of the PRIs, capacity building of DPC and e-Governance.

Dr. Ram has explored the initiatives of the successive governments at the Centre towards democratic decentralisation through Panchayati Raj Institutions and has also analysed the emerging problems and challenges in delivering good governance at the grassroots in particular.

While Dr. Bhardwaj has highlighted the negative impact of globalisation on good governance and emphasised the need for democratic decentralisation to contain them. Dr. Malhotra has made an analysis of the concepts of democratic decentralisation and good governance and discussed its operation at the grassroots level in the form of Panchayati Raj Institutions. He has also suggested the adoption of the concept of human governance for overcoming its inadequacies.

Prof. Singh has examined through his empirical study on Rajasthan how far the Right to Information can be helpful in the process of good governance at the local level, with special reference to Panchayati Raj, and made some expressive suggestions for this purpose.

III

The Section on 'The Conceptual and Operational Dimensions of Democratic Decentralisation' includes the papers of Prof. S. Bhatnagar,

Ms. Saroj Malik and Dr. Shamim Qureshi, Prof. Ranbir Singh and Dr. B.K. Kaushik, Ms. Sunita Dhaka and Yogmaya, Dr. O.P. Bohra and Dr. Chaitali Pal and Anupama Arya.

Prof. Bhatnagar has demystified the concept of democratic decentralisation by drawing a distinction amongst deconcentration, delegation and devolution. He has also discussed the genesis and development of Panchayati Raj in India.

Ms. Malik and Dr. Qureshi have deliberated on the evolution of decentralised rural governance in the country. According to them, it all started as a scheme for democratic decentralisation but subsequently, the 73rd Amendment (1992) added the dimension of good governance to it because of the adoption by India of the New Economic Policy in 1991.

Prof. Ranbir Singh and Dr. Kaushik have discussed S.K. Dey's paradigm of democratic decentralisation. According to them, he had emphasized the need for linking the Gram Sabha to the Lok Sabha and the involvement of voluntary organisations in the Panchayati Raj Institutions. They have also brought to the sharp focus the issues raised by him.

Ms. Dhaka and Yogmaya discussed the paradox of political decentralisation introduced through the introduction of Panchayati Raj and the promotion of economic centralisation through emphases on centralised planning and heavy industries. They contended for the promotion of Khadi and Village industries and strengthening of cooperative movement to achieve the aim of economic decentralisation which is the *sine-qua-non* for the success of political decentralisation.

Dr. O.P. Bohra highlighted the issues and challenges being faced by the third-tier of governance and discussed the conceptual and operational dimensions of the problem that emerged in the local democracy after the 73rd and the 74th Constitutional Amendments (1992). Whereas, Drs. Pal and Arya have, after analyzing the concept of good governance, suggested some steps for the strengthening of Panchayati Raj Institutions for this purpose.

IV

In the Section 'Experiences of Democratic Decentralisation in States', the contributors are Professors P.P. Balan and Yatinder Singh Sisodia, Dr. Kesar Singh and Paramvir Singh, Dr. Mridula Sharda and Ms. Vimlesh Rathore and Dr. Parmod Chand. They respectively presented case studies of Kerala, Madhya Pradesh, Punjab, Himachal Pradesh and Haryana.

Dr. Balan has narrated the success story of Kerala. According to him, the cornerstone of the decentralisation in the state has been people's participation. The processes have been designed in Kerala to facilitate intervention by the interested citizens at all stages of the development process, right from the generation of developmental ideas through project planning, project implementation, upto monitoring.

Prof. Singh has alluded to the amendments carried out in the Madhya Pradesh Panchayati Raj Act (1994), from time to time for making PRIs more

1

Democratic Decentralisation and Good Governance : Retrospect and Prospect

URVASHI GULATI

Governance is the process whereby public institutions conduct public affairs, manage public resources and guarantee the realization of human rights. Good governance accomplishes this in a manner which is essentially free from abuse and corruption, and accords due regard for the rule of law. Its true test is the degree to which it delivers the human rights: civil, cultural, economic, political and social rights. The key question is: Are the institutions of governance effectively guaranteeing the right to health, adequate housing, sufficient food, quality education, fair justice and personal security?

Good governance is a term that is, as a matter of fact, often used to describe the desired objective of a nation-state's political development. According to the United Nations, the good governance is accountable, effective and efficient, participatory, transparent, responsive, consensus-oriented and equitable governance.

The World leaders had aptly concluded at the 2005 World Summit that good governance is integral to the economic growth, eradication of poverty and hunger and sustainable development. If it is to be achieved, the views of all oppressed groups must be heard and considered by the governing bodies because they are the ones who need good governance the most for the alleviation of their deprivations.

Notes and References

1. *Local Government Glossary*: http://www.idea.gov.uk/idk/core/page.do?pageID=1115894.
2. *Local Democracy Campaign*: http://www.lga.gov.uk/lga/core/page.do?pageID=462884.
3. T.M. Thomas Isaac, with Richard W. Franke, *Local Democracy and Development, People's Campaign for Decentralized Planning in Kerala*, Left Word Books, New Delhi, 2000.
4. Girish Kumar, *Local Democracy in India: Interpreting Decentralization*, Sage Publications, New Delhi, 2006.
5. Partha Nath Mukherji, 'Participatory Democratisation: Panchayati Raj and the Deepening of Indian Democracy', *ISS Occasional Paper Series 34*, Institute of Social Sciences, New Delhi, pp. 12-18.
6. Ranbir Singh, 'Genesis and Development of the Concept of Panchayati Raj', in Surat Singh (ed.) *Decentralised Governance in India, Myth and Reality*, Deep and Deep Publications, New Delhi, 2004, pp. 60-72.
7. Harsukhjit Kaur, 'Panchayati Raj Institutions and Deepening Democracy', *Punjab Journal of Politics*, Vol. XXXI, 2007, pp. 104-05.
8. *Report of the Committee on Panchayati Raj Institutions*, Ministry of Agriculture and Irrigation, Government of India, New Delhi, August 1978.
9. Mohinder Singh, Working of Panchayati Raj Institutions in India: Issues and Challenges, in Surat Singh (ed.), *op. cit.*, pp. 108-09.
10. Bidyut Chakrabarty and Rajendra Kumar Pandey, *Indian Government and Politics*, Sage Publications, 2008, pp. 273-81.
11. For an excellent analysis of the impact of the 73rd Constitutional Amendment on the working of Panchayati Raj Institutions, refer B.S. Baviskar and George Mathew, *Inclusion and Exclusion in Local Governance: Field Studies from Rural India*, Sage Publications, New Delhi, 2009.
12. For suggestions on the functional and financial empowerment of Panchayati Raj Institutions, see Fifteenth Anniversary Charter on Panchayati Raj Inclusive Growth through Inclusive Governance (24 April, 2008), *The Grassroots Governance Journal*, Vol. VI, No. 1, 2008, pp. 142-61.

PART I

The Theme Papers

effective as genuine structures of local democracy. However, the Gram Sabhas are yet to perform their expected role in the Panchayati Raj System of the State. He has also emphasized the need for greater financial autonomy, better coordination among the three tiers, greater role clarity in their functions and reduced governmental interference in the day-to-day functioning of the PRIs.

Drs. Singh and Singh presented an analytical picture of the Panchayati Raj Institutions of Punjab in the context of the economy of the State and discussed their present status on the basis of an empirical study, identified the problems that emerged in the working of the PRIs and made copious suggestions for tackling these.

Dr. Sharda presented a dismal picture of the major trends in the Panchayati Raj System of Himachal Pradesh but she concluded with a note of optimism as the Government of Himachal Pradesh and the German Technical Mission have since started the process of drafting a Document on Activity Mapping.

Ms. Rathore and Dr. Chand described in detail the structure and working of Panchayati Raj in Haryana. They concluded that although the institutional framework of the Haryana Panchayati Raj follows the letter of the 73rd Constitutional Amendment Act (1992) yet it grossly violates its spirit. They hold that Haryana continues to have centralised decentralisation instead of democratic decentralisation. This dismal situation has been ascribed by them to the lack of political will, highly centralised and personalized political system and the weakness of the civil society in the State.

V

In the Section, 'Democratic Decentralisation and Women Empowerment', contributions have been made by Professors Jagroop Kaur and S.K. Singh, Ms. Neha Kirti Prasad, Prof. M. Padalia and Dr. Rekha Chaudhary.

Prof. Kaur discussed the evolution of the process of empowerment of women in India after the institutionalisation of the scheme of democratic decentralisation in the form of Panchayati Raj (1959) and traced the impact of the 73rd Amendment (1992) on it. She found, on the basis of secondary sources, that there has been greater empowerment in Kerala, Tamilnadu, Assam and Rajasthan than in Punjab and Haryana because of the historical and cultural factors.

Prof. Singh demystified the concept of empowerment and discussed the findings of the studies of Ministry of Panchayati Raj, Government of India on the *State of Panchayats—A Mid-Term Review and Appraisal* (2006) and the *Study on Elected Women Representatives in Panchayati Raj Institutions* (2008). Somehow, he has concluded on a very optimistic note.

In their paper Ms. Prasad and Dr. Padalia mapped the extent of empowerment of the women of Uttarakhand through the Panchayati Raj Elections held in 2008-09 during which the reservation was enhanced to

50%. They have found on the basis of participatory observation, that not withstanding their glorious role in the Chipko Movement and the Movement for Uttarakhand, the women could not be really empowered.

Dr. Rekha Chaudhary compared the representation of women in the Panchayati Raj Institutions in the Pre-Amendment and the Post-Amendment periods and also presented the findings of an empirical study on the empowerment of women in the Rohtak and Mewat districts. She too has found that women empowerment remains elusive till date inspite of a quantum jump in their representation. However, all the contributors in the Section have laid stress on the capacity-building of women.

An overview of the scholarly articles included in this volume makes it amply clear that the agenda of local democracy remains un-finished even after five decades of Panchayati Raj and more than seventeen years of the enactment on the 73rd Constitutional Amendment (1992) which sought to institutionalise the dream of late Rajiv Gandhi, the then Prime Minister of India (1984-89) for setting up inclusive local democracy for inclusive growth.

The 3 Fs, (functions, functionaries and funds) have not been genuinely devolved in most of the states. There has been a quantum jump in the representation of women as a result of one-third reservation for them. But the objective of women empowerment remains elusive in all the states except a few. Likewise, the objective of decentralised planning remains unfulfilled. Although the District Planning Committees have been constituted in almost all the states as per the mandate of the 74th Constitutional Amendment (1992), the role of planning in the districts continues to be performed by the bureaucracy and the technocracy. Even the enactment and implementation of the Right to Information Act (2005) has failed to ensure good governance through local democracy.[11] Transparency and accountability are still a far cry in decentralised rural governance.

Therefore, earnest attempts should be made for the functional and financial empowerment of the PRIs, for the capacity-building of the members of Gram Panchayats, Panchayat Samitis, Zila Parishads and the District Planning Committees. Besides, the foundation of the Panchayati Raj, i.e. the Gram Sabha, needs to be activated through a systematic campaign. The concerted efforts should also be made for the empowerment of women representatives. Last but not the least, the deficit of politics needs to be overcome and conceptual clarity is needed on the nature of Panchayati Raj Institutions. E-governance too needs to be introduced. Otherwise, the local democracy can not become inclusive. These challenging tasks can be performed only through the combined and coordinated endeavour of the Government of India, the State Governments, the Academics, the NGOs, the Media and the other constituents of the civil society.[12]

SURAT SINGH

Good governance depends on the responsiveness to the needs of people. It is composed of the mechanisms, processes and institutions through which citizens and groups can articulate their interests, exercise their legal rights, meet their obligations and mediate their differences. It also implies democratic decentralisation.

In the above context, the concept of democratic decentralisation has acquired increased legitimacy and new dimensions in India over the years. It was brought to the centre stage of political debate by Mahatma Gandhi during the national movement: He made it an important component of his vision of 'Gram Swaraj'. The Father of Nation stood for the democratic decentralisation in India because he favoured complete political and administrative decentralisation in his ideal polity which was to be a commonwealth of politically independent and economically self-sufficient villages. He, therefore, favoured maximum powers with the Gram Panchayats and minimum powers with the provincial and the central governments. He strongly believed in the dictum; "that government is the best which governs the least". In fact, his concept of democratic decentralisation aimed at creating a political system based on truth and non-violence.

The enactments of legislations for the creation of Gram Panchayats by various states in 1952-53 were steps in the direction of implementation of the mandate of the Article 40 of the Directive Principles of the State Policy which is based on Gandhian ideas. It provides that the State shall take steps to organize village Panchayats and endow them with such powers and authority as may be necessary to enable them to function as units of self-government.

However, the genesis of the concept of democratic decentralisation in its present sense of devolution of powers to the democratically elected and organically linked Panchayati Raj Institutions can be traced to the failure of the Community Development Programme launched on October 2, 1952 with a great fanfare and hope for the social, cultural and economic development of rural society which proved to be the proverbial 'god that failed' as its objectives could not be realized owing to lack of popular participation in it. Since it did not succeed in achieving its objectives, the Government of India appointed a Study Team, popularly known as the Balvantray Mehta Committee, which recommended democratic decentralisation of rural governance in 1957. The Team was of the view that the Community Development Programme was unsuccessful due to its bureaucratic implementation. Therefore, it suggested devolution of powers to a three-tier structure comprising of Gram Panchayats, Panchayat Samitis and Zila Parishads, for the mobilization of human and material resources for the Community Development Programme. This scheme was re-christened as "Panchayati Raj" by the first Prime Minister of India Pandit Jawaharlal Nehru, at the time of its inauguration on October 2, 1959.

As reported by the Asoka Mehta Committee (1978), the Panchayati Raj underwent three phases—the phase of ascendance (1959-64), stagnation

(1964-71) and decay (1971-77). The Committee recommended a two-tier structure consisting of Zila Parishad and Mandal Panchayats for the rejuvenation of Panchayati Raj System in India.

Though few initiatives were taken for reviving Panchayati Raj in the states of West Bengal, Karnataka and Andhra Pradesh, the situation remained unchanged in the remaining states. Elections were never held at time, powers were eroded, functionaries were withdrawn, resources depleted and parallel institutions were created. It was in this scenario that Rajiv Gandhi, the then Prime Minister of India, moved the 64th Amendment Bill in the Lok Sabha in 1989.

It is a mere co-incidence that this Bill which sought to strengthen the Panchayati Raj Institutions for giving power to the people was synchronous with the emergence of the World Bank's recipe for Good Governance.

It is also a matter of chance that the 72nd Amendment Bill (1992), which was enacted as the 73rd Amendment Act (1993), followed the adoption of the New Economic Policy to implement the World Bank Agenda of economic reforms based on the processes of liberalisation, privatisation and globalisation through the Structural Adjustment Programme by India in 1991. This had to be done on account of the foreign exchange crunch on the one hand and the economic crises on the other hand. Whereas, the 72nd Amendment Bill aimed at institutionalising the unfinished agenda of Rajiv Gandhi for the empowerment of people which was as follows:

1. According constitutional status to the Panchayati Raj Institutions.
2. Setting up a uniform three-tier structure of Panchayati Raj in all the states except those having a population of less than 20 lacs.
3. Providing for the reservation of one-third offices and membership for the women at all the three levels.
4. Making provision of reservation in both of these for the scheduled castes/tribes in proportion to their population.
5. Setting up State Election Commissions for timely elections to the Panchayati Raj Institutions.
6. Providing for the appointment of State Finance Commissions to ensure resources to these bodies.
7. Inclusion of the 11th Schedule in the Constitution of India for the devolution of powers pertaining to 29 items listed in it by the State Legislatures on the Panchayati Raj Institutions to enable them to function as Institutions of Self-Government for making and implementing the plans of economic development and social justice.

Therefore, it would be incorrect to believe that the 73rd Amendment was made on the directions of the World Bank. On the contrary, it aimed at promoting the Gandhian ideal of Gram Swaraj and fulfilling the mandate of the Constitution.

As required by the 73rd Constitutional Amendment Act (1992), the states enacted new Panchayati Raj Acts within one year and the new Panchayati Raj System was set-up in all the states in 1994-95. Haryana did not lag behind and enacted the Haryana Panchayati Raj Act, 1994 for implementing the 73rd Amendment. The State Election Commission was set-up in 1994 and the Panchayati Raj Elections took place in 1994, 2000 and 2005. Three State Finance Commissions had been appointed. The reports of the First and the Second State Finance Commissions have already been implemented and that of the Third State Finance Commission is under consideration of the State Government. This Commission has made some concrete suggestions for the functional and financial empowerment of the Panchayati Raj Institutions.

Almost, all the 29 items listed in the 11th Schedule have been included in the powers of the Gram Panchayats and Panchayat Samitis under the Haryana Panchayati Raj Act, 1994. The Zila Parishads have been given the role of supervision and coordination over the Gram Panchayats and the Panchayat Samitis and to perform such other functions as may be assigned to them by the State Government from time to time by its executive orders.

Additionally, the functions of planning, monitoring and supervision pertaining to 16 departments were assigned to the Panchayati Raj Institutions at all the three levels by the Haryana Government Notification of 1995. Moreover, instructions were issued by the State Government in 2000-01 for extending these in as many as 12 departments. The Document on Activity Mapping too was enacted by the Government of Haryana to implement the recommendations of the Seventh Round Table Conference of the Ministers of Panchayati Raj organised by the Ministry of Panchayati Raj, Government of India in 2005 for building a consensus on the empowerment of Panchayati Raj Institutions, and as an outcome of the Memorandum of Understanding (MoU) between the Hon'ble Union Minister of Panchayati Raj and the Chief Minister of Haryana, on August 22, 2005. Subsequently, it was formally issued by the Union Minister of Panchayati Raj, Mani Shanker Iyer, and the Chief Minister of Haryana Bhupinder Singh Hooda on February 17, 2006. The Key-Activities were dully identified for the devolution of functions, functionaries and funds of pertaining the Departments of Food and Supply, Health, Water Supply and Sanitation, Social Justice and Empowerment, Irrigation, Animal Husbandry, Education, Women and Child Development, Agriculture and Forest. In response to the letter of the then Financial Commissioner, Development and Panchayats, the administrative instructions were issued by the heads of the various departments to their district and block level functionaries so that the devolution of three Fs to the Panchayati Raj Institutions by the Document on Activity Mapping becomes a reality and do not remain un-implemented. However, no Gazette Notification was made for this purpose.

Moreover, the Panchayati Raj Institutions of the State have been given key role in the implementation of various rural development schemes and programmes of the Government of India such as the National Rural

Employment Guarantee Scheme, Swarnajayanti Gram Swarozgar Yojana, Haryali, Indira Awas Yojana, Total Sanitation Campaign and National Health Mission, etc.

Furthermore, these have been made agencies for implementing rural development schemes of the Panchayat and Development Department of the Government of Haryana. These include, in the first instance, the PRI scheme under which the State Government gives grants to Panchayati Raj Institution from the central funds for primary education, health, drinking water, street lighting, and sanitation and for such other works as had remained uncovered by other rural development schemes. Secondly, the Government gives interest-free loans to the PRIs for the installation of tube wells in *Gaon shamlats* (Village Common Lands) for leveling and reclaiming land and for the construction of shops. Thirdly, it gives matching grants to the Panchayats for the construction of school buildings, veterinary hospitals, primary health centres, entertainment centres and the *chaupals* for the Scheduled Castes and the Backward Classes. Fourthly, it gives grants to the Panchayati Raj Institutions from Haryana Rural Development Funds (HRDF) for improving the rural infrastructure. Fifthly, it also used to give funds to the Panchayati Raj Institution under the Local Area Development Tax (LADT) scheme for the primary education, drinking water supply system, sanitation, construction and repair of rural roads and other developmental works. However, it has now been discontinued on the orders of Punjab and Haryana High Court and would be restored in case the Supreme Court accepts the appeal of the State Government against that order. Sixthly, a new scheme, Mahatma Gandhi Gramin Basti Yojana, has been launched from the year 2008-09 under which 100 sq. yds. residential plots are being allotted to the eligible families of the Scheduled Castes and Backward Classes (A). Seventhly, another new scheme—Mukhyamantri Anusuchit Jati Nirmal Basti Yojana—has been launched by the Government of Haryana from the year 2008-09 under which all such villages as have more than 50 percent Scheduled Castes in its population will be provided basic infrastructure subject to the limit of Rs. 50 lacs. Moreover, Haryana Renewable Energy Development Agency (HAREDA) has launched a scheme in 2006-07 under which SPV street lighting system is being provided to such villages. Last but not the least, on the pattern of Haryana Urban Development Authority (HUDA), the Government of Haryana has set-up Haryana Rural Development Authority (HRDA) for the planned housing in rural areas.

As stipulated in the 74th Constitutional Amendment, District Planning Committees too were constituted by the Government of Haryana on December 4, 2007 for preparing the District Plans by consolidating the plans of Gram Panchayats, Panchayat Samitis and Zila Parishads and Municipal Committees. Here, it will be quite pertinent to recall that the Expert Group on Grassroots Planning appointed by the Government of India in 2005, had recommended that the Annual Plans under the 11th Five Year Plan be based by the State Governments on the District Plans prepared by the District

Planning Committees. This necessitated that the Deputy Commissioner (DC) be made the Chairperson of the District Planning Committee to ensure healthy interface between the elected members and the officials as also for ensuring cooperation among the line departments and the Panchayati Raj Institutions and for balancing and coordinating the interests of the rural and urban areas in the district plan. The State Government has also appointed experts in planning on these bodies for giving guidance to members in making plans. The Additional Deputy Commissioner-*cum*-Chief Executive Officer of the District Rural Development Agency (DRDA) has been made its Member-Secretary for ensuring convergence between the Panchayati Raj Institutions and the DRDA. The MLAs and the MPs have also been associated with the District Planning Committees so that they could guide the members of the DPCs and ensure linkage between the DPCs and the State Legislative Assembly on the one hand and the DPCs and the Parliament, on the other.

To enable the elected representatives of the Panchayati Raj Institutions to perform their functions in a more effective manner, the Government of Haryana has sanctioned monthly honorarium to various functionaries entitling: President Zila Parishad to get Rs. 4000, Vice-President Zila Parishad—Rs. 3000, Member Zila Parishad—Rs. 1000, Chairperson Panchayat Samiti—Rs. 3000, Member Panchayat Samiti—Rs. 500, Sarpanch—Rs. 1000 and Panch—Rs. 200.

Furthermore an increase has been made in their daily allowances under which President Zila Parishad (Grade-1) will be paid Rs. 160, Vice-President Zila Parishad (Grade-2)—Rs. 130, Member Zila Parishad (Grade-2)—Rs. 130, Chairperson Panchayat Samiti (Grade-2)—Rs. 130, Vice Chairperson Panchayat Samiti (Grade-2)—Rs. 130, Member Panchayat Samiti (Grade-2)—Rs. 130, Sarpanch (Grade-3)—Rs. 105 and Panch (Grade-3)—Rs. 105.

The State Government has also formed "Sakshar Mahila Samoohs" consisting of educated women in every Gram Panchayat with a view to mobilise women to participate in the meetings of Gram Sabha and to guide the illiterate women Sarpanches and Panches. Efforts have also been made to provide healthy interface between the Gram Panchayat and the Rural Youth by linking the Nehru Yuva Kendras to the elected representatives, so that Youth Power could be mobilized for strengthening decentralised rural governance and streamlining Rural Development Administration.

Other steps of the State Government for strengthening the PRIs include an appreciable increase in the number of Gram Sabha meetings in a year from two to three, and appointment of Sarpanches as (State) Public Information Officers to ensure greater transparency and accountability in the functioning of the Gram Panchayats. The State Government has also organised district, divisional and state level Panchayati Raj Sammelans for networking the Panchayati Raj leadership. The Chief Minister of Haryana has also been personally interacting with them to know about their problems, and to provide solutions for the same.

In addition to the above measures, the State Government had organised capacity-building programme for the benefit of the elected representatives of all the three levels in 2003-04 and 2005-06. A State-wide Training Campaign had been conducted by it in 2007-08 under the Rashtriya Gram Swaraj Yojana of the Ministry of Panchayati Raj, Government of India. It has also been organising Orientation Courses and Refresher Courses on National Rural Employment Guarantee Scheme, Swarnajayanti Gram Swarozgar Yojana, Total Sanitation Campaign and Public Distribution System. Besides, it has also organized Functional Literacy Programmes for illiterate Sarpanches and Panches of Gram Panchayats. Training-*cum*-exposure visits of the elected representatives to other states too were conducted. Special programmes have also been organised by it for the capacity-building of women and scheduled castes elected representatives. Programmes on interface between elected representatives and officers of the line departments have also been organised at various levels. A few months ago, the State Government organised a capacity-building programme on 'Right to Information' for the Sarpanches of the Gram Panchayats. The Haryana Institute of Rural Development has been acting as the Nodal Agency of the State Government in organising these programmes.

However, despite all these measures and efforts, there is still a great deal of scope for improvement. The functional and financial empowerment of the Panchayati Raj Institutions needs to be increased. It is sincerely hoped that the recommendations of the Haryana Administrative Reform Commission will go a long way in ensuring the needful. A gradual and incremental approach is needed in this context. The capacity-building and empowerment exercises will have to be done simultaneously. The training programme for capacity-building will have no meaning if the powers are not given to the elected representatives of the Panchayati Raj Institutions. On the other hand, they will not be able to use these powers properly in the absence of capacity building through proper training.

Besides, the empowerment of women still remains an unfinished agenda. We have a lot to learn from success stories of states like Kerala. But at the same time, we will have to keep in view specificities in term of historical, social, cultural, economic and political milieu of Haryana and make modifications accordingly. Concerted efforts will have to be made by the State Government as well as the Civil Society to change the mindset of the people in rural society of Haryana where the conservative and neo-feudal values continue to assert despite rapid modernisation and economic development of the State. Our aim should be to achieve good governance through democratic decentralisation. What we need is the formulation and implementation of a strategy for promoting inclusive growth through good governance. Concrete suggestions should be made by the social scientists and experts for this purpose.

For good governance to exist both in theory and practice, the citizens must be empowered to participate in meaningful ways in decision-making processes. They have the right to information. Although widespread accessibility remains a barrier for many countries including India, one of those ways is the application of Information and Communication Technology (ICT) for this purpose. The e-Governance too has emerged as a viable mean to address development issues and challenges. It can empower citizens through access to information.

2

Democratic Decentralisation and Good Governance : The Theoretical Perspective

RAMASHRAY ROY

The concepts of democratic decentralisation and good governance have assumed central importance today. They are important not only as a theme of academic relevance and discussion, but also as a pragmatic concern involving the need to undertake structural rearrangement of the political system. This is necessary for allowing the fulfilment of the promise that democracy holds out to the people. As a theme of academic discussion, both these topics evoke as well as provoke the articulation of different philosophical perspectives. Looking from different ideological vantage points, scholars take positions that are quite divergent and often give expression to contrary views.

Contrary viewpoints articulated and canvassed about the two themes engender a thick cloud of doubt and uncertainty about the real significance of democratic decentralisation and good governance. It is therefore, essential to disperse the clouds of ambivalence, doubt and uncertainty through an in-depth discussion on philosophical/theoretical implications of these two seminal symbols of political life and relations. The practical aspects of these symbols will also have to be taken into account in this context.

Coming to the substantive themes let us begin with the symbol of good governance. The reason for this lies in the fact that no matter what the political structural arrangement we may choose for organising our political life, the principal objective invariably is the assurance of good governance. Involved with good governance is not only an appropriate institutional format; also involved are the rulers and the ruled as well as the mode and pattern of interaction between them. Also important in this regard is the socio-cultural and politico-economic milieu in which the political system operates. But prior to all this there is the substantive meaning of the symbol of good governance. Only after that we can judge the kind of institutional arrangement that is appropriate for facilitating good governance.

If this argument has any validity, the questions we must raise are, one, what substantively does good governance mean and, two, how can good governance be realized? To take the first question, the concern for good governance is not in any way of recent origin, although it became a buzzword after the World Bank imposed it on India, during Mrs. Indira Gandhi's regime, as one of the conditions of advancing its loan that India sorely needed. However, what does it mean? Does it mean efficiency and effectiveness in realising governmental policies? Or, does it mean democratic accountability in policy formulation and programme implementation? Or, should we understand by the term 'good governance' a situation in which the people, the common man, the demos are made active participants in formulating policies and programmes? There are other senses in which this term can be understood. However, let us confine ourselves to these different significations of the term 'good governance'.

We must reject the first meaning since politico-administrative efficiency in realising policy objectives of the centralised political authority is not enough to ensure good governance. This is so for the reason that this sense of the term completely loses sight of the question whether policy objectives aim at promoting the well-being of the people or not. If the criterion of good governance is democratic accountability, and this must be the criterion, we have to ask whether the present system of representation fulfils this condition or not. What is distinctive about the formal, representative democracy is the divorce, as Habermas notes, between politico-administrative decision-making process and the process of legitimating political will formation that is conducted through periodical elections.

What this divorce means is that the role of the demos, the citizens, is restricted to the casting of their votes once in five years or so. They are expected then to sit back and suffer from or smile at what the people who they have elected as their rulers do or do not so. They have no active role, except when they are pushed to come out in the street to show anger or exhibit support for the regime, which rules over them as their titular head. Devoid of any active role in governmental decision-making, they become passive subjects and affirm, and that also very vaguely, the party manifesto and later on what the government does. However, manifestoes represent a document of intentions—the party or a coalition in power can achieve. It is a document that proposes to do what would attract the voter or what realistically. Moreover, as experience shows, party in power does not usually do what it has promised; it usually does what is convenient and what promises to enhance its power base.

Add to this also the fact that citizens lack the mechanism of articulating their own policy preferences or to publicise if they articulate their preferences. Citizens then do not act, they only react whether favourably or negatively depending on the effect on them of what the government does or does not do. This situation does not in any way augur well for the promotion of democratic accountability. Democratic accountability has further been eroded because of certain developments, both within and beyond the national borders. They have impinged upon the autonomy of the state in making decisions without being influenced by certain extraneous factors, influences that stem from its external environment. I refer here to the process of globalisation. Globalisation signifies the inter-connectedness of states and the proliferation of trans-national and international functions and organisations. These organisations, both governmental and non-governmental, take decisions that impinge on some vital issues that have great relevance for national political communities. However, these decisions are beyond the ken of national governments. They have become fragmented arena of decision-making. As such, democratic accountability has suffered.

Thus, to the extent the decisions taken beyond the border of the nation-state affect its policies and programmes, they curtail state sovereignty. Also, the intensification, especially after Second World War, of interconnectedness of states has eroded the distinction between internal and external affairs and between domestic and foreign policy. As a result, the state has become a fragmented arena of decision-making. It is permeated by international groups and by domestic agencies and forces. With the intensification of global interconnectedness, the number of political instruments available to individual governments and the effectiveness of particular instruments now show a marked tendency to decline. National communities and their governments do not exclusively make and determine decisions and policies for themselves.

It is this state of affairs that has also been instrumental in the erosion of democratic accountability. Decisions made by quasi-regional and quasi-international organisations, for instance, the World Bank, diminish the range of decisions open to given national majorities. The idea of 'national community of fate', that is, a community that rightly governs itself and determines its own, the idea that stands at the root of liberal democracy, has been greatly eclipsed and become problematic today. The impingement on national decision-making process by extra-national bodies and forces is just one factor that corrodes the idea as well as the process of self-government. It is just one factor in the growing dissipation of democratic accountability.

There are other factors also. To mention just one such factor, it is the expansion of economic activities across national borders that have been responsible for the rapid advance of the process of globalisation. The expansion of economic activities has helped the government to assume the responsibility of safeguarding and promoting economic well-being of the people. Towards this end, the state has taken the responsibility of producing goods and services that are necessary for ensuring the well-being of the people. The state is also responsible for correcting the distortions engendered by the working of the market forces. This has also increased the power of the state immensely introducing additional factors, institutions, and processes that affect the autonomy of the individual. This has culminated in what Tocqueville calls 'a new type of despotism which is popularly elected'.

This despotism arises out of the paradox embedded in modern democracy. It is true that politics celebrates freedom and equality. However, as a result of rising aspirations, fed upon the liberal promise of plenty for all, on the one hand, and the strong desire to emulate the life-styles of those who are fortunate to have better access to societal resources, on the other, democracies have become vulnerable to what Tocqueville calls 'permanent social revolution'. The diffusion of democratic ideals has fostered a widespread passion for the equalisation of power, wealth and prestige within the spheres of the state and civil society. The passionate struggle for equalisation has reached dizzying heights. However, this struggle has not yet led to the securing of social and political liberties as well as equality. While the struggle for equalisation is never ending, its outcome is far from what is expected. In the meantime, the struggle for equality goes on unabated. But complete equality slips from the hands of the people at the very moment, they seem to have grabbed it.

This state of affairs has led to a situation where the ideal of freedom from despotism has been replaced, bit-by-bit, by the goal of state-secured equality. The consequence is that people surrender their independence; this paves the way for the state to acquire more and more power over the lives of the people. They become dependent on the state; this opens the field for the state to intrude more and more in different aspects of the people's life. The more the state gets involved in providing public services on a progressively larger scale, the less the civil society is able to cope with the everyday problems of life without state intervention and direction. As a result, the need for state intervention constantly grows. The hands and eyes of the state intrude more and more in the daily life of the people. In the name of freedom and equality, the state emerges as the regulator of social life. It functions as a tutelary power, a type of 'state despotism which is absolute, differentiated, regular provident and mild'. Unlike its older version, modern despotism does not destroy life or tyrannise. It only perfects, as Tocqueville points out, and civilizes its techniques of control. It is, therefore, rendered less odious and degrading in the eyes of its subjects. "It transforms citizens into passive subjects who invest their trust in benevolent power and busy themselves with their humdrum life, the life of everydayness".

It is clear, then, that democratic accountability turns out to be a vacuous term, especially in a representative democracy that is saddled with the responsibility of promoting economic development for satisfying the ever-increasing hunger of the people for goods and services. This brings me to talk about the third meaning of the term "good governance". If we mean by this term effective participation of the people in making the decisions that have a vital bearing on their life conditions and life chances, then, we encounter a paradox. This paradox underlines the fact that while the ideal of democracy has been universally accepted, certain institutions have become obstreperous and prove a stumbling block to the realisation of the ideal of universal participation.

Three different stages mark the journey of the substantive idea of democracy. The Athenian democracy under Pericles is considered to be the best example of direct democracy. However, the claim has no solid ground to stand on. Pericles himself admitted that citizens of Athens enjoyed *isonomia,* equality before law but not equality in politics or socio-economic conditions. He also indicated that in politics, aristocracy of talent was supreme. Aspasia, his wife, put it more emphatically when she observed that Athenian democracy under Pericles was aristocracy under the kingship of Pericles; she also emphasized the fact that "it is and always was the rule of the best with the consent of the people." The tradition of underlining the need of the rule by the best is very well reflected in Plato's idea of the philosopher-king and Aristotle's idea of *spudaios,* the mature man.

In modern times, the tradition has been kept alive in the distinction between elite and mass. It is always the elite who is supposed to rule over the mass. In the process, the very definition of the mature man has undergone a sea change. If traditionally the mature man was identified as a wise man, he is now treated as capable of governing even if he lacks wisdom but enjoys political popularity and is a mature player of the game of politics. The trouble is that the distinction between elite and mass creates an unbridgeable gap between the two and condemns the mass to eternal servitude. Also, the rulers make policy decisions more for consolidating their power base than for promoting collective good. They usually seek to please and appease the voters who can make or mar their aspirations to control power apparatus of society. Moreover, the idea of collective good itself is flawed insofar as we have no clear understanding of what constitutes the collective good. If we say it is the good of the people, it is tantamount to indulging in a generality since we do not specify who constitutes the people at any particular moment. Like many words, the term 'people' too is a twistable word because it can assume different meanings at different occasions for different purposes.

There are some factors that terribly distort the meaning and practice of democracy. The basic reason why the operation of democracy is distorted, is its similarity to market operations; that is why Fred Hirsch calls it 'market mode democracy'. The adjective 'market mode' is apt because society itself has come to take on the basic traits of the market when people do not share anything in common except their desire to rise materially in the world. In such a situation, there is nothing else than private valuations that can provide the basis for constituting the state. Given the central importance of individual choices, democracy does not, Max Weber points out, serve any moral purpose; it is simply a mechanism for arriving at procedurally correct decisions; these decisions must conform to legal-rational norms. The most important task of formal democracy is to transform individual choices into collective decisions; it is concerned with decision-making process alone; it does not concern itself with not what decisions are morally right or wrong, or, for that matter, with whether it is beneficial for the people or not. These decisions must be made in an environment in which divided and fragmented opinions of separated individuals constitute a central fact; it is process of decision-making that produces non-unanimous decisions. It is in this environment that private valuations need to be transformed into consistent and socio-politically effective collective choices.

It is here in this political environment characterised by the lack of unanimity about what collective decisions are appropriate that political parties become crucially important. Political parties are supposed to make or help in making collective decisions in a non-partisan manner. However, the need to win elections compels the competing parties not only to mobilise electoral support on a wider scale. It also requires them to modify their ideal political principles to become pragmatic in their policies and programmes. Parties compete among themselves for controlling power apparatus of society. For this, they present to the voters alternative sets of policy frames as well as candidates for selection as rulers. What formal democracies symbolise then is, as Hirsch notes,

Essentially a choice exercised periodically by the mass of the people among alternative and open ruling elites, who, in turn, are induced by the force of competition (from rival elites) to offer policies tailored to attract political support. The political arena in this approach is akin to market mode for the fulfilment of personal wants. It is an extension of the departmental store –and the problem is to find managers who can undersell the rest of the street.

The reduction of the ideal of democracy to the simple act of creating a mechanism through which citizens can do nothing better than express their choice about who should rule over them has taken place over a long stretch of time. This reduction symbolises what Manicas calls the victory of democratic ideology against democracy. This reduction has also meant the hypertrophy of the government. It signifies the institutional embodiment of the radical separation of civil society and the state. Now civil society is the realm of private persons engaged in the pursuit of private concerns. As a result, it loses its integrative, educative and prescriptive role. It also loses its integrative role; the state emerges as the central authority, which becomes the primary, even exclusive, instrument of integration, cohesion, and coherence in society. With it, politics ceases to be a ground of acquiring and expressing virtue; it becomes the instrument of the protection of private interests.

This reduction has passed through three major landmarks. After the collapse of the Athenian democracy there is a long gap before the advent of the modern, formal representative democracy signifying the consent of the people as the bedrock of democracy. It is this variety of democracy that has been universally embraced. However, the first stage of this idea was articulated as the contract theory. Contract theory took the consent of the people as given once the contract to install a government was made. The second stage is characterised by the acceptance of the mechanism of elections for registering the choice of the people regarding the periodical selection of rulers. However, this device does not allow the citizen to play an active part in political process. We are now in the third stage, which demands full participation of the people in decision-making process.

'By the people, of the people and for the people', best express the ideal in Abraham Lincoln's apt phrase. This ideal has, however, yet to be realised. It is very doubtful that this ideal can ever be realised if the conditions detrimental to its actualisation persist. And the persistence of these conditions is exemplified by representative democracy, which transforms people's sovereignty into state sovereignty meaning the sovereignty of a part of the people that is their rulers. It concentrates all power and authority at the apex of the system and reduces citizens into subjects. It is here that the link between good governance and decentralisation is forged.

The forging of this link intellectually and pragmatically is forced upon us because of the increasing pressure on the system for more and more goods and services when its capacity to perform has been greatly attenuated. It is also called for because the denial of real participation to the people from having a say in the making of collective choices creates a situation in which people tend to lose interest in public affairs. As a result, insufficient support comes forth to protect democracy from a variety of potential threats. This is symptomatic of the mismatch between individual concerns and collective goals. As a direct consequence of this, we have now reached a stage where public choices cannot be made rationally or electorally. Likewise, there has come about a divorce between the individual and the community he lives in.

The combination of these factors has also laid the intellectual foundation for viewing the state, as Weber puts it, as enjoying the monopoly of violence as well as the arena where struggles for power take place. Power, for Weber, implies the exploitation of every chance in social relationship for asserting one's will despite opposition. Exercise of power in this sense amounts, as Aristotle tells us, to violence. Politics then stands for the legitimation of every instance of successful violence. The hypertrophy of the government that this situation promotes also implies that the state enjoys auto-legitimation. This evokes the judgment that power does not emanate from the community of the people. Power, too, then, enjoys auto-legitimation; as a result, it frequently turns tyrannical. In order to prevent tyranny, it is necessary to embed power in the community, an intimate political association that is the local community. It also calls for creating conditions matched by appropriate political institutions so that people are appropriately disposed towards power, instead of being exposed to its vagaries, and become vulnerable to exploitation and oppression.

The only viable way of empowering the people lies through restoration of power to them. Here Mahatma Gandhi's insistence on creating a political system in which the people may develop the capacity to resist tyranny and defy oppression assumes the highest significance. This capacity cannot be developed if the people's participation in making collective choices is restricted to the simple act of voting periodically. But once the people develop the capacity that Mahatma Gandhi talks of, power as violence is sure to be transmuted into power as collective will. Then power is transformed into human ability not just to act but also to act in concert with one's fellowmen. Power would then mean the consent of the people that is mobilised for formulating collective goals in contradistinction to power as disposition to gain control over resources and means of coercion.

For this to happen, the transformation of democratic ideology into real, substantive democracy, participation of the people in political process is *sine qua non*. But for participation to be meaningful, people must have control over decisions that affect their lives as well the resources they happen to have locally. This further means that units of political organisation must be manageably small; this means the local community. Participation, especially within the framework of democratic decentralisation will not simply mean taking part in periodical elections; it will also mean organising or initiating cooperative action with others. This will allow everyone to become a political power centre and assure the generation of the capacity for developing into beings who know and value what it means to participate and be responsible for the care and improvement of their common collective life.

The question can, however, be raised: Why do we need the transformation that we have been often talking about, after the 73rd and 74th constitutional amendments have already ensured democratic decentralisation? That we have to go beyond them is justified for a very good reason. These amendments offer no real and authentic democratic decentralisation since people are still starved of resources and power as well as the control over the resources they have locally available. Moreover, without complete economic decentralisation, politico-administrative decentralisation has no meaning, no real impact on people's civic life. Therefore, let us think of the ways and means for the achievement of real democratic decentralisation so that the good governance could be made a reality.

3

The Dialectics of Democratic Decentralisation and Good Governance

ASWINI K. RAY

Good Governance has now become a buzz word. It has received wide-ranging endorsement. The need for "Good Governance" is being increasingly recognised in all political systems not only for administrative efficiency but also for economic development and social justice. This explains why India also embarked upon the goal of good governance. It became all the more necessary for us to do so due to the general crises of governability.

It was on account of the above scenario that the late Rajiv Gandhi had perceptibly realized that good governance can be made possible in India only through democratic decentralisation. He aptly arrived at the conclusion that the programmes for poverty alleviation, employment generation and other schemes of rural development have not been able to achieve their objectives because of the weakness of the Panchayati Raj Institutions. On the basis of extensive consultations, he found that out of every one rupee spent on rural development, only 15 paisa reached the targeted beneficiaries. He rightly diagnosed that it was the absence of transparency, accountability and responsiveness in the rural development administration which was responsible for this dismal situation. In other words, it was the lack of good governance which had created the malady. And, the only remedy was the strengthening of Panchayati Raj Institutions. The 64th Constitution Amendment Bill that he had moved in the Lok Sabha, on the basis of the LM

Singhvi Committee Report of 1989, for the constitutional incorporation of Panchayati Raj Institutions will have to be viewed in this perspective. But, the vested interests foiled his attempts and the Bill failed to get the requisite two-third majority in the Rajya Sabha.

The unfinished agenda of his vision was ultimately institutionalized through the enactment of 73rd Constitutional Amendment (1992). This Amendment has been hailed as a landmark in the evolution of democratic decentralisation in India. It has not only accorded a constitutional status to the Panchayati Raj Institutions but has also sought to make them institutions of self-government by empowering them to make and implement the plans for economic development and social justice pertaining to the 29 items listed in the Eleventh Schedule which are to be devolved on them by the State Legislatures. The Amendment has also sought to ensure inclusive growth through the empowerment of women and the weaker sections in the Panchayati Raj Institutions by giving them adequate reservations.

The 73rd Constitutional Amendment Act was implemented in all the states of Indian Union through conformity legislations by 1994. But, the experience of the working of the Panchayati Raj Institutions now for more than 15 years clearly shows that the goal of good governance still remains elusive because democratic decentralisation has not been done in the true spirit of the Amendment.

An attempt is being made in this write-up to discuss the concept of good governance and to relate it to the evolution of democratic decentralisation in India.

I

The idea of "good governance" is as old as the discipline of Political Science. Plato's *The Republic* aimed at providing an ideal framework for good governance through the concept of justice, rule of philosopher kings, an elaborate system of education and communism of wives and property. It was the same quest that made Aristotle to suggest the rule of middle class, humane system of slavery, rule of law, small size of the state and steps for preventing revolutions. As a matter of fact, the basic objective behind the ideas of all the political thinkers from Plato to Marcuse had been the pursuit of good governance.

But in more recent times, the concept of good governance, in its mystified new incarnation, has been appropriated by the World Bank. The Bank made a distinction between the government and governance. While the government was viewed in a narrow sense as the mechanism for performing the executive functions of the state, governance was perceived by the Bank as a broad term including the form of political regime, the process by which authority is exercised and the capacity of the government to design, formulate and implement policies. In other words, good governance was conceptualized by the World Bank as a dependent variable on the following criteria:

(i) The degree of democratization to establish the legitimacy of the state. In other words, the higher the degree of democratization, greater the degree of good governance.
(ii) Freedom of media is another determinant of good governance. The larger the freedom of media, higher the level of good governance.
(iii) Accountability of the government too is an important pre-requisite of good governance. Its presence promotes it but its absence obstructs it.
(iv) The status of individual and group rights is also among the important criteria of good governance. In other words, it is only when the rights of the citizens, the minorities, and the marginalised sections, have been ensured that the claim of a political regime to good governance can be accepted.
(v) The level of adherence to the rule of law instead of arbitrary rule and the provision of human rights are the other yardsticks of measuring the degree of good governance.
(vi) Last but not the least, the recognition of a regime to good governance has to be measured in terms of its capacity to formulate well-defined policies and deliver services to the people.

In sum, good governance could be described as effective and efficient administration in a democratic framework.

The above parameters of good governance have been drawn from the experience of the western liberal democracies, operating within the capitalist market economics. The aim is to globalise their relevance for the rest of humanity after the end of the cold war, collapse of the communist regimes in Eastern Europe and disintegration of the USSR, culminating in the hegemony of the United States over the global system. Under these circumstances, the media-savvy agenda of 'good governance' as designed by the World Bank has caught the imagination of the global 'Think Tanks', at any rate, if possible to be operationally replicated in the asymmetrical political economy of the erstwhile 'Third World' of the post-cold war era. The goal of 'good governance' within the aforementioned broad parameters appears to be generally unexceptionable. But it has its critics also within the western liberal intelligentsia. According to one, like democracy, governance remains a particularly difficult variable. 'Good governance', to this critic, is now defined in terms of a 'check-list of criteria', like transparency and accountability in public sector management, 'governance must satisfy to qualify for loans and aid'. It provides no prioritisation, or criteria of measurement and comparison, which invites sharp criticism from the author. Governance is not a binary variable and cannot be defined in terms of 'on'/'*off*' or 'present'/'absent' criteria. There is little clear guidance as to how well or badly a government must perform in the above categories before it is granted or disqualified from funding. If quality of governance is to represent a standard for making vital decisions about international lending, there is a need for greater clarity about what this actually means in practical terms.

II

But, interestingly, while the economic component of the structural reforms to ensure 'good governance' may have been a sharp departure from the entire trajectory of the earlier policies in India based on a political consensus, the political component of the agenda has a striking resonance with post-colonial India's developmental politics since the inception of the Republican era. This is particularly so in case of the emphasis on democratic decentralisation as part of the package of good governance.

In fact, the decentralisation agenda, as such, even predates India's post-colonial democratic transformation. For example, the Bengal Self-government Act (1885) setting up District Boards and Union Councils and Bengal Village Self-Government Act (1919) creating District and Union Boards for developmental activities were implemented in the colonial era without the democratic component of adult suffrage; only those paying land-revenue voted and, consequently these local units of administration, dominated by the rural landlords, were not the best examples of self-government. At any rate, India under colonial rule could not have had self-government at the level of local administration.

India's Republican constitution, in its Chapter IV, containing the Directive Principles of State Policies, emphasized upon the need for the creation of village-level administration as the basic units of self-government, as Gandhiji had envisaged in the post-colonial era. But, instead of Panchayats, the Community Development Programme (1952) with technical specialists assisting the administration was adopted as the mechanism for rural development. However, the Balvantray Mehta Study Team, appointed in 1957 to suggest reforms on local government, recommended the need for local initiative and administrative decentralisation for making the programme successful. It conceptualized the 'Panchayat Raj' as a three-tier structure at the village, block, and district levels for this purpose. But, by the mid-sixties, these institutions remained largely still-born, or became moribund, with elections either scuttled or the local bodies superseded. The operational emphasis was on centralised planning and political centralisation and bureaucratic control of developmental activities, despite lip-service to decentralisation. The Emergency regime of 1975-77 epitomised these general trends within Indian politics; and, at any rate, with the country's democratic institutions of governance in moratorium, and held under siege by the Emergency regime, the institutions of local self-government could not have functioned any better.

The Janata regime voted to power in 1977 showed renewed interest in the revival of the Panchayat Raj system, and appointed the Asoka Mehta Committee (1978) to recommend measures of reform. The Committee recommended additional devolution of powers and functions; empowerment of the citizens particularly in the rural areas; better financial support and representation of the weaker and disadvantaged social groups in the Panchayat Raj administration.

Based on these reforms, the 'new look' Panchayat elections were held in 1978 in some states like West Bengal, Andhra Pradesh and Karnataka which have been described as 'second generation' Panchayats in the historiography of India's democratic decentralisation. But, unfortunately for these institutions, the re-election of Mrs. Indira Gandhi in 1980 heralded the re-emergence of centralised political authority in India. Many states withdrew financial and administrative support to the Panchayat Raj institutions; in states like Bihar, Tamilnadu and Uttar Pradesh, no election to these institutions were held.

The Congress Government under Rajiv Gandhi gave a new impetus to the Panchayati Raj Institutions. The youthful new Congress leader, elected with a massive majority of 'sympathy votes' after her mother's assassination, and hyped by the western media as a new political icon along with his coterie of managerial technocrats and computer whiz kids as his principal advisers, projected the 'West Bengal model' of Panchayat Raj Institutions as the national role-model to revive the experiment of democratic decentralisation. This led to the intense democratic political debate in India which paved the way for the 73rd and 74th constitutional Amendments in 1993 making local self-governments mandatory with assured financial support and statutory representation of women and other disadvantaged groups in Panchayat Raj institutions. By then, as we know, the Fund-Bank 'conditionality' of democratic decentralisation as a component of 'good governance' had given the agenda a new legitimacy in the transformed Indian political economy of the era along with the changed global system following the disintegration of the Soviet Union.

This brief historical narrative would underscore the basic point that the agenda of democratic decentralisation, both as a component of political self-government, as well as the basic unit of developmental planning and administration is rooted indigenously in India's political culture of the national liberation movement, incorporated within the Republican constitution, and given periodic political thrusts through institutional reforms. This part of the package of 'good governance' was certainly not externally induced. But, admittedly, the Fund-Bank endorsement has given a new political legitimacy to the indigenous agenda in India's new political economy more receptive to such endorsements.

III

But it must be admitted that, despite the periodic political thrusts to promote democratic decentralisation—in fact, underscored by the need for such periodic thrusts—the overall national record on this score, prior to the

$73^{rd}/74^{th}$ Constitutional Amendments has been somewhat lackluster. This is where the Fund-Bank endorsement of this aspect of India's indigenous agenda has been useful, particularly in the context of the weak political leadership running coalition regimes in the centre and many of the constituent states.

Not long after the World Bank formulation of 'good governance', the Conference of Chief Secretaries convened by the Government of India (20 November, 1996) made three recommendations: (i) It admitted a crisis in administration, (ii) it underscored the need for administrative reforms to make it 'people-sensitive, efficient and cost-effective'; and (iii) it underscored the concept of 'governance'—as distinct from 'government'—now including citizens, consumer groups and elected local bodies, thus envisaging state-market-civil society interface in managing the collective resources of the community. In May 1997, the Conference of Chief Ministers, convened by the Government of India, endorsed the same agenda. It recognised governance to extend beyond the bureaucracy to involve citizens and consumer groups in the task of empowering disadvantaged groups and to ensure delivery of public services and execution of programs through autonomous elected local bodies.

In the context of the general atrophy of public order and services, it is quite evident that there is an emerging national consensus, dialectically linked with the politics of the Fund-Bank agenda, around the programme for decentralisation and devolution of power and administration, participation of citizens in local decision-making, empowerment of disadvantaged groups by protective discrimination to ensure adequate representation in decision-making institutions at all levels of governance; efficient and cost-effective implementation of schemes affecting people's livelihood and quality of life; and institutional machinery for popular grievance-redressal at all tiers of the administration. Along with these goals, there is also the need for accountability, transparency, efficiency and integrity of the public services, and the right to information of citizens to monitor them within these parameters of the national consensus. There is also a consensus around the sphere of the core-functions of the state, consisting of security, law and order, social services, infra-structure and macro-economic management, which cannot be left to the vagaries of the market.

These goals, consisting of the new package of 'good governance' are not strikingly new, at least in the Indian context. But the Fund-Bank endorsement has given them a new legitimacy. It has now facilitated the pursuit of our indigenous democratic agenda with a new leverage in contemporary India's anomic politics. It is a new opportunity to complete the indigenous agenda of democratic nation-building, aborted by the global cold war and Funding Agencies' promotion of their earlier version of 'modernisation' in the Third World in that era. In the intervening period, while we have defaulted, the global funding agencies have changed priorities by learning from their earlier experiences.

IV

This new emphasis on democracy as part of good governance calls for some de-mystification of the concept itself as popularly perceived, and to contextualise it in the Indian case. While democracy is often defined as a government 'of the people, by the people, and for the people', representative democracies are always governed by regimes elected by the majority party, and of the majority party; and, it is the task of democratic institution-building to ensure that a government of and by the majority party does not become also for the majority party, but remains as for all the people. That makes the need to ensure the democratic rights of all citizens a crucial determinant of democratic governance and as a check against the endemic proclivities of such regimes towards majoritarianism, and majority tyranny. In Indian democracy's multicultural social base, the majority-minority divide is both political/ideological as well as sociological consisting of its myriad ascriptive identities of religion, language, caste, and ethnicity. Within such a social base of India's inevitable multi-party system, this concern is particularly important in view of the fact that, since the inception of the Republican constitution, all the regimes in India's federal centre and most of the constituent states, have been governed by elected regimes with a majority of seats in the legislatures but with only a minority of electoral votes in their respective constituencies. This has been the inevitable consequence of the Westminster electoral system of first-past-the-post with winner-take-all in a multi-party system. In such a system, the political party which rules by majority vote is not necessarily the majority of the electorates in the constituency but simply a majority among the contesting political parties; yet, the ruling parties take seminal policy-decisions with the heady notion of their majority support base, often stoking extra-parliamentary oppositions, including violent protests. Hence, there is a case for considering the proposal to include 'negative voting' in the electoral system, which gives opportunity to the voters to express their disapproval against all the political parties and candidates that are contesting. This would at least partially reflect the ruling parties' level of majority support base before embarking on critical policy-decisions, and possibly make them a little more modest on this score. As of now, the voters have the option of either voting from among those actually in the fray or abstain; this is not ideal democratic options aimed at good governance. Besides, in the Indian context, democratic governance has to reckon with the empirical reality, that roughly about 50% of the people are either not aware of their basic rights or their options of redressal when they are violated or transgressed. This makes the case for democratic decentralisation as a component of good governance so much the stronger in the Indian case, so that the instruments of actual exercise of the authority of state power is brought closer to the citizens. What we are witnessing now within the politically orchestrated chorus of decentralisation is the replication of the Indian *'Rail Compartment Syndrome'* in which the occupants of each of the three tiers demand power to be devolved down from the higher tier, but is reluctant to devolve it lower down to the next. This approach must be institutionally contained to promote good governance through the institutions of democratic decentralisation like the Panchayati Raj, and complemented by the civil society initiatives against their misuse or atrophy.

4

The Conceptual and Substantive Issues of Democratic Decentralisation

PARTHA NATH MUKHERJI

That the theories and concepts are for the 'arm chair' academics that have little relevance for practical application, is a widespread and strongly held belief by many in our part of the developing world. Nothing could be more deceptive, dangerous and removed from reality than this. In fact, as a consequence of such a widely held notion, we have often got driven by 'received' concepts and theories that are formulated elsewhere, generally in the context of Western realities and interests. Such is the level of internalisation of this belief that many of the best and genuine minds become *captive* to 'received wisdom' especially from the West, more often than not, unconscious of the implications.

The universality of Western modernity as 'development', for example, was one such paradigm that swept the developing world following the period that witnessed the dismantling of colonialism. No less a person than Prime Minister Jawaharlal Nehru, an outstanding intellectual and patriot, could not grasp the significance and logic of an indigenously derived polity based on the Panchayati Raj, as was being put forward by Mahatma Gandhi. Nor did the giant intellect of Babasaheb Ambedkar who scripted the Indian Constitution swayed by the fundamentals of the Westminster model of representative parliamentary democracy even as he dismissed the Panchayati Raj with utter disdain before relenting to its inclusion in the Constitution under great pressure from the Gandhians among the members of the Constituent Assembly.

Only when the US-inspired programme of Community Development and Rural Extension modelled on the Tennessee Valley Authority in the United States failed comprehensively, that is a full decade later, Nehru realised the significance of the premises of Panchayati Raj. Clearly, the evolution of democratic decentralisation in India had an *indigenous* legacy that went back to Gandhi's efforts to reconfigure the traditional rural panchayat that had a run through the millennia, within the contemporary democratic framework. Leaders such as Vinoba Bhave, Jayaprakash Narayan, S.K. Dey, Balvantray Mehta, Asoka Mehta, E.M.S. Namboodiripad, Siddhraj Dhadha, Narayan Desai, Rajiv Gandhi and others contributed to its conceptualisation until its final incorporation in the Constitution as the third tier of the Indian Government in 1992.

Considerable amount of confusion surrounds the concept of *decentralisation*. It has sometimes mistakenly conveyed the idea that decentralisation by a central government to its subsidiary levels of administration and governance, reaching out to the local level, means extension of democratic practice.[1] Authoritarian regimes too can attempt to consolidate their centralised structure of power by decentralising, as it happened under Nepalese monarchy and Pakistani military regime. Decentralised governance can take place no matter what is the form of the state that introduces it—authoritarian or democratic. It has to do, as Litvack points out, with dispersing 'fiscal, political and administrative responsibilities across different tiers of government and between public and private sector' (1998: 26). Decentralisation is *regime-neutral*.

Interestingly, this unique evolution of Panchayati Raj figured prominently in the conceptual and theoretical discourse in the social sciences only *after* the conceptualisation of 'decentralisation' took place in the West. In the 1980s, many post-colonial developing countries, particularly in sub-Saharan Africa facing bankruptcy of their economies, were desperately in need of World Bank support. One of the 'conditionalities' of the structural adjustment programme of the Bank was that these economies would need to *decentralise* their service delivery system to avoid 'leakage' so that the financial support given to them for poverty alleviation would reach the targeted destination. This set-off a wave of decentralisation in the developing and transitional countries 'decentralising fiscal, political and administrative responsibilities to lower level governments *and to private sector*' (DFID 2007: 1; Johnson 2003; emphasis added). By 1994, 63 out of 75 developing and transitional countries with a population of more than five million claimed to have embarked on some form of transfer of political power to local units of government (Delinger cited in Crook and Manor 1998). By 2007 this number had risen to 78 (DFID 2007: 1).

'De-centering' the role of the central government in service delivery, and transferring it to the civil society and the market, has been the key elements in the conceptualisation of decentralisation in the context of structural adjustment. This conceptualisation has now gone beyond the instrumentalities of efficient service delivery and embraces a variety of situations.

Litvack (1988) identifies seven different contexts of decentralisation:

- Advent of multi-party systems (Africa).
- Deepening of democracy (Latin America).
- Transition from command to market economy (Eastern Europe and former Soviet Russia).
- Need to improve delivery of local services to large populations in centralised countries (East Asia).
- The challenge of ethnic and geographic diversity (South Asia).
- Countries with ethnic tensions (Bosnia, Herzegovina, Ethiopia, Russia).
- Countries attempting to keep centrifugal forces at bay by forging asymmetrical federations.

For a better comprehension of the concept, we need to distinguish analytically between three types of decentralisation—*deconcentration, delegation and devolution* of decision-making authority and power. A central government/authority may decide to *de-concentrate* its power at the centre by assigning more responsibilities to its lower ends of administration. Decision-making remains concentrated at the centre, only its effective execution is passed down the line. Such de-concentration of power may well serve the purpose of further strengthening the central authority. People's participation does not factor into this system of decentralisation.

Decentralisation could also take the form of a central government/ authority deciding to *delegate* decision-making authority and power to lower levels of administration. Major decisions are still taken by the central authority but a space is created for public participation through elections for effective *implementation* of the policies/administration at lower levels of governance.

Only when a central government/authority *devolves* decision-making authority and power to lower levels of governance on the *principle of subsidiarity*[2] can we term such decentralisation as *democratic decentralisation.* The Panchayati Raj system is based formally, constitutionally on the principle of subsidiarity. Such devolution of authority *transcends* the role of efficient service delivery. At the sub-state levels (district and below), citizens are empowered to self-govern within their territorial jurisdictions by not only planning for their needs but in implementing them. In addition, it cooperates in the implementation of macro national level programmes that cover their areas. Decentralisation, therefore, *ipso fact*, is not democratic democratisation. These three forms of decentralisation can provide a useful analytical framework to assess how the different states are performing in transferring (or resisting to transfer) power to local level Panchayat Institutions in the spirit of the Constitution.

Constitutionally, establishing the PRIs as the third tier of governance in the country, does not mean that the panchayat system has been institutionalised. In fact, it is not. In practice, the constitutional breakthrough has unleashed a *new threshold* of contestations and contradictions between the central and state level legislative elites, *and* the emergent panchayat leadership, as well as, between centralised political party systems *and* the premises of a decentralised, bottom-up, Panchayati Raj Institutions.

A moot question that I posed after the recent study of the Panchayat Elections in West Bengal and Punjab is: Can democratic centralism of the party (e.g. CPM), or party centralism as such (e.g. Akali Dal), be consistent with democratic decentralisation through Panchayati Raj? From the West Bengal situation where the Party exercises a tight grip over Panchayat deliberations through its monopoly of power at the state-level, or in Punjab where the party in power at the State exercised coercive power of the state to influence the outcome of the last Panchayat elections held in May 2008, it would seem to suggest that centralism at the state or party level is inconsistent with the democratic decentralisation at the grassroots level. The fact that CPM in Kerala has contributed maximally in the fiscal decentralisation and devolution of the planning process in the Panchayati Raj Institutions in Kerala, proves the falsity of the incompatibility hypothesis.

I have identified 12 challenges facing the PRIs that may be useful in studying the structures and processes that facilitate or impede the progress towards the institutionalisation of the PRIs (Mukherji, 2007: 32-33):

1. There is the high probability of elite capturing of power and resources in the local political economy setting.
2. Central and state-level political elites will have to compete for support from the same bases from which the local level elites may nurse aspirations for promoting themselves for competing at the state and central level legislatures.
3. The resource-rich, non-elected NGO leadership, with their primary accountability to their donor-driven sponsors, operating within Panchayat jurisdiction, could become a parallel structure of power that could complement or undermine leadership in the PRIs.
4. The ruling party elites in the central government bypass state governments to reach out to the rural constituency directly through mega-projects. In such projects the PRIs generally play a supportive rather than a leadership role to the government administration.
5. Likewise, state governments, try to bypass the PRIs by not transferring all the functions the PRIs are entitled to under the Constitution and controlling the bulk of the funds for rural expenditure.
6. Gram Sabhas, the primary units of direct democracy, in many instances meet at irregular intervals with poor attendance.
7. The much talked about proxy Panchayats in which husbands or male relatives usurp the roles of the elected women Panchayat members come in the way of women's empowerment.

8. Similarly, the role of *dalit* leadership in the PRIs is sometimes blocked by upper caste members who are unable to accept working under low caste leadership.
9. Often a resistant bureaucracy is tardy in devolving power to the elected members of PRIs.
10. Political and economic clientelism in an iniquitous agrarian and caste order tries to perpetuate the role of the dominant powers.
11. Ambiguities in the definition of sharing power as between the three tiers of the PRIs create problems of efficient local level governance.
12. More fundamentally, problems of poverty, illiteracy and malnutrition create structural problems for the improvement of life-chances to the marginalised groups

The great achievement is the *formulisation* of the PRIs through constitutional legislation. This has happened after a long process of political engagement at the *national elite* level of democratic politics. The 73rd Amendment to the Indian Constitution has radically altered the formal structure of the polity. This does not mean that this formal structure has undergone *institutionalisation.* It means that the formal structure has provided a new threshold of conflict, structure and change which is expected to lead to its democratic institutionalisation. In this phase of institutionalisation, the *rural masses and the local elites* will have to play the vital role. The pace and extent of the process of institutionalisation will be uneven, and could even be non-linear, with different states going through the process in accordance with the dynamics specific to them. When the major challenges are overcome the nation can proudly proclaim its contribution to democratic theory and practice that can perhaps be universalised.

Notes

1. No less a votary of democratic decentralisation than Jayaprakash Narayan became a victim of this confusion when he lauded the Panchayat System under the Nepalese Monarchy, and Basic Democracy under the authoritarian rule in Pakistan.
2. The principle of subsidiarity holds that the central authority in any society/state should not exercise such functions as can be carried out competently by lower sub-State levels of authority, but rather the former should support the latter and help to coordinate their activities for the benefit of the society/state (Manor 1999 : 4-6).

References

Crook, Richard C. and Manor (1998), *Democracy and Decentralisation in South Asia and West Africa*, Cambridge, Cambridge University Press.

DFID (2007), "Decentralisation and Governance, Policy Planning and Implementation", At http://www.keysheets.org/red_11_decentra_gov.html (Site visited on 23 February 2007)

Johnson, Craig (2003), "Decentralisation in India: Poverty, Politics and Panchayati Raj", *Working Paper 199*, London, Overseas Development Institute.

Litvack, Jennie, Junaid Ahmad and Richard Bird (1998), "Rethinking Decentralisation in Developing Countries", Washington D.C.: *The International Bank for Reconstruction and Development.*

Manor, James (1999), *The Political Economy of Democratic Decentralisation*, Washington D.C., International Bank for Reconstruction and Development, 1999.

Mukherji, Partha Nath (2007), "Participatory Democratisation: Panchayati Raj and the Deepening of Democracy", *ISS Occasional Paper Series 34*, New Delhi, Institute of Social Sciences.

5

Democratic Decentralisation and Good Governance : The Challenge before the Social Scientists

GEORGE MATHEW

It goes without saying that we badly need good governance and one of the main reasons for this deficit is the lack of democratic decentralisation. And, the democratic decentralisation can be achieved only through the empowerment of people. In this context, I must draw the highlight from the contribution of S.K. Dey, the founder of Nilokheri and the Chief Architect of the Panchayati Raj as the First Union Minister for Community Development, Panchayati Raj and Cooperation from 1956 to 1966. He had rightly emphasized that unless we give power to the people, this country will not survive. It was he who impressed upon, the First Prime Minister of India, Jawaharlal Nehru, to implement the scheme of democratic decentralisation, christened by Nehru as Panchayati Raj, for the success of Community Development Programme.

S.K. Dey considered the Panchayati Raj as one of the three pillars of Indian democracy. The other two being the Community Development and Cooperative Movement. But, unfortunately, as S.K. Dey had perceptively apprehended, the Panchayati Raj was weakened in the post-Nehru era due to the logic and style adopted by his successors towards centralisation and de-politicisation of grassroots democracy. This culminated in the concentration of all the powers in Prime Minister's Office (PMO) which ultimately led to the imposition of Emergency in 1975. But people defeated the forces of authoritarianism in the 1977 parliamentary elections. The victory of the Janata Party was, indeed, a victory of the people in the true sense of the term.

It was earnestly hoped that the Janata Party led government in the centre would revive the defunct system of Panchayati Raj. Of-course, it did appoint the High Powered Committee on Panchayati Raj chaired by Ashoka Mehta which made landmark recommendations. But these recommendations could not be implemented due to the political instability during the Janata regime and acute factionalism among its constituents having divergent ideologies and conflicting support bases. Afterwards, it was not implemented at the national level owing to the lack of faith in democratic decentralisation in the Congress (I) government led by Indira Gandhi that came to power after the 1980 parliamentary elections.

But the states like West Bengal, Kerala and Andhra Pradesh took the idea of decentralisation forward. The credit for this primarily goes to Jyoti Basu, the then Chief Minister of the Left Front Government in West Bengal, who not only brought about the much needed land reforms that were needed for the success of democratic decentralisation but also created a system of Panchayati Raj in which there was, to a great extent, genuine devolution of powers. It is this factor that has enabled the Left Front to retain power in West Bengal since 1977.

With the advent of the Janata Party government led by Rama Krishna Hegde in Karnataka in 1983 and Abdul Nazir Sab as Panchayat and Rural Development Minister, their conviction and action made the Panchayats and decentralisation, a central issue not only in the state but all over the country. They established the system of Panchayati Raj in Karnataka which became a model for other states as well. The Chief Minister of Andhra Pradesh N.T. Rama Rao also followed the neighbouring state's pioneering action with the slogan, 'taking the government to the doorstep of the people'.

We must also recognize the contributions of Nirmal Mukherjee, Upendra Baxi, L.C. Jain and others who kept on actively championing the cause of Panchayati Raj. They were, indeed, great champions of the democratic decentralisation and empowerment of people. They were convinced that these were essential ingredients for good governance. It may be mentioned here that because of the intellectual climate they and others created through constant debate, discussion and advocacy, Rajiv Gandhi, the then Prime Minister of India who had succeeded Indira Gandhi after her assassination in 1984, and has received an unprecedented mandate in the 1989 parliamentary elections worked hard to introduce the 64th Constitution Amendment Bill in 1989 in the Lok Sabha to give constitutional status to the Panchayats. It was indeed a historical move. But many critics perceived it as a device for strengthening the support base of the Congress and for reducing the autonomy of the states. Therefore, the Amendment could be enacted only in 1992 after a considerable thinking, working and reworking of the 64th Amendment Bill. The conviction of those who advocated .for the constitutional status to the Panchayats was that they must become institutions of local government which are inclusive by giving reservations to women, Scheduled Castes/Scheduled Tribes and have functional and financial autonomy. The Eleventh Schedule in the Constitution, the provision for the appointment of State Election Commission and State Finance Commission and so on, need special mention here as they were necessary steps to make the Panchayats the third stratum of our federal system.

But where do we stand after 17 years of the enactment of the 73rd Amendment and 15 years after its implementation by the states through conformity legislations? The democratic decentralisation remains elusive because of the reluctance of the political leadership and bureaucracy to devolve powers on the PRIs. In some states, decentralisation of power has resulted in decentralisation of corruption because the checks and balances system is not effective and the social audit mechanism remains weak.

The Right to Information (RTI) regime, which is a welcome step, was the logical outcome of Aruna Roy-led campaign of MKSS against the corruption in the Panchayats of Rajasthan and her innovative *Jan Sunvai* (public hearing) programme. The r ovement for Right to Information is making strides but it is yet to strike roots in all parts of the country. There is an enormous resistance to it because of the culture of secrecy that continues to prevail due to the persistence of colonial mindset of the bureaucracy.

As is well known, the problem of corruption is not confined to the Panchayats. Its tentacles are spread from top to bottom in all the institutions of Indian polity. Even the judiciary is not free from it. The Panchayats cannot be the islands of good governance, in all its aspects, in an ocean of corruption. The elected Panchayat members and Sarpanches have role models at higher levels and what is it that they can emulate from them? Therefore, the corruption as a whole needs to be tackled on a war footing and the role of civil society in this respect is really enormous.

Despite the rapid economic growth that India has made during the past two decades or so, the good governance remains a mirage. The hunger index is rising in our country because we are far away from good governance. We have not been able to imbibe the basic requisites of good governance—accountability, transparency, inclusion and equity—in our system of governance.

The fact that we do not have good governance is evident from the escalation of the Naxalite movement. It has spread over more than one-third districts of India. The Prime Minister, Manmohan Singh, has described it as the greatest threat to the stability of the country. The root causes behind this menace are the widespread poverty, displacement and deprivation from which the tribal population has come to suffer due to our faulty and pro-rich development policies.

The challenges to good governance are going to increase in the near future in India due to the fall out of the economic depression which has started from USA and has begun to affect the entire world by now. It has also begun to affect our country as well due to the processes of liberalisation, privatisation and globalisation that we have been following since 1991 after adopting the New Economic Policy.

This leads us to the question as to what can be done for promoting the democratic decentralisation and good governance.

The most urgent task before the academic community is to strengthen the knowledge base. We have a great potential for it because we are a nation with many unique features. We have to create more knowledge centres of excellence. All the disciplines of social sciences-Economics, Sociology, Political Science, Anthropology, Public Administration, History, Psychology, Gender Studies and so on-will have to come together for this purpose instead of working under water-tight compartments. The Social Science stream could be strengthened only by an inter-disciplinary approach weaving many aspects of different disciplines to understand our complex social, political, economic and cultural problems. When we create a knowledge base, good governance, democratic decentralisation and all the related issues we were deliberating upon from time to time become much easier to comprehend and to implement at various levels through the formulation of appropriate strategies. Lack of such knowledge base and the consequent deficit in awareness building is the root cause of present pathetic condition in the implementation of the 73rd Constitution Amendment in many states. Good governance is not a stand alone matter. Its roots and base begin from local governance.

The university and college teachers of all the disciplines can play an important role in this process. If they can inculcate in their students the values of democratic decentralisation and good governance, they will become important stakeholders for promoting and strengthening the ideals of good governance and local government in future. This is extremely urgent in the face of the threats democratic decentralisation and good governance is facing from various quarters. The melt down of the India economy as a fall out of the recession at the international level and the escalation of the crises in governance as a rest of mounting inflation had made it all the more important for us to achieve good governance through democratic decentralization. The failure of the monsoons has further added to the problem because the Indian agriculture despite more than six decade of economic development, remains a gamble of monsoons. And, we are going to face the challenges posed by reduced agricultural production on the one hand and the crises in Public Distribution System on the other hand. The herculean task of the implementation of the Right to Food Security can not be performed in all effective manner without good governance in a democratic and decentralisation mode.

PART II

The Special Papers

6

Democratic Decentralisation : The Deficit of Politics

K.B. Saxena

The initiative for democratic decentralisation was taken by the Central government through the 73rd Amendment (1992) to the Constitution for ensuring good governance by making Panchayati Raj Institutions empowered and inclusive. It is, therefore, natural that Panchayati Raj bodies have occupied a large space in the discourse on politics ever since. Notwithstanding a short period of their existence, the functioning of Panchayati Raj institutions has attracted considerable attention from the civil society-researchers, activists, non-governmental organizations and the media. Even the lending institutions—national and international—have, of late, taken note of their existence for exploring ways of involving them in their activities. There is a sustained flow of research on the performance of the PRIs. This is on account of several reasons, one of them being the dedicated centres devoted to this subject in the universities and the research institutions, particularly the centres on women development studies. The studies carried out on the PRIs are permeated with a great deal of empathy for the elected representatives and positive concern for the success of these institutions focusing specifically on the participation of the marginalised sections. Understandably, the presence of women members in these bodies has come in for greater scrutiny than their male counterparts, as reservations for them have been effected for the first time in the organs of power. The research on the PRIs has brought out valuable insights into the individual behaviour, institutional performance and dynamics of rural society and politics. There is also a broad consensus on the range of interventions needed for these institutions to function effectively. One feeling is strikingly evident as one glances through some of this material. The organisational reforms in terms of rationalisation of legal and administrative structures and capacity building of its participants are perceived as the prime movers in the onward path of their progressive empowerment.

The intra-organisational processes and the social, political and economic forces which impinge on their functioning and contribute towards the predicament in which these institutions find themselves placed have, however, not attracted the space they deserve. This paper will try to focus on these to see if some insight can be gained about the future trajectory to be followed for their growth and development.

SOCIAL AND POLITICAL CONTEXT

It goes without saying that the laws and institutions are great catalytic agents of change as they create rights and entitlements on the one hand and space for exercise of power on the other. They are often imbued with a strong intention to shift the existing balance of societal relations to pursue the desired political goals. But such initiatives succeed in realizing their objectives only when the larger social, economic and political context permits them to do. The decision to pursue decentralization contained in the 73rd Amendment to the Constitution has to be evaluated in this perspective. This intervention was made essentially to shift the center of authority for local development, widen the arena of participation in decision-making, and create suitable arrangements for people to manage development in their jurisdiction. Some critics would also like to read in this policy engineering the potential blue print of a much larger political role for the Panchayati Raj bodies, i.e., of promoting equitable social relations. However, this momentous decision has been caught in a vortex of circumstances and forces which have circumscribed the growth path of these institutions in the desired directions. The social, economic and political situation which influences the performance of theses institutions can be explained in terms of four key factors—the globalisation, centralisation, alternative mobilisation and contextual conceptualisaiton. The following analysis would briefly highlight some dimensions relating to these factors.

GLOBALISATION

The neo-liberal transformation of the national economy and its integration with the global economic order, usually termed as globalisation, has produced wide ranging effects on the polity and society. Four dimensions of this impact have a bearing on the initiative for decentralised governance.

CONFLICTING NATURE OF TWO REFORMS

The Constitutional Amendment setting up a third-tier of government was initiated in 1989 and carried out in 1992. This was a major political reform in the country after independence and, in the scale of significance, next to the establishment of a republican polity in the country. Around the same time, the state proceeded with the radical restructuring of the national economy. This was also a reform of equal significance albeit in the economic sphere. The two reforms had a built-in contradiction which lay in the opposite direction of their movements. The decision on the Panchayati Raj signaled a pull towards localisation, the deconcentration and deconstruction of authority as it were whether at the central or at the state level. The economic reforms, on the other hand, conveyed a push towards global integration with increasing concentration of decision-making in the global institutions of governance. The two reforms also had opposite implications for the nature and processes of development. The political reform envisaged that the Panchayati Raj bodies would exercise control over local resources, determine the manner of their use for productive activities and settle the distribution of benefits flowing from them. The economic reform transferred this control over productive resources to the capital—national and international, which determined the pattern of their use for productive activities while the distribution of gains from them were left to the market forces to resolve. For the political reformists, the local people were the prime movers of direction of economic growth while for the economic reformists, it was the capital. The political reform implied that the decision on the use of local resources, nature of economic activities to be pursued, their spread and prioritisation would be taken by the local bodies through a process of democratic consensus. The economic reforms entrusted the decision on the exploitation of natural resources, design of economic activities, their spread and prioritisation to the investing corporate. The democratic decision-making in political reforms inevitably envisaged resolution of competing and often conflicting demands from different social and economic groups. For the corporate decision-making emerging from economic reforms, this was not a consideration to be bothered about. It was solely guided by how its interests would be served and had no concern for the adverse impact on others. Faced with the opposition from certain groups, the corporate agencies would build up alliance with dominant interests to consolidate their position and push forward their project. The decentralised democratic bodies cannot afford to ignore such antagonism to any activity and would attempt to strike a balance among conflicting interests. The two reforms, therefore, do not harmonise with each other and follow different trajectories of their growth. This growth path was determined by their respective strength, the strength of forces backing them and the space they occupied in the political discourse for pursuing their agenda. It is evident that the economic reforms commanded far greater clout since they were supported by the dominant elites, pushed by global interests, backed by media and loomed large on the political landscape. The political reforms were no match to them in comparison since they were not backed by people's political mobilisation, evoked little enthusiasm in the elites, totally ignored by the media and occupied insignificant position in the dominant political discourse. Here lies the constraint in the path of the growth of PRIs. This constraint left a narrow and circumscribed space available to them to respond to the pressing needs and growing aspirations of their constituents. This is because they have no role in influencing the nature of economic activities to be pursued and the pattern of social development to be undertaken in their area. The decisions on economic activities are taken by national and global capital while those on social development are influenced by the dominant elites and, in many cases, by global pressures. On the other hand, these bodies have to face the negative fall out of these decisions which have unleashed unprecedented disparities and contributed to the deterioration in the conditions of the poor, particularly the socially marginalised sections. They have little maneuverability to intervene and provide the kind of relief and help which the affected people seek to cope with their adversity. When these institutions resist such activities or seek ameliorative interventions to neutralise their unfavourable impact, they are confronted with strong opposition from the project agencies, elites, as well as the state. As a result, they lose the *raison dêtre* of their relevance. The economic reforms have, therefore, frustrated political reforms. The timing of the political reforms could not have been more inappropriate.

RESOURCES FOR DEVELOPMENT

The conflicting nature of the two reforms had other implications as well. The most significant in this context, is that the development paradigm emerging from economic reforms moved away from an essentially state-financed and supported development efforts and shifted to a primarily market-driven development largely financed by the private capital national as well as international. This further limits the capacity of the Panchayati Raj Institutions to pursue a local development agenda focusing on improving the quality of life of the people in their jurisdiction. The institutional engineering in political reforms essentially envisaged development activities to be taken up with devolution of funds from the central and state projects, transfer of funds from the pool of state resources as a result of the award of the Finance Commission besides, of course, what the PRIs could mobilise by way of taxation or people's voluntary contribution. In the existing development model financed by the private capital, these institutions have no competence, capacity or leverage to attract such investment. They also have a very limited potential to levy taxes for mobilising internal resources. In so far as, bank finance is concerned, the PRIs are dependent upon the state governments to underwrite the loan advanced to them and to guarantee its payment which the state governments are reluctant to do. They also do not have any control over local resources like land, forests, water and sub-soil resources and little autonomy to decide on their use to attract private capital. In this respect, perhaps, the initiative for political decentralisation may have done better if it had been carried out in the early years of independence when it could strengthen the capacity of local institutions through transfer of funds from the state-financed development activities. The capital, in any case, is motivated by the desire to seek the best advantage in terms of returns accruing from investment. The rural areas, by and large, may fail to satisfy this requirement for the kind of development which people seek. These areas lack requisite facilities and infrastructure and the people do not have the capacity to pay for the services. The PRIs are, therefore, confined to a passive role, i.e., the implementation of the central and state programmes whose structures and components are settled at higher levels and on which they have little autonomy to alter as per the needs of their constituents.

HELPLESSNESS OF PANCHAYATS

The other and the more fundamental implication of globalisation for the PRIs relates to their inability to address the most critical problems of their constituents within the subjects transferred to them. One example may suffice to highlight this powerlessness. In the rural areas, agriculture is the most important economic activity which defines the livelihood pattern of a very large section of the people. One of the pressing problems faced by the farmers is the impact of globalisation on Indian economy on their incomes and livelihoods. Lower remunerative prices for agricultural commodities due to drastic fall in prices in the international market, loss of domestic market for their produce due to competition from cheaper commodities resulting from a liberalised trade regime, declining livelihood opportunities and depreciating wages caused by the movement of low paid migrant labour into the area already suffering from surplus labour are the kind of problems which are beyond the competence of the PRIs. They can do precious little by way of market stabilisation of commodities produced in their area, remunerative pricing to farmers for their produce, regulation of cost of inputs for farming, livelihood security of workers etc. in an increasingly open economy with free flow of goods and services and fluctuating demand of commodities. The PRIs cannot even sustain and protect the existing level of economic activities in their areas much less to expand them to provide livelihood opportunities. There are similar constraints in respect of social sector interventions with decelerating state funding in most of them. The enlarging area of private sector provisioning in these sectors implies that even social services are beyond their capacity to regulate when the poorer sections get excluded from their benefits due to lack of purchasing power. This powerlessness leads to indifference of the people to these decentralised rural governance institutions and their consequent alienation from them.

LIMITED AMBIT OF INTEREST

The impact of globalisation can also be seen in the attitude and behaviour of the elected members of the PRIs towards different sectors of development as reflected in their preference for some and indifference to others. The studies have brought out that the village/block Panchayats show little interest in social sector programmes such as education and health while their attention is primarily focused on infrastructure oriented activities such as roads, bridges, buildings and other social facilities such as transport, drinking water etc. The cynics attribute this behaviour to the rent seeking motive of the decision-makers. This may not be a balanced appreciation of their motive. The interest of the elected Panchayat members in the choice of activities is more likely to be determined by the desire to create a visible impact on their constituents so as to sustain their support. In their perception, the construction of infrastructure or a facility satisfies this norm while the activities in social sectors do not. The explanation for this distorted view does not lie in the intrinsic inability of social sector activities to provide visible benefits to the people. It is related to the inability of the elected representatives of the PRIs to influence decisions in respect of them as per the needs of the constituents. The social sector, in fact, can contribute to greater and longer lasting benefits for the people than the infrastructure oriented activities are supposed to do. This, however, does not happen because of two reasons. One relates to the structures of management of many central and state sector programmes in social sectors, particularly those externally funded (more often those financed by the World Bank) which completely bypass the Panchayati Raj Institutions despite the subject falling within the jurisdiction assigned to them. This is on account of insistence of the financing agencies to set-up separate and vertical management structures at various levels consisting of the bureaucrats and experts which has not been resisted by the central and the state governments. The other is rooted in the absence of control over service providers, lack of autonomy in deployment of resources and want of authority to alter schemes and programmes to improve services and enhance access of people to them. Health sector provides a typical example in this respect. But the argument holds good for other sectors as well.

CENTRALISATION

Decision-making Process

The second key factor which constraints the growth and vitality of the PRIs is located in the historical legacy of centralisation in our policy and governance. The centralisation has been an overarching trend in the polity since independence despite a federal constitutional scheme, diversity of cultural groups and assertive provinces. This is manifested in different ways. These aspects of centralisation must be discussed with reference to their impact on the decentralised rural governance.

Centralisation, like globalisation, has several dimensions. One of them relates to the motive behind this historic decision to set up local governing institutions. The timing of this initiative has a bearing on how solid a foundation has been laid for the new institutions. The political history of independent India, short though it is, strikingly brings out that some of the most radical public policy interventions have been pushed at a time when the ruling political leadership of the country was faced with a national crisis or a threat to the survival of its government and, therefore, was motivated by the desire to consolidate its position by widening the social base of support through mobilisation of the masses. This happened, for example, in respect of the decision on agrarian reforms and green revolution during the period of Pandit Jawaharlal Nehru; nationalisation of banks, abolition of privy purses and 'garibi hatao' movement during the period of Indira Gandhi; extending the ambit of reservations in public services to the backward classes during the tenure of V.P. Singh and constitutional amendment for empowering Panchayati Raj Institutions during the period of Rajiv Gandhi which fructified during the tenure of P.V. Narasimha Rao. In all these interventions, there was a distinct attempt to appeal to the larger segments of the people beyond the confines of institutional politics. While not questioning the genuine commitment of the concerned leadership towards the policy decisions taken, their timing throws light on the motives in taking these initiatives and the approaches crafted to give effect to them. In the case of the initiative taken on the PRIs, the purpose obviously was to attract people to the idea of their direct participation in decision-making on development and to garner support across the political, social and territorial divide for the ruling party. This is nothing unusual in politics. But the approach to this move reflected a directional thrust not necessarily conducive to creating firm roots for the PRIs. The distinguishing features of this approach lay in the 'top down' character of the initiative—a kind of benevolent concession from the leader to the masses. The approach represents an element of patronisation and condense-nation. It was and still continues to be a politico-bureaucratically engineered arrangement and does not represent the outcome of a grassroot-level political movement or a demand emerging from organised struggle of the people or advocacy of the interested social groups. In this respect, this decision shared the historical legacy of the colonial rule when the limited local self-governance was introduced to get over the financial crisis faced by the British Government by letting the local bodies to raise funds for local development sought by the national leaders. But the proposal was packaged as an opportunity to provide political education and experience to the natives for managing their affairs. The intervention to provide local self-governance, therefore, essentially constituted an 'organisational' initiative (coming from the existing government), rather than a 'political' thrust emanating from the processes of politics. This trend continued to this day. It also represented the 'top down' direction of the enterprise rather than the result of pressures generated from below through political and social mobilisation or evolution of a consensus among the political parties or groups in the civil society. The timing of this initiative did not relate either to any widespread demand in its favour across the country or a radical vision of decentralised polity articulated by organised interest groups although the subject had been under consideration for a long time and the reports of committees set up by the central government on the subject had been gathering dust without any forward move. This, incidentally, explains why the PRIs have not acquired an autonomous momentum towards a vision of their empowerment and a distinct identity in politics. They are still anchored to and dependent upon the 'top down' periodical interventions even to sustain the existing level of devolution of authority. The point being made here is not that this and subsequent initiatives for strengthening the PRIs hurt the political objective of local self-governance but only to emphasise the absence of a collective expression of intent of people at the grassroot level leading to its demand. The PRIs are, therefore, handicapped by the absence of an autonomously constructed vision of participatory self-governance rooted in the social experience and consciousness of the people which is manifested in their inability to chart out their own growth path.

PATTERN OF GOVERNANCE

The other aspect of the historical legacy of centralisation is the structure of governance inherited by us. We learn from some works of history that the village constituted an autonomous structure of political authority in ancient India which exercised executive and judicial powers besides being a social organisation and a collective entity consisting of all members residing in its domain. This arrangement was given the nomenclature of 'Village Republics' by some colonial historians though contested by others. The functions discharged by this authority included adjudication on civil disputes, matters relating to rights in land, management of common property resources, collection of taxes from agricultural produce to be paid to the government of the day. On the political front, it took decisions on the relationship with the rulers. This village authority existed in addition to the caste panchayats whose jurisdiction was restricted to dealing with social customs such as Jajmani relationship, marriage, rituals and other forms of social intercourse. The relationship of this village organisation with the central authority must have revolved around issues of security against external threats, taxation and upholding of social order. The institutional arrangements may have varied from one period to another and from one region to another. But there is no serious contest on the extent of autonomy enjoyed by the village organization in respect of the village level governance. Some change came about in this arrangement with the land revenue system introduced by Sher Shah Suri. This change was strengthened during the Mughal period which put in place a more elaborate administrative machinery with a hierarchy of officials functioning as revenue collectors. But it was during the period of colonial rule that we see a more drastic shift in the traditional pattern of governance. The village panchayats were deprived of their role as institutions of dispensing justice with the enactment of criminal and civil laws—IPC, CRPC and CPC and setting up of professional courts assisted by advocates credited with the knowledge of these laws. Baden Powel's scheme of land revenue settlement replaced the customary arrangement and introduced individualisation of landholding in the agrarian structure against the village-based mahalwari system. A centralised administration of the country with district as the focal point of authority was put in place for handling revenue and judicial powers which got fully crystallised with the assumption of power by the crown after 1857. These changes in governance produced centralised and verticalised hierarchical structures in the administration of the country most of which exist even today without any radical alteration. This pattern of governance is so deeply institutionalised and so firmly embedded in the psyche of those in authority that it has developed resilience to change. It has even acquired a degree of autonomy from the institutional arrangements introduced for limiting its power and enforcing its accountability after independence when democratic institutions came into being to exercise formal political control over it. The elected representatives in the early years were very critical of the autonomy and power enjoyed by the bureaucracy despite its subordinate position in the institutional arrangements. Though this problem has ceased now and the bureaucracy, by and large, has become more responsive to the members of the state and central legislature, the problem continues to be experienced in relation to the elected representatives of the PRIs. This is because the cadres of various officials which provide services at various levels in the jurisdiction of the PRIs are managed by the state governments which also exercise control over them. These officials resist any change to transfer this control to the Panchayati Raj institutions. The problem involved here is not merely that of delegating sufficient power and authority to the PRIs but a more fundamental one, that is, to radically change the existing organisational arrangement of the bureaucracy serving in the rural areas. This change would involve restructuring of recruitment, placement, discipline, control and other aspects of the management of different cadres with a view to transferring this responsibility to the appropriate level of the PRIs–virtually a very major surgery of the apparatus. State governments have not shown any inclination to effect this change.

PLANNING PROCESS

The distinct tilt towards centralisation is also reflected in the constitutional scheme as well as the processes of politics and development. Despite the provision of a federal polity with separate jurisdictions for the central and state governments in the Constitution, federalism has been under strain from the beginning. The jurisdiction of states has often been encroached upon and the central sphere of powers expanded under various pretexts whether of security, development or environment. The structures and processes of politics have also emulated this arrangement. The political parties in the country display extremely centralised structures with little genuine autonomy for units at state level and below. From ticket distribution to formation of the government and discipline and control over the members, the final decision-making lies with the central authority of the party. This is so deeply ingrained in the political culture that the local political leaders lack both the confidence and courage to assert and look up to the High Command of the party for resolving local level problems.

The maintenance of law and order is the responsibility of the states. But the central government has encroached upon this jurisdiction through deployment of central security forces and, lately, through a central investigation agency for terror-related cases. The central government's legislation on forest conservation is an example of how the ambit of central list has been enlarged on grounds of environmental conservation. In the field of 'development', centralisation penetrated the state domain through the process of planning. The centralized planning apparatus, although without any constitutional and statutory sanction, settles not merely the broad direction of the economy but also the growth of various sectors many of which fall in the state list. The process is facilitated by the control which the central government exercises over distribution of development funds. This trend has been further strengthened by a large number of the centrally sponsored schemes in respect of subjects which fall in the state list. This leaves limited untied funds available to the states for development interventions of their own choice. The state governments follow the central directions to prepare their state level plans. The globalisation of economy has reinforced and even intensified this arrangement. The state governments are further weakened from charting out their own growth path because in the existing political economy, even the national government's autonomy to design development as per the needs of the people has been highly circumscribed due to the pressures from global institutions and interests. What is significant to note here is that in the earlier decades of independence, there were distinct signs of assertion by the state governments against the growing centralising tendencies which led to the review of centre-state relations by the commissions of enquiry (Sarkaria Commission for example). This protest has virtually faded away now and the state governments are meekly submitting to the central directions. Many state governments do not even favour dismantling of the centrally sponsored schemes which they used to do earlier. They have grown so dependent upon the Central government for transfer of resources that the assertion of autonomy does not constitute a major agenda of political discourse. The externally aided projects which now constitute a major source of funding for development programmes have only added to this centralising process. The fragility of state governments in resisting this trend is nowhere reflected more glaringly than in the meek acceptance of the management structures introduced in externally aided projects. These projects have laid parallel institutional arrangements for implementation at all levels bypassing the existing institutional arrangements at the state, district and block levels and even the PRIs which have been meekly accepted and operationalised by the state governments so as not to lose access to external finance.

CONSOLIDATION OF HIGHER LEVEL POLITICAL ORGANS

The other dimension of centralisation is related to the late entry of the Panchayati Raj institutions in the arena of governance by almost four decades. During this period, the higher level organs of governance have had the opportunity to consolidate their position and, therefore, to acquire the strength and primacy in the political process. The state and the central governments have had the advantage of distinct jurisdiction demarcated in the Constitution and the autonomy bestowed on their organs to function within these allocated areas. The Panchayati Raj Institutions have suffered on both these counts. Though they have been brought into existence by the same Constitution, they do not have the advantage of a neatly demarcated jurisdiction and a clearly defined autonomy—the Weberian legal rationality—in terms of structures and processes which have been carved out for the other two levels. The result is that even in matters broadly falling in the jurisdiction of the Panchayati Raj Institutions, they have to contend with the more crystallized powers of the organs at the higher level and find it difficult to compete with them or resist their encroachment into their sphere and other mechanisms of control. Much worse, in the existing scheme of constitutional engineering, the PRIs are dependent upon the very same organs of state legislature and executive to empower them and sustain their autonomy. This creates an obvious clash of interests represented by the unequal power relations between the organs at two levels. The state level organs they are pitted against are in a much stronger position whatever may have been the intention behind the constitutional amendments. The PRIs as decentralised institutions of governance do not have a comparable neatness of jurisdiction and the areas of operation in which they can exercise exclusive powers. Only the broad subjects to be transferred are indicated in a separate schedule. The extent of transfer of work relating to these subjects has to be demarcated by the state level institutions. The conflicting signals, therefore, emerge from the ways in which the state level governance structures get patronised at the cost of the PRIs. One obvious example is to be found in the huge funds allocated to the MPs and state legislators, called the 'Area Development Fund'. The money is to be spent by them in their constituencies/specific areas as per their individual choices. This arrangement came into existence after the enactment of the 73rd Constitutional Amendment and has been continued and even strengthened despite the fact that the activities undertaken through these funds, by and large, fall in the jurisdiction of the Panchayati Raj Institutions. These institutions are also nowhere in the loop in the decision making on how this money is to be spent. They are not even consulted, let alone having a voice in its utilisation. The MPs and the MLAs of the ruling parties and coalitions in the states are also in a position to influence the transfer and posting of officials who work in the jurisdiction of the PRIs but the latter are not even consulted in the matter. In respect of the location of development projects, they exercise a significant and, at times, decisive influence. Many a time the state legislatures have passed resolutions or state governments have issued directions that the local implementing agencies should consult their concerned MLA in such matters as installing a hand pump or locating an irrigation project or a public facility in a village falling in his constituency—a decision which should essentially rest with the local Panchayat. The MPs and the MLAs have been empowered through the directives issued by the central/state governments to attend meetings of the PRIs even though they are not the elected members of these bodies. But the office-bearers of the PRIs have no such privilege in respect of higher level legislative organs. Studies have brought out that the elected members of the Panchayat feel overawed by the presence of MPs and MLAs when they attend such meetings. The decisions taken in such meetings would, obviously, be influenced by their presence. Besides, encroachments have also been made into the decision-making powers of the PRIs by them by taking advantage of their influence in the central and the state level governance structures. For example, it has been observed that the MPs in the Consultative Committee of the Parliament, attached to the Ministry of Rural Development, have insisted on issuance of directives to the DRDAs (District Rural Development Agency) that they should be consulted in the implementation of various development programmes initiated by the central government in their jurisdiction and should be invited to all crucial meetings in this regard. A number of MPs have demanded that the beneficiary selection for these programmes be done with their consent. Similar demands have been made by the MLAs. They do not hide their hostility to the powers conferred on the PRIs which, in their view, make them irrelevant. There has been no strong resistance to such demands by the central and the state governments. This consolidation of power by the central and state organs has shown no perceptible dilution or decline and runs counter to the ethos of the constitutional amendment concerning the PRIs. More important, the existing political processes have also failed to neutralise this trend or to resolve it in the spirit of what has been termed as 'Cooperative Federalism'. Though some tension also prevails between the central and the state governance structures, these are not of the same order and intensity as exist between the PRIs and the central/state institutions. This is entirely because the Constitution has provided a distinct and exclusive jurisdiction to the central and state governments which the sphere of activities earmarked for the PRIs cannot match. This has permitted consolidation of power in the higher level representative bodies.

PARALLEL INSTITUTIONAL ARRANGEMENTS

The initiative for decentralised rural governance is facing even greater strain on account of other modes of centralisation which provide contradictory signals about the sincerity of the Government to empower the PRIs. This is reflected in the emergence and growth of several institutions parallel to the Panchayati Raj bodies which are not merely officially recognised but also empowered through legal sanction and transfer of resources. Thus, on the one hand, there is an expression of political commitment to the decentralisation of rural governance for development and participation and, therefore, of strengthening the structures and institutions of the PRIs for this purpose. On the other hand, through these parallel institutional arrangements, an implicit distrust is conveyed about the capacity of these institutions to meet the requirements for achieving this objective. The parallel institutions, which include the Users' Associations, NGOs, Community-based Organizations, Self-Help Groups, Public-Private Partnerships, Registered Societies, Project Development Authorities and the Special Purpose Vehicles (SPV), are mushrooming all over the country. The DRDA is a classic example of how the Ministry of Rural Development which fathered the initiative for decentralised rural governance and enacted the constitutional amendment concerning the PRIs has itself neutralised them through such parallel arrangements. These institutions are taking up programmes of and drawing resources from the central and state government—precisely in areas which constitutionally belong to the domain of the PRIs. What is striking is that these arrangements have come into existence not clandestinely but very openly and assertively and, in some cases, even by law. Still worse, none of these institutions have been brought under the control of the PRIs which are the only legitimate political institutions at the local level constitutionally entitled to demand accountability from them. These arrangements have also received immense encouragement from the international financial institutions, mainly the World Bank which supports and promotes them in projects financed by it. It is not surprising, therefore, that the NGOs aggressively demand that they be directly dealt with and funded by the central government and resist being brought under any structural control of or accountability to the concerned state government not to speak of the Panchayati Raj Institutions.

ALTERNATIVE MOBILISATION

The Radical Movements

One aspect of the institutional legacy we have inherited relates to the agrarian and social structures and power relations reflecting them that have survived from the colonial times and could not be altered by the reforms undertaken since independence. The social relations, therefore, are sharply characterised by domination of a few caste and class-based nexus and exploitation of a large section of people have been excluded from the benefits of democracy as well as development. It was expected that the PRIs as institutions of decentralised rural governance would help in loosening these relations and facilitate participation of the marginalised sections excluded by caste, class and gender. This does not seem to have been realised. The mere reservation of seats for SCs, STs and women in the PRIs is insufficient for ensuring genuine participation of these sections unless factors responsible for their exclusion such as livelihood insecurity, lack of access to productive resources, social discrimination and subjugation, dependence on their exploiters for survival and atrocities committed on them are eliminated. These sections continue to be alienated from the existing institutions of governance as well as processes of political participation. The unequal power relation makes institutional democracy whether at the national, provincial or local level meaningless for them. In fact, the nature of politics over the years has increased their alienation from its institutions and processes. This vacuum is finding an expression in radical movements (called by different names) in many parts of the country, particularly central India, the north-eastern region and some of the border state. These movements are challenging all that is represented by politics and its institutional arrangements including electoral democracy. More important, they are also contesting the whole 'paradigm of development' which ignores their concerns, impoverishes them and unleashes forces which have the effect of destroying even their identity and dignity. They are, therefore, struggling for a more inclusive ideology of democracy, development and governance. In pursuance of this inclusive vision, they are boycotting elections and refusing to allow state structures of governance and development to operate in areas under their influence. The movements operating in these areas have replaced the state structures of governance with *de-facto* alternative arrangements as well. Even state monopoly of use of coercive power has been challenged by resort to counter violence. The Panchayati Raj Institutions in these areas face even greater stress when compared to the other parts of country since their legitimacy itself is not recognised. The decentralised model of rural governance and participation represented by the PRIs does not conform to the vision of democracy nurtured by these movements and would, therefore, be confronted with the same degree of passivity which the other structures of state power face. Sufficient information is not available on how the PRIs relate themselves to these movements whether the PRIs in such areas represent a social reality different from the one observed in the other areas. In short, their impact on the structure and processes of the PRIs is not known. But this is the most challenging area of exploration as these movements claim to have accomplished in their own way much of what the PRIs were expected to do in terms of loosening the structures of exclusion, discrimination, domination, exploitation, and could provide a lead in designing a different model of decentralised rural governance, development and participation. The political discourse on the PRIs has not taken note of this experience which goes beyond the trajectory of organisational reform and capacity building.

CONTEXTUAL CONCEPTUALISATION

Multiplicity of Visions

Another facet of the crisis with which Panchayati Raj Institutions are faced concerns the varying visions of their role and expectations from them in terms of what they should deliver. These visions perceive the Panchayati Raj Institutions as structures of self-governance, decentralized development and planning, arena for deepening democracy and increasing participation and as instruments of social transformation, all at the same time. The conceptual framework of the Panchayati Raj Institutions and structures created to operationalise them do not lend sufficient clarity on which of these visions conform to the intentions of the law-makers. The official statements and declarations tend to use these varying visions interchangeably as if there are no distinct meanings attached to them and each one of them is inclusive of what is represented by others. The prerequisites which are needed to discharge a role conforming to each of these visions are also not the same. This deficit of clarity also influences varying expectations. These expectations range from more efficient and effective delivery of programmes designed by the central and state governments, local level planning and resource management, collective decision-making for harmonised and inclusive resolution of local problems, to loosening structures of dominance and exploitation for ensuring social justice. In this context, the backdrop to the initiative for decentralised rural governance may be recalled in the famous statement of the then Prime Minister, Rajiv Gandhi (though officially denied later) that hardly 15 paisa worth of benefits out of a rupee reach the people from various development programmes. The government at all levels repeatedly faces complaints of poor delivery of services due to the bureaucratic indifference, unresponsiveness and corruption. The expectation in the official discourse, therefore, is focused on the efficient execution of the central/state development programmes and delivery of the desired benefits to their target groups to check the growing cynicism among people and their alienation from the government. This expectation does not in any way signal self-governance as the goal though the PRIs may have been conceived as institutions of self-governance in Article 40 of the Constitution. The latter goal would require decisions about what is to be delivered to be taken by these institutions and not by other political formations and other forms of autonomy. This, in turn, would demand restructuring of these institutions in terms of powers and resources to discharge this role and would also imply shedding of considerable powers and control over decision-making and resources by higher level organs of governance. There is no indication that this seems to be the intent. Self-governance from the point of view of the government, central or state, merely implies transfer of programme management to these institutions on the basis of design, structures, and norms laid down by the higher level formations. But the central and state governments also advocate local level planning and encourage the Panchayati Raj Institutions to prepare plans for their area based on the needs articulated by their constituents, taking into account resources available to them or which can be mobilised. This is apparently done so that the concerns of the local people are reflected in central and state plans. As per this understanding, the plans prepared by the PRIs would constitute a chain in the hierarchy of the planning process culminating in the finalisation of the National Plan. But this rhetoric is not matched by supportive arrangements such as control over local resources, sufficient untied funds, autonomy to reject schemes and programmes imposed from the above, etc. More important, the planning process has not changed a bit from its top-down direction and resource driven orientation since inception. The local level planning by the PRIs is, therefore, unachievable unless radical changes are introduced in the existing structure and processes of planning besides effecting corresponding empowerment of the PRIs.

Similarly, the objective of deepening democracy and widening of participation cannot be met unless the PRIs have the capacity and strength to remove social exclusion. Across the country, there is a very low level of participation by the poorer and marginalised sections in the Gram Sabha. The agrarian and social structures further constrain their spontaneous participation. Even, when people belonging to these sections attend Gram Sabha meetings, they rarely speak their mind due to the fear of facing reprisals. A recent Kerala study brought out that even the rich are indifferent to the processes of rural local governance and do not participate in the activities of the PRIs though for different reasons. There is also a cluttering of multiple structures of participation within the confines of a small democratic space of the PRIs which creates dissatisfaction because there is too little to distribute and benefit from this effort. The participation in the PRIs also creates disappointment, as much of the deliberations therein pertain to the central and state programmes in which they have limited role for taking initiative. Some state governments have sought to remedy this situation by making interventions from the top to facilitate greater participation, particularly of the weaker sections. Besides directions from the state level, capacity building efforts by non-governmental agencies have also sought to neutralise these constraints. These measures may have shown some improvements in the level of participation in individual Panchayats or in some pockets. But, this has not substantively changed the existing problems relating to participation and assertion even in the PRI bodies headed by the members of the social groups empowered with reservation.

The goal of achieving social transformation is even more distant because the PRIs have shown neither the capacity and will to break the structures of domination and exploitation nor placed this item on their agenda. This is, in fact, the toughest task. When even higher organs of political power have failed on this score, it would be unrealistic to expect the

PRIs to show results in this direction. More relevant in this context is the fact that the PRIs do not even have powers in the domain of regulatory governance such as implementation of land reforms, adjudication on complaints relating to the violations of labour laws, protection of people from harassment by police which would have given them some leverage to pursue this task. Even if they do intervene in these matters, the dominant sections may take recourse to legal action and invoke courts' intervention to defeat such an attempt. The PRIs can only proceed through persuasion, social mobilisation and building support for social justice in a large section of the society by isolating the hardcore elements and meticulously using their existing powers to deliver the entitled benefits to the affected sections. There is no indication that this agenda has any space in their scheme of action and order of priorities, if any. This is true even of Kerala where peoples' planning campaign has carried out capacity building on a scale unknown elsewhere and the delegation of powers and resources effected are also of a much higher order.

GROWTH OF THE PRIS : LOCATING THE CONSTRAINTS

Deficit of Politics

How weak is this position of the PRIs and how can their failure to grow into a formidable political force is to be explained? This leads to the central part of the argument. It is not by enacting laws and setting up structures and institutions that people can be motivated to think how they would like to shape their lives and change society around them and accordingly strive to achieve this vision, though admittedly, such interventions may contribute to enhancing their consciousness and efforts in this direction. It is only when people are mobilised collectively to bring about change in the existing situation that such a transformation occurs. The context in which the PRIs as decentralised rural governance institutions were established, reflects the absence of such a collective political mobilisation. What is more surprising is that no such mobilisation has emerged even after these institutions have become functional for more than 15 years. There is no visible urge in them to struggle for resolution of many problems that block their growth and progress not in any organised form, any way. This massive initiative has failed to produce a distinct country-wide movement for assertion of their power in the realm of local self-governance defined in the Constitution. Kerala state may be an exception where the PRIs show a great degree of political vitality and handle close to one-third of the development programmes. These institutions, if sufficiently mobilised, have the potential to constitute such an irresistible force that various political formations would be compelled to come to terms with their demands since they preside over the local political space and continue to be the vital link with the higher organs of power. In the absence of such an assertion, aggressive defence of their jurisdiction and a forceful articulation of their vision, the Panchayati Raj arrangement has remained anchored to and dependent upon the benevolent concessions from the higher organs of power. The PRIs have not been sufficiently internalised in the processes of politics since the issues confronting them do not figure prominently in the agenda of national political parties. The essentially centralised structures of political parties have failed to reflect on the constraints affecting their performance, accommodate their concerns in their manifestoes and prioritise them in the agenda of electoral battle. The political parties do participate in the elections to the PRIs in some states and even where they are disallowed to do so, they sponsor candidates covertly, make vigorous efforts to capture positions in the PRI structures and also use them for consolidating their position in the larger arena of politics. But these democratic bodies are not integral to the preoccupation of national political parties which essentially look up to the state and central structures of governance for satisfaction of their political ambitions. In the highly politically conscious states of Kerala and West Bengal, the bastions of left political parties, and to a lesser extent in Karnataka, where a higher degree of politicisation of these institutions has been achieved, the situation may be different. But in most other states, there is little enthusiasm to take up their agenda and create pressures on the higher level organs for resolution of problems confronting them. Equally, the political parties have not demonstrated a qualitatively better level of governance and social mobilization in the areas where they have captured executive positions in the PRIs. This is an indication that the PRIs, perhaps, do not matter very much beyond a point and certainly do not occupy a central place in the vision and activities of the political leaders and in the growth path of their politics. This outcome can only be attributed to the way these institutions came into existence and have functioned thereafter.

The other implication that emerge from the foregoing, is that though some devolution of powers, authority and resources has taken place, the PRIs have shown no internal momentum to carve out a niche for their activities within the limitations they operate through a process of intensive and widespread social mobilisation. They may not have the powers to create infrastructure, solve livelihood problems and promote access to health and educational facilities outside the domain of central and state schemes. But what cannot be denied to them is the democratic space to mobilise people for a great deal of social transformation which could counteract the exclusion of the marginalised groups, gender discrimination and forces of domination and exploitation. What they still can do within the limits of their powers is to coordinate with different agencies at the local level to benefit weaker segments of the community and pave the way for more equitable political participation which, at present, is severely lacking. But the PRIs have shown no inclination, not to speak of efforts, in this direction. The laws, structures and institutions of the PRIs have, therefore, not been able to neutralise the impact of agrarian and social structure and its distribution of power despite the reservations provided to such groups.

The PRIs have also not been able to show any initiative in taking up activities which do not necessarily depend upon transfer of funds or cooperation of and control over officials. There are areas where the PRIs, by virtue of their status, sheer force of the strength of the people behind them and available powers, can achieve some change for betterment. Such initiatives would have enhanced their powers, increased the ambit of activities and made other organs of power to attach importance to them. The lack of vision to pursue this route to empowerment can also perhaps be attributed to their passive dependence on the bureaucratic-legislative interventions rather than optimal realisation of their internal power and strength.

Why has all this not happened? Why have the laws, structures and institutions not created, even belatedly, a movement for consolidation, assertion and not led to efforts towards innovation and for deepening of democracy in the PRIs? This is because the emergence as well as the evolution of the PRIs as institutions of decentralised rural governance have been constrained by what I would call 'deficit of politics'. The mobilisation of people for any task is essentially a political task and it is much more so when such a major political goal as local self-governance is in the reckoning. The absence of meaningful mobilisation of the people for this purpose is at the very centre of the identity crisis which the PRIs face today. This mobilisation cannot be carried out by the civil society outfits such as the non-governmental organisations and the social activists. It requires that the whole issue of decentralised rural governance should become not only integral but central to the political processes of the country and find a space of priority in the structure and operations of the political parties, their agendas, strategies of political struggles and articulation of paradigms of development. This has been singularly missing notwithstanding the limited interests shown by the political parties in capturing power in the Panchayati Raj Institutions. The vision of decentralised rural governance, whether in terms of widespread participation, equitable distribution of benefits, elimination of social exclusion or consensual development, cannot be achieved without intense political mobilisation. The vision has to be clearly and forcefully articulated and intensively fought for and cannot be obtained through concessions from the higher organs of power. Similarly, the agenda of intra-PRI democracy has to be outlined and vigorously pushed internally against strong resistance of those who preside over the structures of dominance and exploitation. This objective cannot be achieved without a struggle particularly, when even strong laws and coercive power of the state has failed to subdue these structures. Much deeper political involvement is required than what exists today in this respect so that the concerns of decentralised rural governance constitute the focus of advocacy of all political parties. The PRIs would be able to influence their growth path and future only when the competitive politics are forced to internalise the importance of decentralized rural governance for national and state level democracy.

A vigorous political mobilisation alone would extricate the PRIs from the culture of dependence on 'top-down' concessions, remove their inferiority and subordination to higher political formations, generate greater confidence and assertion in them to exercise control over bureaucracy, enable inclusion of their agenda in the national and state political processes, help in pushing through social transformation, relate them more meaningfully to the radical movements alienated by the existing pattern of representative democracy, develop a distinct strategy for checkmating centralisation and, above all, contribute to the designing of approaches to deal with the impact of globalisation.

The advocacy of more politics that is suggested here may come as a surprise or even as shock to many readers. The middle classes and the better-off sections have developed indifference to and even despondency for politics due to the aberrations that are witnessed and reported every now and then in the media. This has taken extreme form of politician-bashing and anti-politics. Understandably, there is a lot that is not very heartening about our politics today but it was not always so and hopefully would not be so for ever. The bad episodes in the current patch of politics are no ground for secession from politics. Rather, it provides a stronger reason for much deeper involvement in it. This is because politics cannot be washed away from any organised society, much less a democratic one. It only has to be reformed through a higher level of consciousness and deeper level of peoples' mobilisation and participation. Wishing away politics also does not make for absence of politics. It only makes room for less accountable and more authoritarian politics. What is, therefore, necessary is to deliberate on how the 'deficit of political mobilisation' for decentralised rural governance, development and participation through the PRIs and removal of deep-rooted political and economic inequalities can be made up so that it becomes integral to state and national level political processes and deepens the democratic ethos. Otherwise, the ideal of good governance through democratic decentralisation would remain a mirage.

7

Good Governance or Self-Governance? Prospects of Economic Revitalization of Panchayats in Post-1991 LPG India

P.C. MATHUR

In this paper we argue that as the 'Services' sector of the Indian economy grows· by leaps and bound and its Industry sector is increasingly becoming globalisation-driven, India's fast-diminishing 'Agriculture' sector would find it increasingly difficult to sustain its 'rurality' as the 21st century advances and 'modernity' extends its urban tentacles into India's half-a-million village communities whose rural future would become uncertain if not becoming a matter of history text-books. The extinction of India's age-old 'reality can, however, be prevented if a systematic effort is blue-printed to usher in what Prof. M.S. Swaminathan calls 'Ever Green Revolution' which would become a reality only if the term 'Institutions of Self-Government' used for the 'Panchayats' in Article 40 as well as Chapter IX becomes a clear policy-goals.

II

As an exercise in 'futurelessness', this paper departs radically from the conventional analyses of prospects of rural development in India which has, in quantitative terms, enjoyed an unprecedented dynamism during the second half of the 20th century, the quantum of growth-rate appearing to be magnified on account of near-stagnation during to first half of the 20th century.

The last 10 to 15 years have, indeed witnessed an impressive economic growth in up scaling India into a emergent economic power-house with a PPP-based GDP rank amongst the top five economies of the world; but this shining economic achievement has virtually bypassed India's agriculture posing many questions about the rural future of India with its vast populous agricultural sector fast approaching a single-digit growth-rate and the size of the agricultural GDP dropping precipitously from over 66% of total GDP to in 1950 to below 20% within 60 years. The travails of Indians agriculture are not only economic but also technological and even cultural as global modernity is making fast inroads into the ancient religious-cultural norms of village traditions which were regulated, mainly, by the daily seasonal, annual and cyclical rhythms of agricultural activities.

While the Planet Earth has been sporting a variety of vegetation for hundreds of million years, agriculture as an organised enterprise for crop husbandry is certainly not more than 8,000 to 10,000 years old, but even in this short span in the total history of human life, it has created a deep imprint in the psychology, sociology and cultural traditions of homo sapiens all over the world. To be sure, this agricultural imprint on human traditions has been overlaid by cultural ideas and ideologies embedded in spirituality and religiosity, an amalgamation which in the case of South Asia has survived major vicissitudes including emergence of fortified as well as unfortified urban centers whose political and economic glories out-shone most contemporaneous cities, the most outstanding example being Patliputra which was, for nearly 800 years the most magnificent city in the world.

Hence, notwithstanding the glitter of urban centers, throughout the entire pre-Gupta history (i.e. before 550 CE), the rurality of culture and civilization ethos of ancient India has been a widely accepted axiom of political life in India which is, more often than not, portrayed, somewhat utopian, as a vast conglomeration of multitudinous small villages inhabited by farming and non-farming people living in interactive harmony and autonomy *vis-à-vis* even such gargantuan political systems as the empire-states of the Mauryans and the Imperial Guptas, not to mention even more ancient times, in which pastoralism was the dominant form of economic systems. Although direct evidence, whether in form of monuments or documents, about the way of life prevalent in such villages is scanty, the utopia of 'village republics' has come to dominate the political and cultural discourse in post-Mughal India specially after several British scholar-administrators heaped a lot of praise on the village life in ancient and medieval India as displaying an extra-ordinary vitality which enabled the Indian villages to cope with scarcities and adversities of diverse origins and dysfunctional ties through the time-honored device of self reliance, self-governance and self-sufficiency.

Over the years, the utopianism of the idea of existence of 'self-sufficiency' prevailing in Indian villages at any point of time in the past two or three millennia has been clearly established, but the ideal of perfect harmony prevailing amongst village communities which were ever-ready to come together and display communitarian interaction has continued to occupy a special place in hagiography of rurality with no less of a person than Mahatmas Gandhi firmly articulating the thesis that India's soul lies in its villages.

This idea had, indeed, gained some academic and intellectual currency during the first quarter of the 20th century and the research studies of scholars like Radhakamal Mukherjee, Radha Kumud Mukherjee and A.S. Alteker had been profusely quoted at the annual and other INC deliberations but while Mahatma Gandhi did not dwell upon the theme of the village communities being the cradle of Indian civilization, he did give instances of the wisdom and virtues of Indian villages in his *Hind Swaraj* in support of his thesis that Indians were fully ready for maintaining consensual and harmonious political order going to the extent of appending a longish quotation from an Englishman (Sir William Wedderburn) to buttress his views and including main *Villages Communities* in an appendix listing 20 books which he 'Recommended for personal study to follow-up the study of the foregoing (text of *Hind Swaraj*)'.

In any case, Gandhi was fully aware of the true state of affairs prevailing in Indian villages of his times and never even tried to rebut the strong anti-village tirade let loose by B. R. Ambedkar in the Constituent Assembly when it was presented with a Gandhian proposal for utilising the village(s) as the building-blocks of architectural design of the constitutional edifice of free India in 1946-49, However nearly one and a half decade later, the proposal was re-articulated by Jayaprakash Narain but even his plea attracted little interest including a rebuttal from a deep scholar of Indian politics, W.H. Morris-Jones, who described it as a case of 'JP in wonder land'. However, while the Gandhian pleas for conferment of constitutional status upon villages (or Village Panchayats) could be ignored by free India's constitution-makers, Mahatma Gandhi's galvanisation of millions of villages men, women and children for anti-British 'freedom struggle' could neither be doubted nor discounted and many Gandhian projects for economic re-construction of Indian villages were grafted into the successive Five Year Plans and other cognate development policies of the Union and State Governments. These plans for enlistment of villages life culminated in Indira Gandhi's 1971 'Quit Poverty' call which resounded in India's half a million villages.

III

Indira Gandhi's spectacular election victory in 1971 Lok Sabha polls elevated 'Rural Development' firmly to the centers-stage of Indian economic development policies. Its earlier overemphasis on mega-projects of industrial capital-formation led to severe droughts in the mid-sixties and the specter of starvation death began to loom large even upon some sections of urban population as the country began to enter a ship-to-mouth scenario of food supplies as far as staple food grain were concerned. A re-prioritization of Plan matrix towards agriculture was thereby generated putting into motion the Green Revolution strategy which quickly defused food shortages at least as far as wheat is concerned. However while the Green Revolution dispelled the clouds of starvation doom, it did little to improve nutrition profile of the Indian people with the village population being too poor to buy the marketed crop like wheat while the output of nutritionally rich Coarse Grains continued to decline and even the per capita consumption of pulses declined steadily.

The Green Revolution of the 60th and 70th thus, not only created nutritional impoverishment for the rural poor all over India but also began to run out of steam as it needed a large basket of techno-economic inputs like fertilizers, irrigation, energy, new varieties of seed and new crop husbandry equipments, e.g. Tractors, threshers and harvesters to mention only a few which only a small section of better-off farmers could afford. Even more important than the issue of the economic affordability of Green Revolution was its low long-term environmental sustainability with large tracts of Panjab and Haryana experiencing rising depletion in crop productivity on account of overdose of irrigation leading to the Green Revolutions farmers to look for others options like horticulture and floriculture which suits MNCs interested in urban retail marketing of such products like cut flowers and potatoes. Further, the Green Revolution in wheat is slowing down, while efforts to replicate it, i.e. the rice-fields have yet to achieve comparable results while the acreage and tonnage of pulses is declining even faster, making food grain agriculture losing momentum in all the Indian villages situated in diverse ecologies. The worst hit is being taken by dry land agriculture whose coarse grains are increasingly yielding place to animal husbandry portfolio of protein-rich products like milk, meat and eggs.

Free India started its economic life with a deep commitment to enhance 'food security' and the Grow More Food campaign took precedence over agricultural reforms except Land Reforms intended to eliminate tenurial insecurity and conferment of ownership rights upon the actual tillers of the land. With all their implementational loop-holes and definitional gaps, Land Reforms generated an unprecedented economic dynamism in the Indian villages but, as stated above, by the mid-sixties the new owner-cultivators of rural India found it difficult to attain new heights of productivity which, by world standards, remains low even 60 years after 1947 although the total tonnage of food grain had raised more with the aggregate increase in acreage being three fold during the last six decades or so. However, the high priority accorded to long-gestations industrial projects since the Second Five Year Plan (1957-62) onwards has obscured the Indians farmers economics performance, the obscurity being augmented by the disparity and credit profile of Indian incomes which has left an overwhelming of majority village population seeking out a living on less than Rs. 40 per day even though overall GDP growth-rates have been sustained at amazingly unprecedented high levels during the first decade of the 21st century.

It is certainly a fact that during the first decade of the 21st century, the Indian economy has clocked a GDP growth-rate of at least 7% to 8% creating the image of India as an emerging economic power-house set to out-rank all but a few countries in the world during the next one or two decades. Concomitant with the containment of high GDP growth-rate, some of India's emergent economic luster has percolated to the Indian villages many of which have obtained better connectivity with the rest of the country via new communication and transport networks but their agricultural economy is still antiquated except for the small number of owner-cultivators operating large-size farms with modern techno-economic inputs like irrigations, HYV seeds, pesticides, tractors, and chemical fertilizers made available by the Union and State Governments at the subsided rates. However, even this tiny section of farming communities is facing economic distress since the adoption of LPG reforms in 1991 with MNCs and other foreign corporate entities scudding in their campaigns for knocking down the tarring, retail Marketing of fresh vegetables by the introduction of Genetically Modified Crops on the one hand and Retail chain marketing of processed food package on the other hand.

IV

Although the Village Panchayats figured several times in the annual AICC sessions of the Indian National Congress frequently during the first half of the 20th century, practically very little was done to institute and vitalise villages-level institutions of local government, let alone conceptualising and institutionalising village level *institutions of self-government*. Even though the term 'institutions of self-government' was inscribed in the Constitution of India, nothing concrete was done to implement the Article 40 for almost a full decade till the Panchayati Raj Institutions (PRIs) were established in most of the states in 1959 following the recommendations of a somewhat obscure Study Team of a Committee of the National Development Council. The PRIs were not given a constitutional status even by referring to Article 40 in the various state legislations on the subject, the PRIs were in fact, treated as developmental rather than constitutional institutions, let alone being regarded as 'institutions of self-government'.

What exactly does the term 'Institutions of Self-Government' (ISGs henceforth), first used in the Article 40 and later incorporated in the 73rd (and 74th) Constitution Amendment Acts, denote? Even though nearly 15 years have passed after the CAA, 1973 coming into force, the answer remains unknown, rather, the question itself remains unasked even though, the terms ISG now occurs many times in the Chapter IX of the Constitution of India. One thing is, however, clear. *Neither the Union Government nor the State Governments are ISGs while the Panchayats (and Nagar palikas) are explicitly stated to be ISGs in Article 243 of the Constitution of India.* No wonder, the tendency persists, the administrative, political and academic communities continue to treat the Panchayats as institutions of local government (ILGs) rather than ISGs (Institutions of Self-Government).

All those familiar with the 19th century controversy over the Indians rejection of 'Good Government' in favour of 'Self-Government' would readily realise the criminality of the difference between ISGS and ISGs, but even if it is agreed that, with the transfer of power to Indian hands on August 14-15, 1947, the issue of self-government is settled, the question that constitutional pundits must answer is: Are the Panchayats and Nagarpalikas constituted under Chapter-IV of the Constitution Institutions of Self-Government? Does it imply that other institutions like the Union and State Governments are not 'Institutions of Self-Government'?

In an attempt to answer these questions, let us refer to Article 1 which describes the Republic of India as a 'Union of States'. However, since 1956 some Unions Territories have also come into existence which are equipped (or can be) equipped with Legislative Assemblies (as well as High Courts) but there is no equivalent provision for legislative or judicial institutions at Panchayat-level some of which are not only far bigger than many which are by virtue of Article-240, subject to the powers of the President to 'regulation for peace, progress and good government'. Is it not ironical that while its UTs (eg. Andaman and Nicobar Island, Dadra and Nagar Haveli, Daman and Diu and Puducherry), UTs are, constitutionally placed under the authority of the President who is empowered to make regulations for : 'good government', the Panchayats (and Nagar Palikas) are described constitutionality, as 'ISGs'. Yet the UTs are regularly placed at a higher pedestal than Panchayats including the Zila Parishad nearly all of which are more populous and have been in the mainstream of administrative and political development advancement. Further some U.Ts. have been upgraded as full-fledged states while even the best administered Zila Parishads with a long history of existence and conferred a constitutional status as of 'Institutions of Self-Government' are routinely considered to be of less importance than the UTs some of which are even equipped with Legislative Assemblies and High Courts.

V

After moving at a slow pace (the GNP growth-rate climbed only to 4% in the eighties from a low base of 1% during the fifties of the 20th century) for 40 years, India's techno-economic establishment had begun to dream about a 10 percent growth for 10 years within two decades after unfurling the flag of LPG reform in 1991, but this dream has come crashing down in 2008 which saw unpredicted rise in oil prices followed by a steep upward climb in inflation topped by indication of U.S. economic melt-down generating recession in the Indian economy which may result in the Indian economy reaching a low water mark of 6 percent growth in 2009. (cf. Pramit

Paul Chaudhuri, 'Losing the Momentum', *Hindustan Times*, December 29, 2008:8).

India's new-found economic momentum is sustained by an unprecedented rise in the Services Sector which has already crossed the 50% mark of India's total GDP with the share of Agriculture dipping below the 20% mark and likely to attain a single-digit sooner than later. In 1951-52 the share of Agriculture Sector in NDP at 1999-2001 prices was 60% but in 2005-06 it only a shade above 20% whilst in 1951-52 the share of Service was just a shade above 20% while in 2005-06 it had crossed 50% mark and most have upped more towards the 60% by 2008-09, as per the following data:

TABLE 1

Growth-rates of GDP by Sector at 1999-2000 Prices

(% per annum)

Sector	*1991-92 to 1996-97*	*1996-97 to 2002-03*	*2002-03 to 2005-06*	*2001-02 to 2005*
Agriculture, forestry and fishing	4.13	1.63	4.70	2.55
Industry	7.95	4.71	8.98	8.46
Services	7.31	7.73	9.32	8.86

Source : Extracted from Surajit Majumdar, "Investment and Growth of India under Liberalization: Asymmetries and Instabilities", *Economic and Political Weekly*, December 6, 2008, 69.

8

Grassroots Governance in Tribal Area of Chhattisgarh

K. Gopal Iyer

This paper seeks to discuss the functioning of grassroots governance in the Naxalite stronghold of Chhattisgarh state. The analysis given in it is based on both the primary and secondary data. The field work was undertaken by a group of academicians including the author, lawyers, social activists and ex-government officials from 18-22 January 2008. The group visited the tribal areas in the districts of Bastar, Dantewada, and Bijapur. The team also met the Governor of Chhattisgarh and the Director General of Police of the state in connection with the prolonged detention of Dr. Binayak Sen.

The paper has been divided into four parts:

1. The status of Naxalite Movement in Chhattisgarh.
2. The role of Gram Sabha in the tribal areas of the state.
3. The report of the Committee of the Government of India on the Working of Gram Sabhas.
4. Concluding observations

I

Chhattisgarh is a tribal state to a great extent. They account for over 30% population of the state and over half of its development blocks fall under Schedule V. It presents a contrast in richness and poverty. Chhattisgarh is rich in natural resources but there prevails large scale impoverishment of its rural masses. The major minerals in the state are Iron Ore, Limestone, Bauxite, Coal etc. Land alienation and displacement in the wake of development projects have been a major problem in the state. The New Industrial Policy of Chhattisgarh has encouraged the setting up of Sponge Iron, Steel, Electricity, and Coal Washing plants. The State Government has signed several MOU's with private corporate industrialists.

During the last over 25 years, the Naxalites led by People's War Group (CPI-Maoist) have established their *sangams* in the tribal districts of Chhattisgarh, particularly in Bastar and Dantewada. The spread of the Naxalite movement is due to the problem of alienation as a result of tribal land acquisition for industries and forceful displacement. The harassment of the tribals, whose source of livelihood has been forest produce, by the Forest Officials on the charge of felling trees or grazing cattle and the violation of the forest rights have also accentuated the process of marginalization of tribals. Their exploitation by the non-tribal traders has been an another reason for it. Between 1980 and 2000 the CPI (Maoist), a Naxalite outfit, had created substantial bases in the forest areas of Bastar, Kanker and Dantewada.

Chhattisgarh happens to be the gateway to Red Corridor of Central India. Since the entry of Maoist in the area during last two and half decades, the harassment by forest officials and exploitation by the traders has been considerably minimized. That is why the tribals have become sympathetic to the Maoists (so called Naxalites). Another contributory factor in this context is the increase in the price of Tendu leaf. It is pertinent to mention that, the CPI (Maoist) had setup bases in the forested areas of Bastar and Dantewada at the time of formation of Chhattisgarh State in 2000.

Though the economic benefits accrued to the tribals are instrumental in getting the tribals' sympathy for the Maoists, but a real appraisal would lie in understanding the core of Maoist political strategies. The first major political achievement of the Maoists is to declare Dantewada as a liberated zone where the administration of Maoists has replaced the Indian state. The new authority of the village administration is the 'Sangham'. Though the Maoists claim Sangham as the self-organization of the people, it is according to Balagopal (December 2006), the organization established by the Maoists. The monopoly of their power is due to the guns of the Maoist armed squads. There is no freedom to setup a rival organization or to practice one's dissent after a decision is taken.

In order to suppress Naxal violence, a tenuous spontaneous movement got initiated under the leadership of Mahendra Karma, MLA of the Congress Party from Dantewada and was given the nomenclature of 'Salwa Judum'. Now it is primarily supported by Chhattisgarh Government which has appointed 5000 Special Police Officers with a monthly payment of Rs. 1500 to each. They include unemployed tribal youth, minor boys and girls, some surrendered Sangam Members and several criminal elements. The Reports on agrarian violence have cited copious instances of arson, looting and killing of civilians particularly the tribals by Salwa Judum and the security forces. During 2006, there were 250 killings due to Police and Salwa Judum encounters. As many as, 500 persons were killed between 2005-07 and 450 villagers were killed between June 2005 to March 2007, apart from the burning of 700 villages (Campaign for Peace and Justice in Chhattisgarh, August 2007). There are also reports of violence against women including gang rapes, custodial rapes and so on. One of the worst impact on the marginalized tribals and Dalits has been that over 47425 persons are now living in 20 Salwa Judum camps in the district of Dantewada. They have been forcefully uprooted from their social and cultural setting by Salwa Judum to eliminate the Naxalites. As a result, the democratic and indigenous tribal institutions are getting decimated. Most camps have an acute shortage of food. There is no access to livelihood, and the basic amenities.

The tribals and the marginalized are sandwiched between the violence perpetrated by CPI—Maoist and Salwa Judum combined with the paramilitary forces. As per the District Collector of Dantewada, the Maoists had killed 253 persons (228 civilians including 12 SPO's, 25 Police and Para Military Personnel) between June 2005 to middle of May 2006 (Human Rights, Forum December 2006).

There have been attempts in the early 90s to counter the Maoists by mobilizing groups from local people which assumed the form of Jan Jagaran Abhiyan. The activity of the Abhiyan included mobilizing villagers, holding public meetings, spreading hatred against the Maoists, attacking persons sympathetic to the Maoists and handing them over to the police. The Maoists killed quite a few of the Jan Jagaran Abhiyan leaders. The second Jan Jagaran Abhiyan was mainly led by Mahendra Karma during 1997-98 from his native village close to Dantewada. The Abhiyan attacked the Maoists in the Bijapur area where about 180 Sangam members were forcibly handed over to the police.

Similar pattern of attacks against Maoist sympathizers have been followed after the genesis of Salwa Judum in 2005. The Maoists had banned tendu leaf picking in Dantewada in 2005 which created dissatisfaction among the tribals against the Maoists as it was a major income earner for them during the lean months of April and May. It was in this background that initial mobilization against Maoists first took place in the villages. Administration soon entered in the fray. The Salwa Judum activity was supported by Chhattisgarh Government and the CRPF and Nagaland Battalion. The Salwa Judum took to various kinds of atrocities such as burning down of houses, hamlets. *Modus operandi* of the Salwa Judum has been that of organizing meeting in villages having Maoist influence. During the course of these houses and cattle pigs were burnt. They were accompanied by Security forces. The tribals who became the major victims of Salwa Judum violence belonged to the following categories.

1. Those who joined the camps willingly.

2. Those who continued to live in their forest habitations out of reach of Salwa Judum.
3. The families who moved into Andhra Pradesh. Their number rose to over 50000 by 2007.
4. The colossal tragedy of displacement and deprivation affected over one lakh families

The official figures substantiated 472,38 persons staying in 20 transit camps. The Salwa Judum is heavily promoted and funded by Government. Printed posters are pinned to trees along the highway and there are painted signboards after every few kilometer.

According to the Administration of Chhattisgarh, the Maoists had killed 228 civilians including 12 SPOs and 25 police personnel, i.e. 253 in all. A major Maoist attack took place on the 16th July, 2005 in the Errabore Camp. They burnt large number of houses and killed 33 persons including old men and children. The number of persons killed by Maoists between June 2005 and May 2006 comes to 300. From the year 2003, when the CRPF entered Dantewada, the killings on both sides appear to have increased. After the floating of the Salwa Judum in June 2005, the strife has taken a very bloody form.

As per the estimation of Balgopal, the death toll in the Dantewada war could come to about 600 in one and half year. The campaign for Peace and Justice in Chhattisgarh reports that 257 persons were killed in encounters in 2006 as per police reports and 450 villagers were killed between June 2005 to March 2007 and 700 villages were burnt as per Maoists Press release.

- It has been evident to everyone in Dantewada that Salwa Judum is very much an 'official' movement.
- The Chief Minister, Raman Singh, claims that Salwa Judum Movement, that has been going on from June, 2005, is a peaceful non-political movement. As many as 10000 rural Adivasis have been voluntarily participating in it and that it is a tribal revolt to put an end to Naxalite extremism.
- The CPI has been raising questions about the usefulness of Salwa Judum from the beginning and it has been questioning their claim of putting an end to the roots of Naxalism. It has also expressed doubts about the alleged political nature of the movement.
- The District President of CPI has expressed the opinion that brutal atrocities are being perpetrated on unarmed rural Adivasis by the police with the assistance of Salwa Judum and in the process many of them have died.
- Many Congress and BJP leaders too have been openly opposing to the present form of Salwa Judum.

- The State Government has almost made the Salwa Judum movement a Government programme. The people are not joining it on their own but only because they are caught between the presence of Naxalites on one hand and the Police on the other hand.
- The State Government has been giving all types of security to those who are participating in Salwa Judum and has also been bearing all the expenses for the expansion of the movement.
- The extra-ordinary powers given to the Schedule Areas of Bastar under the Vth Schedule of the Constitution and the special rights given to the Gram Sabhas and Panchayats in the Panchayati Raj Act of 1996 have been blatantly violated.
- The obstruction caused by Naxalites to the development works in the area and the killing of unarmed people and their representatives has resulted the development works in halting.
- Barbaric atrocities and inhuman repression of the villagers by the Police in the name of Salwa Judum are taking place in South Bastar, particularly in Bijapur tehsil.

The tragedy of Chhattisgarh is that of massive and forced displacement of Adivasis into the roadside camps, to Khammam district of Andhra Pradesh and into the interiors of the jungles of Dantewada. The estimate of the displaced persons ranges from 70,000 to 1,00,000.

Those in the camps are getting some food from the Government. Those in Khammam are suffering the worst. Many of them are starving. Those displaced into the forests live on the grains left behind but now they have to depend on the abandoned lands by escaping the attention of Salwa Judum and the Police/Para Military Forces. The forest produce has become completely out of reach of those in the camps and to those who have migrated to Khammam. The weekly markets of Dantewada have also been abandoned. Education and health needs of the refugees too are being seriously affected. To enable the displaced to go back to their hamlets and live as before without any fear has become the first and foremost task today. However, there seems to be little possibility of this to happen as the Government of Chhattisgarh and Salwa Judum have decided to build pucca colonies at the camps until the Maoists are driven out of the forests.

It has been amply proved that the Salwa Judum is not a spontaneous uprising of the people but a Government sponsored agency to unleash the unchecked violence against sympathizers and supporters of CPI—Maoists with the assistance of Police and Para Military forces. The violence and counter violence have created a terror ridden situation in the area which has led to major violations of the human rights of the villages. *Hence, agrarian violence by CPI—Maoist and to Salwa Judum (assisted by Para Military forces) should be stopped forthwith and the enabling environment should be created for the safe return of the people from Salwa Judum Camps to their villages.*

II

Panchayats in tribal areas listed in Schedule-V of the Constitution enjoy additional functions and powers to help local communities to preserve their socio-cultural norms and to conserve their natural resources. These additional powers are laid down in the Panchayats Extention to the Scheduled Areas Act (PESA) of 1996. The State Governments are expected to enact laws conforming to the spirit of PESA for this purpose. While Chhattisgarh has made suitable legal enactment, the actual working of Panchayati Raj in its tribal areas has been frustrated by legal anomalies and poor awareness among the people and their representatives about the special provisions of PESA.

Under the PESA Act 1996, the following provisions have been made:

- Gram Sabhas can be held at the *para, majra and tola* levels.
- These are empowered to protect the traditions, beliefs and culture of the tribal communities.
- They have the powers to manage and protect common properties
- Local disputes can be resolved by the Gram Sabha through its traditional systems.
- In case of land acquisition, the administration will have to seek permission from the Gram Sabhas for the rehabilitation of affected families.
- These will have the rights over minor forest produce, powers to restore land to tribals, control money lending to them, control social organizations working for the welfare of tribals and prepare the local plans and sub-plans for the development of tribal areas and communities.
- The Gram Sabhas can exercise control over local markets and *melas* held within their jurisdiction.
- They also have the right to control the distillation manufacture and prohibition of liquor.
- The District Panchayats have rights and powers similar to the District Panchayats falling under Sixth Schedule.

The basic provisions of the PESA were aimed at facilitating participatory democracy in tribal areas by empowering the Gram Sabha to manage and control its own resources. These were given special functional powers and responsibilities to ensure effective participation of tribal communities in their own development in harmony with their culture so as to preserve/conserve their traditional rights over natural resources. The Act restored control of the tribals over their natural resources including land, water, forest and minerals and bestowed ownership rights over minor forest produce to the Gram Sabha.

However, during ten years since the existence of this Act, its implementation on the ground has been full of problems and confusions. Instances of violations of its provisions have been on the increase especially in the states where natural resources are abundant and these are primarily located in the tribal areas. These natural resources are viewed as central to the economic growth of the state and as such acquired at the cost of the tribal communities living in the area. *The question now is whether the Gram Sabhas have any power to intervene in a situation where there is a conflict of interests between the state and the local communities?* How far reaching are the powers and rights vested in the Gram Sabhas in comparison with the powers and rights vested in the Revenue and Forest departments of the state? Are the decisions taken by the Gram Sabhas binding on the state departments? Today these and many more issues have emerged before the tribal communities, state departments and the State Government.

III

On 13 April 2006, the Land Resources Department of Ministry of Rural Development of Government of India and the Planning Commission constituted a Land Committee for providing inputs for the formulation of the 11th Five Year Plan. During the course of a meeting of Land Committee on 9 July 2006, an 'Enquiry Committee' comprising of Rajgopal P.V., Subhash Lomte, Balaji Pandey and Ramesh Sharma was formed for the purpose of investigating the violations of PESA provisions in Raigarh district of Chhattisgarh.

The brief for the Enquiry Committee was as follows:

- To document instances and cases of PESA violations.
- To have dialogue with the concerned local residents and administrative officials.
- To provide suggestions for solution of identified violations.

The members of the 'Enquiry Committee' undertook a field survey of selected villages in Raigarh district from 26-28 July 2006.

The Enquiry Committee has found the following instances of the violation of the provisions of PESA Act, 1996:

Village: Singhanpur, Tehsil Kharsia

21.03.03 The State Investment Enhancement Board, through Notice No. 366/I.E.P.V. dated 21.03.03, directed the Gram Sabha of Singhanpur to submit its objections on acquisition of land (Singhanpur *1.967 hectare,* Neharpali *16.212 hectare* and Salihabhata *12.022 hectare*) by 29.05.03. The land thus marked for acquisition fell under the category of administrative land (grazing land).

28.05.03 *The Gram Sabha of Singhanpur submitted its objection to the proposed acquisition through resolution No. 1. But these were overruled.*

Village: Tamnar, Tehsil: Gharghoda

A Brief No. 1/20 dated 06.03.06 issued by the Collector's Office for the District Planning Committee, Raigarh stated that the villagers of Tamnar, Salihabhata, Godhi, Northern Regaon, Southern Regaon, Kunjemura, Pata etc. registered angry protests after a public announcement for the *acquisition of 29.595 hectares of land in these villages*. The acquisition was intended for Jindal Steel and Power Limited. The land marked for acquisition included main pathway of the village, religious site and a *talab*. It also included *nistar* land such as cremation ground, cemetery and *gothan*. Along with this 0.769 hectares of land was *chote jhad ke jungle. The concerned Gram Panchayats and villagers raised objections against the acquisition of this land. However all these protests were put aside by the State Government in favour of economic development of the area.*

04.03.2004: In a written complaint lodged with the Thana Incharge, the villagers have stated that the 'no objection' letter dated 01.02.03 claimed to have been issued by the Gram Panchayat with the seal of the Sarpanch and submitted before the Raigarh Collector by Jindal Steel and Power Company on 29.01.04 is false. They state that there was no discussion in the Gram Sabha on 01.02.03 regarding the issuance of 'no objection certificate' to Jindal Steel and Power Company and no such certificate was issued. That the submission by it is false is proved by the fact that in the Gram Sabha meeting of 01.02.03 only 1-14 resolutions were discussed and passed. Resolution No. 14 deals with the selection of Antodaya beneficiaries and after its passage there are no signatures in the register denoting the passage of any other resolution. It is clear from the submitted document that the letter was issued by the Gram Panchayat and the word Panchayat has been changed to Sabha by using white ink. Therefore the submission by the Company is unconstitutional and false. The villagers demanded action against the guilty and the company.

31.07.04: On the objections presented by the villagers and Gram Sabha to the Collector, Raigarh stated, *"on the subject of 'no objection' by the Gram Sabha, there is no question as the Gram Sabha is only consulted in the process and is not required to give a no objection certificate"*. He further added 'where the question of rehabilitation and employment of the affected farmers is concerned, it has to be mentioned in the Award Notice. The compensation for acquired land is awarded on the basis of irrigated and un-irrigated land and its quality. This is done as per administrative guidelines. The land acquisition proceedings are being done on the orders of the government and are mandatory in nature. As per the Act and law the objections raised by the villagers and Gram Sabha cannot be accepted".

Village: Rabo, Tehsil: Gharghoda

25.11.04: The following Gram Sabha resolutions objecting to the dam construction on Kurkut River were presented to the District Magistrate, Raigarh and Chief Minister of Chhattisgarh:

07.11.04 Gram Sabha resolution from Charratangar
08.11.04 Gram Sabha resolution from Gadgaon
09.11.04 Gram Sabha resolution from Darradih
12.11.04 Gram Sabha resolution from Dehradih
12.11.04 Gram Sabha resolution from Pakhadraha
12.11.04 Gram Sabha resolution from Vilaskhar
13.11.04 Gram Sabha resolution from Aamapali
14.11.04 Gram Sabha resolution from Dokramuda
17.11.04 Gram Sabha resolution from Rabo

08.10.04: Jindal Steel and Power Limited started the construction of a dam on Kurkut River even before obtaining the permission and clearance from the Government of Chhattisgarh and Ministry of Forests and Environment, GoI.

Ujwalpur, Taraimal, Tehsil: Gharghoda

18.11.02: The Sarpanch of Gram Panchayat Taraimal submitted a written objection stating that the *nistar* land in the village has 2271 small and large trees, shrubs and trees should not be given for industrial use as this would cause disturbance in the *nistar* rights of the people and harm the environment. Later, many residents of the village submitted their written objections alongside the Sarpanch's letter.

IV

It may be argued, on the basis of the above discussion and analysis by way of conclusion that Land Acquisition for corporate sector and multinationals is one of the important reasons for the deep roots of Naxalism and its fast penetration in the tribal regions of Chhattisgarh. This is inspite of the resolutions of the Gram Sabhas against Land Acquisition and goes against the basic spirit of democratic decentralisation pronounced by the Government of India. This is a paradox as the State Government is emerging as a major violator of the provision of PESA and the powers of Gram Sabhas in the tribal areas of the Chhattisgarh. The roots of the Naxal movement lie at the non-implementation of land reforms and dispossessing the triblas from their lands through Land Acquisition. *Chhattisgarh state is a case in point where the tribals have been subjected to worst form of exploitation by the combined violence of the State and the Naxalites.* Their strong traditional institutions are being decimated. They have been displaced and uprooted from the villages and forced to shift in lakhs to transit camps and to migrate to adjacent state of Andhra Pradesh. The democratic decentralisation process in the Bastar Region has virtually been crippled. The grassroots governance in Dantewada and Bastar region can, however, be restored in the near future if the strategy worked out by Planning Commission, for implementing the land and forest problems and for providing an enabling environment for the implementation of PESA in the Tribal areas without intervening in the powers and functions of Gram Sabha, is faithfully operationalised.

References

Azad, "Maoists in India: A rejoinder", *Economic and Political Weekly*, Vol. XLI, No. 41, Oct. 14-20, 2006.

Bhattacharya, Dipankar, "Trail Blazed by Naxalbari Uprising", *Economic and Political Weekly*, Vol. XLI, No. 50, December 16-22, 2006.

"Death, Displacement and Deprivation. The War in Dantewada : A Report", Human Rights Forum, December 2006. Hyderabad.

"Salwa Judum: Civil war in Chhattisgarh"; Campaign for Peace and Justice in Chhattisgarh. 2007; New Delhi.

"The Adivasis of Chhattisgarh: Victims of the Naxalite Movement and Salwa Judum Campaign", Asian Centre for Human Rights, 17th March, 2006.

Ganapathy, in an Interview given on the occasion of the formation of CPI (Maoist). *People's March*, Vol. 5, Nos. 11-12, November-December 2004.

9

Empowerment of Panchayati Raj Institutions

SAHIB SINGH BHAYANA

During the last six decades, the Indian governance scenario has been gloomy, uninspiring and dismal. The system failed on several fronts. There was evaporation of moral values, inadequacy of social reforms, decline in character, integrity and national spirit, failure of leadership, fracturisation of political parities, and mal-governance by three wings of government. Consequently, good governance has been the greatest casualty. That is why India is now being rated as one of the most corrupt countries of the world. The findings of Vohra Committee are a testimony to the notion of triangular nexus amongst politicians, bureaucrats and criminals. To be more specific, the three arms of government and instrumentalities of governance have declined over the years. The legislature and executive have conspired to sacrifice governance at the altar of political expediency. The judiciary, which provided a ray of hope to a common man and seemed to be saviour, has also gone into darkness thereby engulfing the entire system of governance.

Therefore, the time has come to people-ise government and power. Unless people share real power in the government, no strategy for reform can be fruitful. Instead, the fact is that the government is treating people as bothersome clients, not as citizens in the present scenario. But, democracy needs citizens not clients.

The present paper attempts to highlight the conceptual parameters of good governance and various issues involved in the empowerment of the Panchayati Raj Institutions, in the light of the spirit behind the 73rd Constitutional Amendment and to trace how far it has been operationalised in terms of 3Fs (functions, funds and functionaries). The present author is fully conscious of the fact that he is not the first person to raise these issues. Here the intention is to emphasise the need for a re-orientation of the priorities of those academicians, administrators, politicians and citizens who are interested in good governance and want grass root institutions to act as institutions of self government. At the same time, it is intended to suggest how the State Finance Commissions and the Central and State Governments can realistically empower the Panchayati Raj Institutions.

However, concept of good governance has been used differently by different people without reaching to any consensus since both "good" and "governance" have varied connotations. Consequently, there is no single answer to a question: What is good governance? However, whatever makes institutions more effective, transparent, participative, responsive and accountable may be regarded as an element of good governance.

Some have defined the term in the terms of means. Others have focused on democracy, many on decentralisation and others on pre-ordained goals. The remaining perceived it as a phenomenon which leads its people to peaceful, orderly, reasonable, prosperous and participatory lives. However, the World Bank has identified good governance as political accountability, availability of freedom, law abiding citizens and people in power, bureaucratic accountability, transparency, availability of information, efficiency, effectiveness and cooperation between government and society.

Thus, our discussion on the conceptual parameters indicates that it refers to new values of governance that seek to establish greater efficiency, legitimacy and credibility of the system. In simple words, good governance can be considered as citizen friendly and citizen-caring administration. It is also clear that it is not simply something that government can achieve or do by itself; it depends on the cooperation and involvement of a large number of citizens and organisations. Here lies the need for people's institutions (and also of civil society) at the grassroot level. Thus there is a strong case for empowering Panchayati Raj Institutions in this context.

In a democratic country like India, every strategy has to originate from political sphere. Some of the common options available may take the form of strengthening of democratic forces and institutions, allowing and encouraging people's participation in the decision-making process, devolution of political power and certain policy measures such as reservations for women, scheduled caste/scheduled tribes and other backward classes. To operationalise these options, the Government of India initiated the process of democratic decentralisation through the introduction of Panchayati Raj in 1959.

During the initial period of ascendancy (1959-64), the process of democratic decentralisation was introduced with lot of enthusiasm and with high expectations. But after this, its significance started tottering and later crumbled under the heavy weight of political factionalism, scramble for control over patronage among politicians, scarcity of financial resources, general apathy of the people and centralising trends during Mrs. Gandhi's regime. The power hungry bureaucracy also conspired to make grass root institutions ineffective and meaningless. However, good sense prevailed amongst some leaders. Rajiv Gandhi Government took keen interest to revitalise them. The first concrete measure to provide constitutional sanction to Panchayati Raj came in the form of the 64th Constitutional Amendment Bill. But it could not succeed. This reached its culmination during the tenure of Narsimha Rao Government in 1993, when the 73rd Constitutional Amendment Acts of 1992 conferred constitutional legality on the Panchayati Raj Institutions. Thus, started a new era in the process of democratic decentralisation and empowering the people's institutions at the grassroot level.

Thus, any discussion on empowerment of Panchayati Raj Institutions is futile and meaningless if we do not understand the real intentions and spirit behind this Amendment. The issues of local finance and fiscal decentralisation can not be studied in isolation. (a) The fact is that the 73rd Amendment has not only given the Panchayati Raj bodies constitutional protection but also defined them as 'Institutions of Self-Government' (Article 243G). (b) It also mandated the task of planning for economic development and social justice for these. But to evolve as institutions of self-government, the fundamental requirement is to have adequate financial resources to discharge their responsibilities. However, in this context, even the constitutional amendment falls short of expectations as it has not created a clear cut financial provision for the Panchayati Raj bodies. The taxation power of the central and state governments are listed in the Union list (List-I) and State list (List-II). As there is no mention of the local list for local bodies, they can have only those powers which the State Government devolves on them from their own taxation powers listed in the items 45 to 66 of the State List. However, Article 243-H does refer to the empowerment of Panchayats by the State Governments to levy taxes, duties tolls etc. But it is only an enabling provision. The net result is that taxes are assigned to local bodies by the state governments and they do not have independent power of taxation. The only consolation left with the Panchayati Raj Institutions is the provision for the constitution of State Finance Commissions every five years. But again their role is very limited as the implementation of their recommendations is left to the State Governments and they may or may not agree to all the recommendations. It is in spite of the fact that the institution of State Finance Commission came into existence in every state to meet the requirements of Article 243-I of the Constitution of India inserted by the 73rd Amendment.

In conformity with it, all the State Governments have created three-tier structure of Panchayati Raj by amending their respective acts. Therefore, financial resources of Panchayati Raj Institutions in the various states need to be studied in the context of functions and duties devolved upon them. To be more specific, powers and resources need to be matched. Besides, the respective State Finance Commissions should take into account, the progress of devolution of functions, functionaries and funds to them in respect of 29 subjects listed in the 11th schedule. According to the Constitution, it is necessary for every State Government to clearly identify the subjects and the tiers of Panchayati Raj structures to deal with these. However, this urgency does not seem to exist in most of them. Even after 16 years of constitutional amendment, the status of devolution in respect of 29 subjects does not seem to be rosy. The Table 1 is indicative of this fact.

TABLE 1

Status of Devolution of Departments/Subjects with Funds and Functionaries to the Panchayati Raj Institutions

State	*No. of Departments/Subjects Transferred*				
	Funds	*Functions*	*Functionaries*	*Value of Devolution Index*	*Rank*
A.P.	5	13	2	22.98	9
Assam	—	—	—	—	—
Bihar	—	—	—	—	—
Gujarat	—	—	—	—	—
Haryana	—	16	—	18.39	10
Karnataka	29	29	29	100.00	1
Kerala	15	29	15	67.82	2
M.P.	10	23	9	48.27	5
Maharashtra	18	18	18	62.07	3
Orissa	5	25	3	37.93	7
Punjab	—	7	—	8.04	11
Rajasthan	—	29	—	33.33	8
Tamil Nadu	—	29	—	33.33	8
U.P.	12	13	9	39.08	6
West Bengal	12	29	12	60.92	4

From Table 1, it is clear that devolution of powers and authority to the Panchayati Raj Institutions is minimal. The devolution index was calculated by taking into account average of percentage share of devolution in respect of funds, functions and functionaries. It shows that in the index, value was highest in Karnataka and it is zero in Assam, Bihar and Gujarat. However, although Haryana is better than Punjab, it occupies 10th position. On the whole, the present position does not seem to be encouraging.

Similarly, for supplementing the process of devolution of powers to the Panchayati Raj Institutions, the 74th Amendment to the Constitution made provision in Article 243 ZD for the formation of a District Planning Committee. It states as under:

"There shall be constituted in every state at the district level a District Planning Committee to consolidate the plans prepared by the

Panchayats and Municipalities in the district and to prepare a draft development plan for the district as a whole. The state legislature has been given the authority to make laws in respect of the composition, the manner of filling up the seats, the chairperson of DPC".

The experience here too is not encouraging. Out of 15 major states only in 8 states such an arrangement exists. It is through DPC that linkage can be established between the district and local levels. In this way, the needs and aspirations of the local people can be reflected in the district plan.

The community participation is an important step in the decentralisation process as it contributes to more appropriate and cost effective works, lowers costs, checks corruption and ensures the use of local materials. For ensuring people's participation in the activity of Panchayats, Article 243 (A) states that "a Gram Sabha may exercise such powers and perform such functions at the village level as legislature of a state may by law provide". But the realistic situation is that most of the states have not made effective laws for strengthening the Gram Sabha. As per the prevailing legislation in the various states, its meetings are held twice a year, however, the attendance in these is negligible but some how quorum is reached. The Gram Sabha meeting has a definite end in view. This does not involve mere participation of more people in the affairs of Panchayats. It also aims at mainstreaming the women in development activities. The Constitution of India has made it obligatory to reserve 1/3rd seats for women in all the tiers of Panchayati Raj structure. This offers an opportunity to women to change the face of leadership. The basic requirement, however, is to provide them support and build up their capacities for facing the challenges of competitive world.

In view of the above mentioned facts the institution of State Finance Commission of every state should chalk out its strategy in the light of the real intentions enshrined in the Constitution (Article 243 G). It is, therefore, desirable for the Commission to take a holistic view and adopt a wider perspective. This perspective should include legislative pattern of the controlling act, with a view to making it compatible with the constitutional provisions; structural issues and inter tier relationship; financial devolution; staffing pattern and administrative set-up; and desirability of evolving organisational and working systems with view to provide better coordination between State Government and local bodies without sacrificing principles of responsive government, both at the state and local levels. It has also to find out the ways and means for activating the role of civil society in the development effort and in the capacity building of women strata in the power structure. The public–private partnership strategy too should be kept in view by it for introducing citizen charters for civic activities and to give a fillip to the constitutional mandate of involving local bodies in the process of plan formulation. The Commission should as well find ways and means for introducing awareness campaign for decentralised planning.

Thus, in view of the above mentioned reasons/issues, the role of the State Finance Commissions in empowering Panchayati Raj Institutions becomes all the more important. The present author is fully conscious of the fact that State Finance Commission has limitations because some of the issues may not fall within its purview but without touching these areas, realistic solutions seem a distant dream to us. However, to my mind, the wisdom of the State Finance Commissions will have a far reaching impact on the State Governments. It would be a difficult proposition for them to reject their recommendations outrightly. Similarly, the National Finance Commission must come forward and ensure that funds meant for the Panchayati Raj Institutions are not diverted to elsewhere. It is obligatory, for the State Governments to transfer the funds meant for grassroot institutions, to them.

It is desirable that while formulating their recommendations, the following objectives should be kept in view by the State Finance Commissions:

- Identification of such resources for local bodies as could enable them to perform their functions efficiently and effectively.
- Growing mandatory requirements of these institutions and their need for sustainable income.
- Equity and efficiency in allocating taxes amongst Panchayati Raj Institutions along with incentives.
- Provisions of weightage to financially weak institutions while determining their share in grants-in-aid.
- Allocation of funds to meet expenditure on the upkeep and the maintenance of the capital assets as per certain well defined norms.
- Provision of special grants for the development of infrastructure in the changing scenario of information technology.
- Introduction of measures concerning the performance of Panchayati Raj Institution in the matters pertaining to revenue collection, tax administration, expenditure control, efficiency in raising resources, planning and other corrective measures.
- Identification of the parameters of individual performance of Panchayats with a view to giving them special grants.
- Finding ways and means of ensuring expenditure on staff and the administration of rural local bodies in relation to their assigned responsibilities.
- National Finance Commission should stop giving grants to the states which do not transfer the funds to these institutions within a stipulated time frame.
- Exploration of the possibility of direct transfer of funds allocated by the central Government for the development to the Panchayats.
- Association of the universities/academic institutions for capacity building of women and other representatives with a view to

making their representation meaningful and effective in governance.

- Encouraging organisations to play an active role as eyes and ears of the people at the village level. They can make the communities aware of the services to which they are entitled and mobilise them to demand their rights. More importantly they have a role in enabling the community to overcome the dependency syndrome and become self-sufficient in meeting some of their demands.

Since the Central Government has a significant influence in the devolution of 3Fs (functions, funds and functionaries) upon Panchayats because of the large fiscal transfers it makes to the states in the functional domain of the Panchayats, mainly through the centrally sponsored schemes (CSS) and additional central assistance (ACA), its every guideline can be a potential vehicle to carry the message of strengthening Panchayats. The Activity Mapping is also necessary in this context. The empowered Panchayats, with clear role assigned through it, would also begin to demand and get the staff required for effective performance. The strategy should be that of attributing each activity to the appropriate level of Panchayati Raj Institutions. Activity mapping has also to clearly identify accountability and competency. There is no gain or loss of power through it but just role clarity.

This perception is of great relevance for local level. When the local governments are assigned clear task and made accountable for devolved funds and the performance of assigned responsibilities, they would demand the required capacity for effective performance. Several steps to ensure the centrality of Panchayats in planning and implementation have been taken. Major centrally sponsored schemes have been modified to ensure the centrality of Panchayats. For instance, under the National Rural Employment Act, around 50 percent value of the plan is to be implemented at the village Panchayat level. Similarly, Backward Region Grant Fund Programme, which provides for Rs. 4,670 crore to the Panchayats and Municipalities in 250 districts in 27 states, can be used to fill any development gap identified by them through Gram Sabha. Similarly, 11th Plan too seeks to substantially empower Panchayati Raj Institutions as the primary means of delivering of the essential services that are critical to the inclusive growth, and details several steps such as activity mapping, the creations of Panchayats Sector Window, in the state and in the central budgets, and IT enabling to key steps for empowering panchayats.

Within this larger area of concern, the key issues for us are:

- To ensure that CSS and ACA relating to functions in the domain of Panchayati Raj Institutions are actually implemented by them. It is desirable that centrally sponsored schemes related to service delivery should be redesigned to give incentive to states to formulate action plans that bring Panchayats to the centre stage of service delivery.

- They should have two windows–one conventional supply driven window (entitlement based on as at present) which is phased out gradually, and increasing reform linked window (competitive) that rewards states willing to move along the path of empowering Panchayats.
- Autonomous monitoring arrangements that are not subject to the pitfalls of the present system should be seen as critical to this redesign.
- There should be a clear structure of budgeting of the Panchayats and a mechanism for checking how the actual expenditure matches with the budget proposal. This will require creation of head of the accounts of the Panchayats to broadly define the nature of work as well as the source of funds.

Thus, reforming of the entire CSS/ACA system is crucial in creating better incentives for effective devolution to Panchayats. A standard format for those CSSs that deal with the functional domain of Panchayats is being prepared by the Panchayati Raj Ministry.

In nutshell, what is required is an integration of various systems and structures of governance and unification of various development schemes in order to evolve a holistic development paradigm. The strategies to tackle people's empowerment should be multi-dimensional, i.e. social, economic, administrative, and political. Since we have entered in the 21st century, it is high time that pre-requisites of good governance are operationalised. This presumes a strong commitment from decision-makers at the levels of society, social activists and intellectuals who could address the issues of access and affordability in the context of extreme inequality, poverty and hunger in a comprehensive and a forward looking manner.

10

Local Governance and Equity in Public Service Delivery

SUSHMA YADAV

Decentralisation is recognized as a largely positive aspect of democratic political development. It is one of the few developmental concepts that have found supporters even in differing ideologies. It finds support within the neoliberal school because of the latter's emphasis on dilution of central state authority and control, while at the same time it finds supporters in the leftist-Marxist thought because of its inherent potential to distribute power away from the elite and to include the generally marginalised people in decision-making. The realisation that the centralised, bureaucratic system of planning and implementation has failed to deliver much to the developing world, as well as the fact that the common citizens should have a say in the decisions that affect their lives, has brought decentralisation to centre-stage within development discourse.

DEMOCRATIC DECENTRALISATION

Democratic decentralisation[1] is the development of reciprocal relationship between central and local governments and between local governments and citizens. It addresses to the power to develop and implement policy, the extension of democratic processes to lower levels of government, and, measures to ensure that democracy is sustainable. Democratic decentralisation incorporates both decentralisation and democratic local governance.

Some definitional issues are involved at this point. Decentralisation is of three types: (i) Devolution; (ii) Deconcentration, and lastly (iii) Division. Along with this, Decentralisation encapsulates three distinct elements: (1) financial decentralisation, entailing the transfer of financial resources in the form of grants and tax-raising powers to sub-national units of government; (2) administrative decentralisation (sometimes referred to as deconcentration) where the functions performed by central government are transferred to geographically distinct administrative units, and (3) political decentralisation where powers and responsibilities are devolved to elected local governments. This form of decentralisation is synonymous with democratic decentralisation.

Our major concern in this paper is mainly with the impact of democratic decentralisation on public service delivery. Several experiments in decentralised service delivery have also involved the transfer of financial or administrative powers to sub-national units of government that are not subject to democratic oversight through competitive elections. These variations in the form and content of decentralisation have an important bearing on service delivery outcomes, as much as on the processes of participation, accountability and responsiveness.

WHY IS DEMOCRATIC DECENTRALISATION IMPORTANT?

Political and economic changes during the past decade have demonstrated people's interest in democratic ideals of freedom, human rights, and accountable government. Because democratic regimes contribute to peace and security in the world and because democracy and respect for human rights coincide with fundamental liberal values, democratic decentralisation is an important part of the democratic movement and evolution throughout the world. As described in USAID's *Strategies for Sustainable Development, Democratisation is an essential part of sustainable development because it facilitates the protection of human rights, informed participation, and public sector accountability.*[2]

PUBLIC SERVICE DELIVERY

As already discussed, one of the potential impacts of decentralisation is improved service delivery. It is assumed that the Local governments know better about their citizens' preferences; they are better prepared to meet their needs; and the local people might be more willing to pay taxes for services provided in accordance with their needs by their local authorities. Local governments, however, can only be efficient in providing services if: responsibilities are assigned with clarity; revenues are sufficiently available to them to fulfil the mandates; and there are appropriate incentives to improve accountability in service provision.

A better match between local government outputs and local preferences rates makes local service delivery more efficient, unless this situation is outweighed by spillovers or other efficiencies in central government provision.

Theoretical claims may assert that decentralisation may have a direct impact on the capacity of the state to effectively undertake public service delivery abound, but the empirical evidence for this relationship remains largely weak. Using broad measures, we argue that decentralisation appears to have no direct linkage to a potential deterioration of state capacity in most areas/sectors. However, one may come across a robust relationship between developing state's usage of IMF assistance and an improvement in overall state capacity for better and more inclusive public service delivery. This finding is examined in more detail as it pertains to the potential of decentralisation to ensure equity and excellence in public service delivery in the emerging governance paradigm.

The focus of this paper is mainly on equity and social justice concerns, and some elaboration of the meaning and application of these terms is required in the context of service delivery. Equity can be assessed in two ways: access to services across different groups of the population on the basis of income, gender and other categories, and inter-regional equity in terms of disparities in access within and across local government jurisdictions. The provision of affordable, accessible and appropriate services to all categories of a population in equal measure, but with particular concern for the welfare of economically and socially marginalised groups, frames a social justice perspective on service provision.

By bringing governance, decision-making, and delivery of basic services closer to the people, decentralisation promises both greater efficiency and a more responsive government based on transparent and more accurate information. The proximity between people and state can foster greater understanding and a better perception of the needs at the local level. At the same time, the closer contact promises greater transparency of decision-making processes and greater accountability of elected officials to the general populace. Most importantly, it has the potential to allow citizens to play a direct role in decision making and implementation at the local level.

Decentralisation has been criticised on some fronts since it creates a complicated and politically charged relationship between local development plans and national priorities. And, it can also lead to regional inequalities. Unless handled carefully and in conjunction with the centre, it can be financially unstable. Most importantly, the greater proximity between state and citizens can lead to political 'capture of government decision making by special interests, often invoked as a real danger of decentralisation'. Nevertheless, the concept itself enjoys favour amongst different schools of thought.

Whereas decentralisation requires a simple act of legislation to alter the structure of governance, its success depends on much more. When assessed in terms of sustainability, ownership, democratisation, participation and service delivery, it turns out that successful decentralisation is a difficult and seemingly rare outcome to achieve. In fact, it has succeeded only in very few cases around the world. A study, even though quick, of these successes reveals that decentralisation requires a very specific environment in order to succeed in improving the delivery of services.

There may be three 'necessary, but not sufficient' prerequisites. First, a strong central state is required so that 'decentralised despotism' and elite capture at the local level can be avoided. This requires regulation and coordination between various levels of government, as well as between the functions that can be performed by them. A weak central state may end up catering to the needs of the local elite in order to create local power bases to maintain its power at the centre. This may erode the effectiveness of the decentralisation effort as far as power devolution and delivery of services is concerned. Second, a strong civil society and a close connection between the state and the civil society are required, especially in the form of social movements. This is essential for breaking the power-hold of local elite groups, and for allowing an alternate channel of information collection, feedback, mobilisation, and participation for ensuring access to services. Third, an ideologically cohesive political party that has significant ties to grassroots organisations is required.

At times, it is felt that decentralisation, to succeed, needs the left-of-centre political parties that have strong social movement characteristics. This link with social movements is interesting because it highlights the fact that decentralisation succeeds only when it comes as a result of a popular demand, and not as a top-down insertion. It also means that it must deliver on promises made and cannot be reduced to a popularity-gaining gimmick that seeks to create local power bases. Two other prerequisites can also be added. The first is structural reform such as land reform, which breaks the power of the landed elite so that the decentralisation effort can be characterized by social transformation. In the absence of such reforms, decentralisation will only lead to elite capture at the local level. The second is political competition, which opens up spaces for the articulation of citizen's voice.

Exponents of democratic decentralisation base their arguments on widely differing criteria, ranging from expected improvements in allocative efficiency, welfare, and equity through devolution and decentralisation to increased participation, accountability, and responsiveness on the part of local authorities. The former are generally employed by the economists and are framed in terms of the costs and benefits of decentralisation, while the latter are favoured by social scientists and practitioners concerned with democratic aspects of the process of governance (Blair, 2000). The scope for decentralisation to generate improvements in service delivery offers a useful opportunity to employ both sets of evaluative criteria.

However, there is no systematic or comparative evidence on whether increased participation in decentralised local governance generates better 'outputs' in terms of improvements in the provision of health, education, drinking water and sanitation services for poor and marginalised people.

The literature on democratic decentralisation and service delivery generally falls into two distinct categories. The first category focuses on opportunities for enhanced popular participation and the second tries to explore the possibility of increased accountability of local authorities or emergence of new forms of service delivery involving a plurality of actors. Moreover, the available evidence draws either on examples from single countries and sectors, or is anecdotal, temporally specific and highly localised, making the task of generalisation pretty difficult, if not, impossible. Similarly, efforts to measure 'outcomes', in terms of reduced poverty or improved social indicators, as a consequence of devolved powers and resources to local governments and increased participation, are inconclusive and fraught with methodological problems.

These data constraints seem to pose a serious challenge to the advocates of increased accountability and participation in local governance through decentralisation, since the material benefits for the poor arising from improved service provision ought to be a key determinant of its effectiveness. The positive consequences of increased participation, accountability and responsiveness should not be underestimated, especially when political rights have generally been severely curtailed under centralised, authoritarian regimes. However, unless these process changes demonstrably translate into enduring improvements in service provision and material well-being, the claims made for the pro-poor potential of democratic decentralisation remain incomplete and cannot be easily sustained.

Services are often equated with public goods like health, education, drinking water and sanitation and are the most common forms of services provided by local governments. Police, fire, transportation, housing and social welfare services also fall under local government jurisdictions in many countries. Local governments are also given responsibility for a range of other public services, such as infrastructure in the form of roads and bridges, public buildings, and housing. In many developing countries, specialised services for low-income groups are the responsibility of local governments, such as social welfare, credit, and agricultural extension. Local authorities in rural areas often perform a range of functions directed at agricultural and rural development, environmental management, disaster prevention and rehabilitation.

In most countries, public services are largely provided by the state through government departments and specialised agencies, while private sector provision is becoming increasingly common in all areas of service provision as a result of state failure, privatisation, globalisation and legislation that permits market competition. Governments may remain responsible for determining service standards and financing the costs of provision, but private sector organisations, whether for-profit or not-for-profit, deliver the services. These distinctions serve to demonstrate that public service delivery is no longer the exclusive prerogative of state agencies in national and local governments, but involves combinations of state and private actors and civil society organisations that directly engage in the delivery of services.

As already hinted, a leading rationale for decentralisation is that it can generate efficiency as well as financial and quality gains by devolving resources and decision-making powers to local governments for the delivery of services. It is financially attractive to national governments because part of the burden of financing services can be shifted to sub-national units and private providers. The efficiency argument is that productivity of health, education and other services will be maximized by allowing local governments to take decisions on the allocation of scarce resources, since they have a better sense of local priorities. In the process, decentralised units of government can become more accountable in resource-allocation decisions. It is further argued that the quality of service provision can also be enhanced by decentralisation since local governments will be more sensitive to variations in local requirements and open to feedback from users of services.

However, there are some risks involved in decentralisation. First, there is no automatic assurance that increased political autonomy for local governments will lead to improvements in public services. Second, there is also the risk of their capture by local political elites which can worsen the delivery of services. Third, the technical capacities of local government staff may be inadequate. Fourth, decentralisation may widen and get affected by the regional disparities in the provision of public services. Fifth, decentralisation poses macro-economic risks by increasing government vulnerability to financial deficits and over-expanding *vis-a-vis* the size of the public sector.

Governments in Asia and, to a lesser extent, India, have experimented with decentralised service delivery over the past two decades. Initiatives have been taken towards the transfer of powers and resources to lower tiers of government, through a combination of measures centering on deconcentration to state agencies operating under central line departments, and devolution to elected local authorities.

Evidences from India are very limited, largely because experiments of decentralised service delivery in the region are more recent in origin, and because in most of the matters services have only been devolved to them to a limited extent. For instance, drawing on survey data from 33,000 households in 17,000 villages, Mahal demonstrates that decentralisation of public service delivery in primary health care and education services is positively correlated with improved child mortality and school enrolment. (Mahal, A., V. Srivastava and D. Sanan (2000), "Decentralisation and Public Sector Delivery of Health and Education Services: The Indian Experience", Discussion Papers on Development Policy No. 20, Bonn: Centre for Development Research, University of Bonn.)

However, generally health and education services in India are under the jurisdiction of state governments and local councils have limited influence over the use of resources or deployment of personnel. Elected councils have limited discretion over the use of resources for developmental purposes, which are largely earmarked for schemes and programmes determined by central and state governments. It is only in the states of Kerala and Madhya Pradesh that decentralisation of expenditures for basic services has taken place on a significant scale, in the former by placing substantial untied funds at the discretion of local village councils for developmental purposes, and in the latter through specialised missions for primary health and education. Some preliminary evidence from Kerala's Popular Planning Campaign launched in 1996 indicates that local council expenditures reflect local priorities more accurately but it is too soon to determine their equity impact (Isaac, 2000).

By comparison, successive decentralisation schemes in Bangladesh have failed to deliver improved services or outcomes. According to Crook, "Material welfare, in terms of agricultural output, did not increase. There was little evidence of greater equity at grassroot level, and a number of studies indicated that the beneficiaries were the rich and the well-born. Instead, decentralisation was generally seen as a means to channel development resources into the hands of the better off" (2001: 46). Responsibility for implementation of disaster relief programmes was devolved to local councils under the Ershad military regime in the mid-1980s, but with negative impacts. Flood rehabilitation programmes suffered from poor management, maldistribution, corruption, and shortages of resources, while very few poor households received any benefits from rehabilitation schemes that tended to focus on roads, bridges and buildings (*Ibid.*: 46).

This brief review of the experience of decentralised service delivery leads to the following tentative conclusions. First, equity outcomes have generally not been realized for poor and socially marginalised people. Second, the quality of public service provision has not improved under decentralised local government, and variation in the quality of services supplied by the state has widened relative to those offered by private providers. The gap in quality between wealthier and poorer areas has often increased under decentralisation. Third, efficiency gains have been realized, usually as a result of the delegation of financial responsibility for service provision from central to local governments, but resources have not been adequate to ensure effective coverage and quality.

With this kind of studies in background, one can feel tempted to draw the conclusion that equity and social justice objectives are not well served by decentralised service provision, and that centralised provision through deconcentrated state agencies is a preferable approach. At the same time, evidence also suggests that increased participation and accountability do result from democratic decentralisation, and that these benefits should not be underestimated (Crook and Manor, 1998; Blair, 2000). The challenge is to identify the conditions under which increased participation in local governance is conducive to enhanced outputs in terms of the equity, quality and efficiency of services. This may require further comparative research but it is possible to outline a schema in which the potential ingredients for success are political, institutional, financial and technical in nature.

POLITICAL COMMITMENT AND LEADERSHIP

Political factors are of intrinsic importance to decentralised service delivery for several reasons. It is widely accepted that political commitment on the part of the federal or state governments is a *sine qua non* of effective democratic decentralisation, and especially for forms of decentralisation that are specifically geared to the interests of the poor (Crook, 2001; Blair, 2000). Similarly, successful pro-poor decentralisation is associated with governing parties that are politically committed to the democratic empowerment of local governments (Heller, 2001; Escheverri-Gent, 1993).

The Indian state governments of West Bengal and Kerala seem to evince a strong commitment to decentralisation, reflected in supportive legislation and a significant flow of resources to lower levels of government. Effective local/grassroot level leadership also plays an instrumental role in fostering local innovation, in the field of policy as well as service delivery especially in response to political and institutional incentives.

POLITICAL MOBILISATION OF THE POOR

The political impetus for process of democratic decentralisation created by reform-minded political parties as well can create opportunities for collective action from below by mobilising constituencies traditionally excluded from policy-making and participatory arenas. This can entail mobilisation of cadres and supporters by political parties in local constituencies, and mobilisation of the poor by civil society organizations (NGOs, trade unions, social movements) to take advantage of political openings from above and to articulate public protest and dissent. Party-based mobilisation can assume two forms in the context of democratic decentralisation: mobilisation of people through local units of political parties for electoral purposes, and mobilisation of supporters to ensure effective implementation of reform initiatives. Democratic decentralisation usually entails the devolution of power to elected local authorities which widens the scope of political participation at the local level. In many Latin American countries municipalities were traditionally run by non-elected administrators appointed by military or authoritarian regimes. It was only the legislation introduced in the 1980s that led to the creation of elected mayors and local councils.

Civil society organisations also mobilise constituencies in local government jurisdictions to take advantage of increased powers and resources, to mobilise people to take part in consultative arenas (see the following section), and to engage in public protest over public services. In Kerala, a prominent social movement (Kerala Sastra Shitya Parishad—the

People's Science Movement) played a critical role in shaping and implementing the People's Campaign for Decentralised Planning in the late 1990s, which also ensured better and equitable/just service delivery though this has not been replicated elsewhere in India (Isaac, 2000; Chaudhuri and Heller, 2002).

ADEQUACY OF FINANCIAL RESOURCES

The availability of financial resources is a critical determinant of the equity and efficiency of public services and the inadequacy of financial resources often explain poor service outcomes. Devolution of responsibility for service provision to local governments is usually accompanied by some elements of financial decentralisation through resource transfers, usually as a share of central taxation, or enhanced powers to raise revenues through a variety of local taxes. Financial decentralisation often renders local governments vulnerable to macro-economic shocks and remedial measures to control public expenditures and national budget deficits. The financial imperative has been a key factor underlying municipal privatisation initiatives and the introduction of cost-sharing measures in the form of user fees in local governments around the world.

Another dimension of the financing issue centers on the financial powers of local governments. Salaries and recurrent expenditures tend to account for a large share of local government outlays on services, especially in the health and education sectors, with more limited resources available for capital expenditures. Limited scope for discretionary allocations across budget heads further restricts the budgetary autonomy of local governments. Local governments may also receive financial transfers that are earmarked for certain programmes or pre-assigned categories of expenditure.

In India, for example, local bodies receive grants-in-aid from state and central government that are tied to specific anti-poverty and social welfare programmes, while recurrent expenditures account for a very high proportion of health and education budgets. The financial autonomy of local governments is thus highly constrained. A major exception is Kerala, where the local Panchayat councils have discretion over 40 per cent of the state development budget, which can be used for service delivery, subject to broad guidelines on different categories of expenditure.

TECHNICAL AND MANAGERIAL CAPACITY

The provision of public services can be an enormously complex exercise, especially in urban municipalities with large populations, and often requires a high level of technical and managerial capacity. However, decentralisation of responsibility for service provision has not always been accompanied by measures to ensure effective capacity for planning, budgeting, implementation and monitoring in local governments, all of which have a critical bearing on service quality. Efforts to build professional and technical skills of local government employees and to improve the internal organization and management style of local administration are often central to building such capacity.

Managerial and technical capacity is not only a key determinant of the performance of local officials in relation to service delivery, but also influences their behaviour towards users of services. Centralised service delivery through hierarchically organised line departments and deconcentrated agencies gives rise to behavioural norms that may not be conducive to participation and greater responsiveness. Creating an organisational culture in local government that is more citizen-friendly and receptive to active community involvement, as well as performance-oriented, requires a combination of incentives and focused capacity-building measures to complement the strengthening of technical and managerial skills.

CONCLUSIONS

This paper sought to ascertain the impact of decentralised service delivery in terms of equity and social justice outcomes. Subject to constraints of data, two main conclusions arise from a review of available evidence in less developed countries: (1) quality and equity of access have not improved with decentralisation of health and education services; and (2) outputs are closely related to the availability of financial resources and the local government capacity.

These insights tend to give rise to two types of policy prescription, neither of which is closely compatible with democratic decentralisation: (1) health and education services are better administered by deconcentrated public agencies working under the direct control of central line departments, and (2) expanding the role of private providers and introducing user fees can improve quality and efficiency of resource use but not equity.

However, experience suggests that while efficiency gains may be realised, neither of these approaches is conducive to participation, nor are they guaranteed to produce outcomes that are more favourable to equity and social justice objectives. The challenge for exponents of democratic decentralisation is to specify methods and approaches by which equity objectives can be realized under decentralised forms of service delivery. Successful interventions are not premised on participation and accountability alone, but require attention to political factors (commitment, leadership and mobilization), institutional arrangements, financial resources, and technical and managerial capacity.

Greater emphasis should be given to measuring and monitoring service delivery outcomes under decentralised forms of provision, to ensure that participation produces real gains for the poor in terms of improved access and quality of [Fiszbein (1997: 1031)] governance which use the concepts of production and allocative efficiency as a basis for assessing capacity. Capacity for production efficiency is manifested in the presence of a performance-oriented government. It requires that the government must have the tools to optimise the use of resources in the production or provision process. Capacity for allocative efficiency is manifested in the presence of a customer-oriented government. It involves the existence and adequate functioning of mechanisms through which the community can voice demands, channels by which authorities can translate these demands into actions and instruments through which the government is accountable for its services. Failure to do so will undermine the lure of democratic decentralisation and encourage policy alternatives that run counter to the ethos of participation in local governance.

Notes and References

1. Historically, the word 'decentralisation' has been used to refer to many a quite different institutional reforms. To the public finance economist, decentralisation usually means *fiscal decentralisation* where reforming the inter-governmental fiscal system is usually the first priority. To the political scientist, decentralisation usually means a set of *policy* issues, a focus on who has authority and responsibility. The political scientist tends to focus on the structure of power and authority and how it is wielded. To the institutional economist, decentralisation usually involves getting an *incentive system* in place so that individual behavior meets the expectations. To the sociologist, decentralisation usually means *participation*, and the role of informal organizations and community groups is a major focal point. The urban planner or economist may stress yet another element—decentralisation as a strategy for enhancing *local economic development*. Finally, the civil society expert sees decentralisation as a path to *democratic local governance*. From *The Wikipeadia*, www.wikipeadia.com.
2. *Strategies for Sustainable Development* (Washington, DC : USAID 1994), p. 17.

References

Astiz, M.F., A.W. Wiseman, and D.B. Baker (2002), "Slouching Towards Decentralisation: Consequences of Curricular Control in National Education Systems", *Comparative Education Review*, Vol. 46, No. 1, pp. 66-88.

Biacchi, G. (2001), "Participation, Activism and Politics: the Porto Alegre Experiment and Deliberative Democratic Theory", *Politics and Society*, Vol. 29, No. 1, pp. 43-72.

Blair, H. (2000), "Participation and Accountability at the Periphery: Democratic Local Governance in Six Countries", *World Development*, Vol. 28, No. 1, pp. 21-39.

Burki, S.J., G.E. Perry and W. R. Dillinger (1999), *Beyond the Center: Decentralizing the State*, Washington, D.C.: The World Bank, World Bank Latin American and Caribbean Studies.

Chaudhuri, S. and P. Heller (2002), "The Plasticity of Participation: Evidence from a Participatory Governance Experiment", mimeo.

Crook, R.C. and J. Manor (1998), *Democracy and Decentralisation in South Asia and West Africa: Participation, Accountability and Performance*, Cambridge: Cambridge University Press.

Crook, R.C. and A.S. Sverrisson (2001), "Decentralisation and Poverty-Alleviation in Developing Countries: A Comparative Analysis or, is West Bengal Unique?", *IDS Working Paper 130*, Brighton: Institute of Development Studies.

Dillinger, W. (1994), "Decentralisation and its Implications for Urban Service Delivery", *Urban Management and Municipal Finance, 16*, UNDP/UNCHS/World Bank Urban Management Programme, Washington, D.C.: The World Bank.

Escheverri-Gent, J. (1993), *The State and the Poor: Public Policy and Political Development in India and the United States*, Berkeley and Los Angeles: University of California Press.

Fiszbein, A. (1997), "The Emergence of Local Capacity: Lessons from Colombia," *World Development*, Vol. 25, No. 7, pp. 1029-43.

Forero, H. and M. Salazar (1991), "Local Government and Decentralisation in Colombia," *Environment and Urbanization*, Vol. 3, No. 2, pp. 121-26.

Francis, P. and R. James (2003), "Balancing Rural Poverty Reduction and Citizen Participation: The Contradictions of Uganda's Decentralisation Program", *World Development*, Vol. 31, No. 2, pp. 325-37.

Fung, A. and E.O. Wright (2001), "Deepening Democracy: Innovations in Empowered Participatory Governance", *Politics and Society*, Vol. 29, No. 1, pp. 5-41.

Gideon, J. (2001), "The Decentralisation of Primary Health Care in Chile", *Public Administration and Development*, Vol. 21, No. 3, pp. 223-31.

Heller, P. (2001), "Moving the State: The Politics of Democratic Decentralisation in Kerala, South Africa, and Porto Alegre", *Politics and Society*, Vol. 29, No. 1, pp. 131-63.

Isaac, T. with R.W. Franke (2000), *Local Democracy and Development: People's Campaign for Decentralised Planning in Kerala*, New Delhi: LeftWord Books.

Johnson, C. (2001), "Local Democracy, Democratic Decentralisation and Rural Development: Theories, Challenges and Options for Policy", *Development Policy Review*, Vol. 19, No. 4, pp. 521-32.

Klugman, J. (1994), "Decentralisation: A Survey of the Literature from a Human Development Perspective", *Occasional Paper 13*, New York: United Nations Development Program, Human Development Report Office.

Livack, J., J. Ahmad and R. Bird (1998), *Rethinking Decentralisation in Developing Countries*, Washington D.C.: The World Bank, Poverty Reduction and Economic Management Network.

Mahal, A., V. Srivastava and D. Sanan (2000), "Decentralisation and Public Sector Delivery of Health and Education Services: The Indian Experience", Discussion Papers on Development Policy No. 20, Bonn: Centre for Development Research, University of Bonn.

Manor, J. (1999), *The Political Economy of Democratic Decentralisation*, Washington, D.C.: The World Bank.

Mills, A., J.P. Vaughan, D.L. Smith, and I. Tabibzadeh (1990), *Health System Decentralisation: Concepts: Issues and Country Experience*, Geneva: World Health Organization.

Montoya-Aguilar, C. and P. Vaughan (1990), "Decentralisation and Local Management of the Health System in Chile", in Mills *et. al.*, pp. 55-63.

Mwabu, G., C. Ugaz, and G. White (eds.) (2001), *Social Provision in Low-Income Countries: New Patterns and Emerging Trends*, Oxford: Oxford University Press.

Nickson, R.A. (1995), *Local Government in Latin America*, Boulder, CO: Lynne Rienner.

Parry, T.R. (1997), "Decentralisation and Privatization: Education Policy in Chile", *Journal of Public Policy*, Vol. 17, No. 1, pp. 107-33.

Prawda, J. (1993), "Educational Decentralisation in Latin America: Lessons Learned", *International Journal of Educational Development*, Vol. 13, No. 3, pp. 253-64.

Rakodi, C. (2002), "Decentralisation: Does Local Democracy Improve Responsiveness to the Poor?", Institute of International Development, University of Birmingham, mimeo.

Robinson, M. and G. White (2001), "The Role of Civic Organizations in the Production of Social Services", in Mwabu *et. al.*, pp. 79-100.

Schneider, A. (2003), "Who Gets What From Whom? The Impact of Decentralisation on Tax Capacity and Pro-Poor Policy", *IDS Working Paper*, 179, Brighton: Institute of Development Studies.

Sixth Administrative Reforms Commission Report on "Local Governance: An Inspiring Journey into the Future", (2007, Government of India).

Smith, B. (1985), *Decentralisation: The Territorial Dimension of the State*, London: George, Allen and Unwin.

Stewart, F. and G. Ranis (1994), "Decentralisation in Chile", *Occasional Paper 14*, New York: United Nations Development Programme, Human Development Report Office.

Tankersley, W.B. and Cuzán, A.G. (1996), "Privatization and Decentralisation in the United States and Chile", *Journal of Developing Societies*, Vol. XII, No. 1, pp. 104-18.

Ugaz, C. (2001), "The Role of the State in the Provision of Social Services:
Decentralisation and Regulation," in Mwabu *et. al.*, pp. 142-53.

Wunsch, J.S. (2001), "Decentralisation, Local Governance and "Recentralization" in Africa", *Public Administration and Development*, Vol. 21, No. 4, pp. 277-88.

De Souza, Peter R., 2002, "Decentralisation and Local Government : the 'Second Wind' of Democracy in India". In *India's Constitution : Ideas, Practices, Controversies*. Edited by Zoya Hassan, E. Sirdharan and R. Sudarshan, New Delhi: Permanent Black, pp. 370-404.

Blomkvist, Hans, 2003, "Social Capital, Civil Society and Degrees of Democracy in India". In *Civil Society and Democracy in India*. Edited by Elliott Delhi: Oxford University Press.

Bogdanor, V., 1999, "Devolution, Decentralisation or Disintegration?" *Political Quarterly*, 70, No. 2, 185-94.

Widmalm, Sten, 2001, "Decentralisation and Development—The Effect of the Devolution of Power, July-December 2001, *Madhya Pradesh Journal of Social Science*.

Dreze, Jean and Amartya Sen, 1995, *India: Economic Development and Social Opportunity*, New Delhi, Oxford University Press.

Mitra, Subrata K., 1992, *Power, Protest and Participation: Local Elites and the Politics of Development in India*: London and New York: Rutledge.

Kohli, Atul, 1990, *Democracy and Discontent*, Cambridge. Cambridge University Press.

Bird, Richard and Thomas Stauffer, eds., 2001, *Decentralisation of the Socialist State*, World Bank: Washington D.C.

Horvarth, Tamas M., ed. 2000, *"Decentralisation: Experiment and Reforms", Local Government and Public Service Reforms Initiative*, Budapest: Hungary.

Lister, Stephen and Mary Betley, 1999, *Approaches to Decentralisation in Developing Countries*, World Bank: Washington D.C.

Rondielli, Dennis, J.R. Nellis, G.S. Cheema, 1983, *Decentralisation in Developing Countries: A Review of Recent Experience*, World Bank.

Gaventa John, 2002, "Towards Participatory Local Governance: Six Propositions for Discussion", Discussion paper at the Institute of Development Studies, Sussex, U.K.

Harris, John, 2000, "The Dialectics of Decentralisation", *Frontline*, Vol. 17, issue 13, 24 June, 27 July, 2000.

11

A Study of the Gram Panchayats in Haryana

A.S. Malik and Sahib Singh

The search for good government has always been advocated by many scholars in their writings. Its objective has always been to establish qualitative relationship between the government and the citizens as Mahatma Gandhi wrote: "The measure of a country's greatness should be based on how well it cares for its most vunerable population". He may be referring to the 'good governance'.

Thus the governance is good governance when it is carried "as per the constitutional and legal framework and rules and regulations framed to that effect and is also legitimately driven in accordance with and democratically decided policies in order to ensure developmental objectives and social harmony in the society".

The United Nations Development Programme (1997) enunciates the legitimacy and voice (focus on participation and consensus orientation); direction (focus on strategic vision); performance (focus on responsiveness, efficiency and effectiveness); accountability (focus on accountability to public and transparency) and fairness (focus on equity and rule of law) as the components of good governance. The sixth report of the Second Administrative Reforms Commission on Local Governance : An Inspiring Journey into the Future (October, 2007) stated that participation, rule of law, transparency, responsiveness, consensus orientation, equity, effectiveness and efficiency, accountability and strategic vision must be there in the institutional set-up of good governance.

GOOD GOVERNANCE AND DEMOCRATIC DECENTRALISATION

The Second Administrative Reform Commission (SARC) identifies subsidarity, democratic decentralisation, delineation of functions, and devolution in ideal terms, convergence, and citizen centricity as the principles of local governance. Thus any attempt to ensure good governance in local governance means the observance of the above stated principles in a practical manner. But as the assessment of the application of all the principles is an elephantine affair, the scope of the present paper is restricted to the democratic decentralisation only.

The Commission (SARC) expects that democratic decentralisation should be guided by: (i) a clear link in citizens' minds between their votes and the consequences in terms of the public good it promotes; (ii) tends to promote fiscal responsibility, provided there is a clear link between resource generation and outcomes in the form of better services; (iii) the asymmetry in power and the imbalance in its exercise need to be eliminated; and (iv) the need for greater citizen participation and ownership which are illusory despite national citizen sovereignty, need to be ensured. Therefore, if democracy is to be real and meaningful, the locus of power should shift as close to the citizen as possible in order to facilitate direct participation, constant vigil and timely intervention.

RESEARCH METHOD

An empirical study was conducted in five villages (Bandrana, Dadwana, Jajanpur, Solumajra and Kaul) of Kaithal district of Haryana mainly to find out the status of accountability at Gram Panchayat level. A small population of 30 respondents comprising of Sarpanches (16.7 per cent), Panches (33.3 per cent), and other knowledgeable persons (50 per cent) was purposively drawn for eliciting empirical information (Table 1). The sampled respondents were interviewed with the help of an unstructured interview schedule and information obtained from them has been processed and analysed with the help of SPSS.

TABLE 1
Position

	Frequency	*Valid Percent*	*Cumulative Percent*
Sarpanch	5	16.7	16.7
Panch	10	33.3	50.0
Other knowledgeable person	15	50.0	100.0
Total	30	100.0	

The sample of the study comprises of both male and females; however, the proportion of females is only 13.3 per cent (Table 2). Further, half of the

TABLE 2
Sex

	Frequency	Valid Percent	Cumulative Percent
Male	26	86.7	86.7
Female	4	13.3	100.0
Total	30	100.0	

sample is in the age group of 20-50 years and the other half is above 50 years (Table 3). The other knowledgeable respondents have a higher proportion of elder/aged people (about 60 per cent) in comparison to elected Sarpanches and Panches. The sample has also been drawn almost in proportion to the caste composition (general castes—53.3%, backward castes—23.3% and scheduled castes—23.3%, Table 4). The respondents are not much educated (66.7 per cent have primary to matriculation level of education). Besides, 20 per cent of them are illiterate and only 13.3 per cent could acquire education higher than matriculation (Table 5). Majority of them are agriculturists (56.78%), followed by agricultural labourers (13.3 percent), housewives (10 percent) and the remaining are shopkeepers, and those professing other occupations.

TABLE 3
Age

	Frequency	Valid Percent	Cumulative Percent
Up to 30 years	2	6.7	6.7
31-40 years	7	23.3	30.0
41-50 years	6	20.0	50.0
51-60 years	12	40.0	90.0
Above 60 years	3	10.0	100.0
Total	30	100.0	

TABLE 4
Castes

	Frequency	Valid Percent	Cumulative Percent
General castes	16	53.3	53.3
Backward castes	7	23.3	76.7
Scheduled castes	7	23.3	100.0
Total	30	100.0	

TABLE 5
Education Level

	Frequency	*Valid Percent*	*Cumulative Percent*
Illiterate	6	20.0	20.0
Primary	6	20.0	40.0
Middle	8	26.7	66.7
Matriculation	6	20.0	86.7
Graduation	1	3.3	90.0
Others	3	10.0	100.0
Total	30	100.0	

ACCOUNTABILITY : NEED AND ITS ELEMENTS

The experiences indicate that democracy, including local democracy, is by no means a perfect tool to improve governance. The only antidote to imperfections in democracy is more and better democracy. It has also been experienced that the evolutionary process of governing institutions, including the institutions of local governance in a democracy, has always been plagued with many kinds of negative tendencies. The Second ARC report also supports this view-point and states: "Experience over the last decade shows that, in many cases, local governments are beset by the same problems of corruption, patronage, arbitrary exercise of power and inefficiency which have bedevilled governance". Thus, the power is prone to corruption and the local institutions of democratic decentralisation are more susceptible to this malaise. Therefore, there is an urgent need to ensure "effective instruments of accountability to check abuse of power and to give citizens a voice in improving the quality of services". In simple words, the local governance needs to be accountable if it wishes to qualify as an instrument of good governance. It is also evident from the responses of the

TABLE 6
Occupations

	Frequency	*Valid Percent*	*Cumulative Percent*
Labour/Agri. labour	4	13.3	13.3
Agriculture	17	56.7	70.0
Shopkeeper	2	6.7	76.7
Agriculture and business	2	6.7	83.3
Housewife	3	10.0	93.3
Others	2	6.7	100.0
Total	30	100.0	

sampled respondents that a large majority of them wish to review the working of the Panchayats after two years (Table 7). However, more than one-fifth of them wish that these must be sovereign within the village and should be accountable to the villagers rather than to any outside agency including the state or legislature which enacted law for establishing the Panchayats (Table 8).

TABLE 7
Perceptions on Willingness to Review the Working of Panchayats

	Frequency	*Valid Percent*	*Cumulative Percent*
Yes	24	80.0	80.0
No-response	6	20.0	100.0
Total	30	100.0	

TABLE 8
Perceptions on the Agency to Review the Working of the Panchayats

Institutions for reviewing the performance	*Frequency*	*Valid Percent*	*Cumulative Percent*
Committee (unknown composition)	2	6.7	6.7
Government	7	23.3	30.0
Committee of villagers	6	20.0	50.0
PR officials	4	13.3	63.3
Gram Sabha	1	3.3	66.7
No-response	10	33.3	100.0
Total	30	100.0	

Democratic accountability is the touchstone of democracy and the ultimate goal of many administrative reforms. Generally speaking, accountability of public institutions has focused almost wholly on two issues namely, (a) prevention of activities not specifically authorised by law or any subordinate legislation, and (b) integrity of the public system or maintenance of financial propriety, which is often equated with adherence to financial rules. The information collected from the respondents indicates that only a simple majority of them (53.3 per cent) affirmed that the Panchayats are working as per the law/rules laid down for the purpose. Many (16.7 per cent) were uncertain about it (Table 9). Thus about one-third (30 per cent) find their working as improper. Further the respondents who rated it as per law, are higher among the Sarpanches and lower in case of the knowledgeable persons of the concerned villages. The Panches found it

TABLE 9
Panchayat's Functioning as Per Law/Rules

	Frequency	Valid Percent	Cumulative Percent
Agree	9	30.0	30.0
Fully Agree	7	23.3	53.3
Uncertain	5	16.7	70.0
Disagree	8	26.7	96.7
Fully disagree	1	3.3	100.0
Total	30	100.0	

to be uncertain in comparison to the other categories of respondents Table 10).

TABLE 10
Perceptions on Panchayat's Functioning as Per Law/Rules

Categories of respondents	Panchayat functions as per law/rules					Total
	Agree	Fully Agree	Uncertain	Disagree	Fully disagree	
Sarpanches	1 11.1%	4 57.1%	0 .0%	0 .0%	0 .0%	5 16.7%
Panches	3 33.3%	2 28.6%	4 80.0%	1 12.5%	0 .0%	10 33.3%
Other knowledgeable person	5 55.6%	1 14.3%	1 20.0%	7 87.5%	1 100.0%	15 50.0%
Total	9 100.0%	7 100.0%	5 100.0%	8 100.0%	1 100.0%	30 100.0%

There are certain other elements also which influence the extent and quality of accountability of an institution. These are the responsiveness, efficient and effective performance particularly in meeting legitimate demands of people and fair play, adherence to rule of law.

The accountability of local bodies manifests and focuses on the followings:

1. Institutional mechanisms to ensure propriety.
2. Measures to improve responsiveness of the local bodies to the people.
3. Evaluation of local bodies by measuring their performance in terms of efficiency, effectiveness and other indicators.

In other words, the accountability is ensured in the form of state control which is preventive and through maintaining propriety/integrity, increasing responsiveness by developing some institutional mechanism and by measuring performance *vis-à-vis* some established standards.

I. State Control

The institutional mechanism for state control is mainly exercised by state legislature, executive and accounting and audit system.

The SARC is of the view that howsoever independent the third tier of governance may become, it should still be responsible to the State Legislature. The Commission is of the considered view that legislative supervision can be ensured by institutionalising a separate Committee on Local Bodies in the State Legislature.

There are valid reasons for this as a large chunk of resources is currently being devolved to the local bodies for the implementation of various centrally sponsored schemes called eight flagship programmes. The policy envisages that the funds both from the Union and State Governments for various schemes would flow directly to the nodal agency designated by the states and funds for identified projects would be disbursed to the local institutions executing programmes or spending units. It is true that the rural local institutions are yet to be devolved with these functions but quantum of funds is increasing year after year. Thus, with the large flow of funds under various socio-economic development programmes to the local bodies and the growing realisation of the importance of the third tier of government, accountability concerns assume critical importance and this accountability may be best discharged by the people of the village itself.

Owing to the large number of local bodies in the country, it is necessary to address the concerns regarding maintenance of accounts and audit. Article 243J of the Constitution provides for the audit of the accounts of Panchayats in the following way: "The Legislature of a State may, by law, make provisions with respect to the maintenance of accounts by the Panchayats and the auditing of such accounts". Even though various states have incorporated general provisions regarding audit and maintenance of accounts in their Panchayati Raj Acts, detailed guidelines have generally not been issued. The Eleventh Finance Commission (EFC) had an occasion to comment on this:

> "Article 243J and 243Z of the Constitution expect the states to make provisions by way of legislation for maintenance of accounts by the Panchayats and the Municipalities and for the audit of such accounts. Following this, most states' legislation do make general provisions for these purposes, but detailed guidelines or rules have not been laid down in several cases. In many states, the formats and procedures for maintenance of accounts by these bodies prescribed decades ago are continued without making any improvement to take into account the manifold increase in their powers, resources and responsibilities".

Besides this, empirical information reveals the absence of financial propriety. As many as 30 per cent of respondents were uncertain about the observance of financial propriety and another 13.3 per cent clearly stated that there is some sort of impropriety (Table 11). Moreover, the respondents who were uncertain were Panches and the knowledgeable persons of the village. But, all of them except 13.4 (who were uncertain and disagreed) a large majority of the respondents stated that grants are being spent on right and need-based activities (Table 12). In simple words, this shows that the financial resources are being properly utilized on the rightly identified works but there may be a chance of not following the financial rules or of misappropriation. This is evident from the data in Table 13 which indicates that 60 percent of them feel that their Panchayats are honest and remaining 40 per cent did not respond.

TABLE 11
Panchayat Functions as per Financial Rules

	Frequency	*Valid Percent*	*Cumulative Percent*
Agree	6	20.0	20.0
Fully agree	11	36.7	56.7
Uncertain	9	30.0	86.7
Disagree	3	10.0	96.7
Fully disagree	1	3.3	100.0
Total	30	100.0	

TABLE 12
Panchayat Spends Grants on Right and Need-based Activities

	Frequency	*Valid Percent*	*Cumulative Percent*
Agree	17	56.7	56.7
Fully Agree	9	30.0	86.7
Uncertain	2	6.7	93.3
Disagree	2	6.7	100.0
Total	30	100.0	

TABLE 13
Perceptions Regarding the Incidence of Panchayat being Honest

	Frequency	*Valid Percent*	*Cumulative Percent*
Yes	18	60.0	60.0
No-response	12	40.0	100.0
Total	30	100.0	

Most village level Panchayats do not have any staff except for a full or a part-time Secretary because of financial constraints. It would, therefore, be rather too much to expect them to have a trained person dedicated exclusively to the upkeep of accounts.

As regards audit, the legislation leaves it to the State Government to prescribe the authority. In some states, the Director, Local Fund Audit or a similar authority has been given the responsibility for the audit of accounts of Panchayats. The C&AG has a role only in a few states and that too for the audit of district level Panchayats. In our view, this needs to be set right through the supervision of the C&AG and by specific earmarking of funds from the grants recommended to the local bodies.

The audit in traditional sense is applied only in financial context and in that context it means 'an official examination of accounts'.[13] But, now-a-days, it has also been frequently applied to governance/public governance. The most general definition of an audit is 'an evaluation of a person, organisation, system, process, project or product'. Audits are performed to ascertain the validity and reliability of information and also to provide an assessment of a system's internal control.

The purpose of undertaking audit has always been improving the governance or the working of an institution by making 'suitable recommendations to improve transparency, accountability and ethical behaviour' of the governance or institution audited. In wider context, depending upon the subject matter of the things to be audited, the audit comprises of three categories namely: compliance audit, financial audit and performance audit. However, as audit is a *post facto* control mechanism therefore many a times it has not been found effective to the desired level. Hence, the measures to reform audit system have been felt necessary in the Panchayats.

One of these measures may be the "the appointment of an Audit Committee by the State Government with independent members of proven integrity and professional competence and with appropriate oversight powers". These are expected to play a significant role in improving all aspects of governance, including transparency, accountability and ethical behaviour. In the case of local bodies, such Audit Committees may be constituted at the district level.

2. Measures to Improve Responsiveness of the Local Bodies to the People

In order to ensure efficient service delivery, accessibility and reach, there is need for improving the responsiveness of the local bodies to the citizens. Such responsiveness could be enhanced through:

(i) Delegation of functions.
(ii) In-house mechanism for redressal of grievances.
(iii) Social audit.
(iv) Transparency.

(i) Delegation of Functions

The delegation of functions should be made to the lowest functionary or the unit of governance. This is the level where frequent interface of citizens takes place. This level is real and effective for performing developmental function or delivering basic/welfare service to the people. Besides it helps to make the lowest functionary accountable and to inculcate responsibility at the cutting edge level. This would make the local bodies responsive in their interface with the common man. It is at this level where a clear link between votes and their consequences can be established.

The sampled respondents were asked to respond the question: Is there any benefit of electing your representatives or Panchayats? All of them stated that this has resulted in infrastructural development of the village. Naturally there is a benefit of having a representative body. Thus there is a link between the vote and its consequences. It is realised but perhaps in rudimentary form.

The public policy on local governance intends wider and effective people's participation. However in practice, the government is restricting the Panchayats to certain limited traditional activities which they used to perform collectively for community use. There has been nothing new except linking it with the democratic politics and extending grants for various purposes, but mainly for poverty alleviation programmes. The intellectual capacity and moral virtues of government official at the village level are not high enough to influence the Gram Panchayats' leaders and people to follow them. The democratic politics can not ensure real involvement and participation as everyone does not desire to join democratic politics (except at the time of elections when every one wishes to participate). Only personal benefits or social recognition motivate the people to join it. Hence the real involvement and participation remain confined to elected representatives and to those who contested elections. But devolution of more functions to local institutions may widen the scope for involvement if not for participation. Therefore, it is again stressed that more functions be entrusted to the Panchayats in order to promote people's participation. More participation means more accountability. The sampled respondents were probed about the nature of their involvement and we found that about half of them (46.7 per cent) are active participants and the others (53.3 per cent) were active only at the time of election (Table 14). It is important to state here that election time involvement is also found in elected Sarpanches, Panches and in some of the knowledgeable persons of the village who held these offices earlier but could not contest the last election because of reservations or who had been defeated in it.

The demand to devolve functions to Panchayats has been stressed by the majority of respondents (76.7 per cent). They stated that these need to be entrusted with more functions than the existing ones. Only 10 per cent of them disagreed with the need to devolve more functions to the Panchayats (Table 15). Further, it is not merely the devolution of functions, they

TABLE 14
Participation in Panchayati Raj Institutions

	Frequency	*Valid Percent*	*Cumulative Percent*
Casting vote	10	33.3	33.3
Voting and motivating candidates to contest	6	20.0	53.3
Many levels of involvement	14	46.7	100.0
Total	30	100.0	

TABLE 15
Panchayats and Other Functions

	Frequency	*Valid Percent*	*Cumulative Percent*
Agree	13	43.3	43.3
Fully agree	10	33.3	76.7
Uncertain	4	13.3	90.0
Disagree	2	6.7	96.7
Fully disagree	1	3.3	100.0
Total	30	100.0	

(although 70%) are also confident that the Panchayats shall perform in much effective way in comparison to government agency. There are a substantial proportion of respondents who are uncertain (16.7 per cent) or who disagreed (13.3%) on this. However, the respondents do not agree with the view that the Panchayats can perform these functions in a more economic way than the government.

(ii) In-house Mechanism for Redressal of Grievances

An independent grievance redressal body is needed to provide the citizens with an instrument for enforcing accountability. This body can make the Panchayats realize their lapses. No doubt the Gram Sabha can perform this responsibility but it could not become effective. Therefore, there is a need to provide an effective institution to play the role of an in-house watch dog.

It is urgent as devolution of funds, functions and functionaries is inevitable because of political, administrative and technical reasons. Even if this devolution has not taken place as yet, it is certain that there will be an enormous increae in the services to be delivered and the funds to be spent by the Panchayats. And, naturally that will give rise to the incidence of complaints and other grievances and hence there is need to have an independent grievance removal mechanism.

The absence of such a mechanism has been creating many kinds of problems. This has not only been hampering smooth functioning of Panchayats but has also been draining lot of human and financial resources. Otherwise, those might have been utilized for rural development. The conflicts and complaints, when reported to the officials under present institutional framework, are delayed intentionally. It reflects the indecisiveness of the present system. This state of affairs has made the local leaders to believe that nothing is likely to happen in the name of reforms and hence they can not become active participants unless they safeguard their vested interests.

The need for institutionalising a grievance redressal mechanism has also been felt to address the complaints regarding elected functionaries and officials of the local bodies. The basic purpose is to provide a platform to the citizens for voicing their complaints and also for bringing out the deficiencies in the system for suitable remedial action.

Therefore, the SARC recommended the setting up of Ombudsman by making appropriate changes in the local governance related legislations. But the experiences of the working of this institution in Kerala indicate that its success story has been a limited one. Therefore, it is suggested that a proper enquiry needs to be conducted before arriving at a decision on this issue.

(iii) Social Audit

The creation of an effective system of social audit is essential for improving local service delivery and for ensuring compliance with laws and regulations. An effective system of social audit will have to be based on two precepts; first, that service standards are made public through citizens' charters and second, that *suo moto* periodic disclosure is made for the attainment of service delivery standards by the local bodies. The formal audit should give due consideration to the findings of social audit and *vice-versa*. It is also stressed that operational guidelines of all developmental schemes and citizen centric programmes should provide for a social audit mechanism. Usually there is belief that whatever service is provided by the government, it can not be supervised by the body of citizens or the Panchayats. This misconception has been dysfunctional for the empowerment programmes being undertaken by the Panchayat leadership for the government.

The operational guidelines stipulate that there should be a Local Vigilance and Monitoring Committee, composed of members of the locality or village where the work is undertaken, to monitor the progress and quality of work. The Gram Sabha has to elect the members of this Committee and to ensure adequate representation of SC/ST and women on it. However, as indicated earlier, it is difficult to build a culture of social audit at Gram Panchayat level owing to rigid and traditional social-cultural traditions. But this is necessary for strengthening accountability of the local democratic institution.

(iv) Transparency

Right to Information has made the functioning of Gram Panchayats open to all. Not only this, there is a provision to make *suo moto* disclosure of information, especially with regard to duties, functions, financial transactions and resolutions of the Panchayats. This is an instrument which can ensure their more real accountability. Therefore, it is suggested that every thing in the Panchayats must come under *suo moto* disclosure provision. Several local bodies have developed their own transparency mechanisms. Such practices may also be adopted by other local bodies. This may save the resources of local government and also infuse confidence among the citizen. It can help in the establishment of a qualitative relationship between the state and citizens. This may also link the votes to the public goods.

EVALUATION OF PERFORMANCE OF LOCAL BODIES

In general, improving government performance and facilitating citizen participation are the two fundamental requirements for local governance. Therefore, performance measurement and citizen participation have been the important reform streams in recent years. However, the link between performance measurement and citizen participation has not been fully emphasised.

Local bodies have to be evaluated in terms of efficiency, effectiveness and resource mobilisation. For example, the Union Ministry of Panchayati Raj has also instituted an Awards Scheme for the Panchayats (in 2005). One important criterion for determining the best Gram Panchayat under this Scheme is 'efficient service delivery tested against specifically identified benchmarks and range of activities'.

Apart from the above, the evaluation of the performance of local bodies may also be attempted from the viewpoint of the citizens. This brings the concept of 'feedback mechanism' to the fore. The feedback could be on legal and procedural conformity, services and amenities, public works and projects and on the planning and vision.

12

Democratic Decentralisation and Good Governance : The Need for Realistic Empowerment of Panchayats

V. Eshwar Anand

The democratic decentralisation has been widely recognised as the key to good governance because it is considered necessary for ensuring its essential ingredients–transparency, accountability and responsiveness. It had been institutionalised in India through the establishment of Panchayati Raj Institutions (PRIs) in 1959. The powerful support to these by the then Prime Minister of India, Pandit Jawaharlal Nehru, led to the rapid development of these institutions of decentralised rural governance. But, these gradually lost their shine and virtually became shadows without substance after his demise in 1964 because Nehru's successors did not share his faith in democratic decentralisation. Even the recommendations of the High Powered Committee on Panchayati Raj, popularly known as Ashoka Mehta Committee (1978), failed to revitalise these due to the same reason. However, Nehru's grandson, the Late Rajiv Gandhi who succeeded Indira Gandhi as the Prime Minister in 1984 after her assassination, recognised the need of democratic decentralisation for good governance and therefore, moved the 64th Constitutional Amendment Bill in the Lok Sabha in 1989. This aimed at the strengthening of the PRIs by according them a constitutional status and by making them inclusive through adequate representation for the women. Although, he did not succeed in his mission due to the opposition from the vested interests, his unfinished agenda was completed by the 73rd Constitutional Amendment Act (1992) and the 74th

Constitutional Amendment Act (1993). These Amendments are important milestones in the annals of the Panchayati Raj.

The PRIs have made a big headway since then. Today, there are 23293 Gram Panchayats, 6094 Panchayat Samitis and 537 Zila Parishads in India. There are 265647 members of Gram Panchayats and out of them 975116 are women. In the Panchayat Samitis, there are 156609 representatives. Out of them, 58095 are women. The Zila Parishads have 15698 representatives. Out of which, 5779 are women. (*The State of Panchayats, A Mid-term Review and Appraisal*, 22 November, 2006, Vol. III, Ministry of Panchayati Raj, Government of India).

This is gender empowerment at its best, unparalleled in the world. Clearly, this makes the world's largest democracy the most representative democracy. Significantly, women's participation in the panchayat elections has been increasing every year. Though the 73rd Constitutional Amendment Act mandated only 33 percent seats to be reserved for women in many states they far exceed the mandated quota. According to the Union Ministry of Panchayati Raj, women members in the PRIs constitute over 37 percent of the elected representatives. In states such as Karnataka, the proportion of elected women members is as high as 45 percent.

Despite considerable progress of the PRIs in the country, the results have been uneven in states. In Kerala, for example, over 40 per cent of development expenditure of both planned and unplanned budget is utilized by the PRIs. But situation in the states like Punjab and Haryana is far from encouraging in this context.

It is pertinent to mention that the purpose of the PRIs is to encourage popular participation not only in the management of local affairs but also in the implementation of developmental plans and programmes. The founding fathers of the Constitution were fully convinced that without popular participation, no democratic system of government could be successful. From this point of view, the Panchayati Raj experiment is a commendable effort.

However, there is no denying of the fact that it has not been as successful as it was expected to be. Some of the shortcomings are as follows:

- The local government functions and the development functions have been mixed up although these two functions are vastly different in nature. They are rather incompatible with each other. While development functions require expert knowledge and a certain measure of centralised planning and control, the management of local affairs requires maximum freedom of action. The mixing up of the two functions has created confusion. There is an impression that neither the local affairs are properly managed nor are the developmental programmes effectively implemented.
- There is no clear cut demarcation of functions between the Gram Panchayat, Panchayat Samitis and the Zila Parishads. This absence of role differentiation has led to conflict among them. The elected

representatives of the Gram Panchayats feel that the higher level bodies often make undue interference in their working. The members of Panchayat Samitis feel that the Gram Panchayats do not bother about them. The representatives in the Zila Parishads have a feeling that neither the Gram Panchayats nor the Panchayat Samitis care for them.

- The paucity of funds is a big problem in the way of successful working of the PRIs. Moreover, they have very limited powers to levy taxes and cesses and the funds doled out to them by the state governments are meager. Furthermore, the PRIs are generally reluctant to raise necessary funds through taxes for fear of losing popularity with the masses.
- The PRIs suffer from excessive bureaucratisation. The main objective of the Panchayati Raj was to offer opportunities to the people for maximum participation in the management of the affairs that concern primarily to them. However, in reality, the key administrative and technical positions are manned by government officials who are under the administrative control of the state government. For the success of the Panchayati Raj System, it is imperative that the administrative personnel are under the direct superintendence and administrative control of the local institutions themselves. But this is easier said than done in the present scheme of things.
- The PRIs are also accused of having an undemocratic character. This cuts at the very root of democratic decentralisation. In many states, both the Panchayat Samitis and Zila Parishads are packed with *ex-officio* and associate members. This vitiates the working of the system.
- The state government's absolute control over the PRIs is repugnant to the concept of democratic decentralisation. Though a certain amount of state control and supervision are required, excessive control has retarded the PRIs' healthy growth. The state government constitutes the PRIs, delimits their jurisdiction and assigns them specific powers and functions. It arbitrates in all inter-local disputes, i.e. disputes between the Panchayats, Panchayat Samitis and Zila Parishads as also between the rural and urban local governments. It associates its officials with the local bodies at all levels. The Deputy Commissioner (DC) or the District Collector (DC) exercises extensive powers *vis-a-vis* the PRIs.
- And finally, infiltration of party politics has considerably vitiated the PRIs working. The active involvement of political leaders and parties in the day-to-day functioning of the local bodies has brought into play partisan considerations which adversely affect the unity and harmony of the village communities.

Let us now focus on three critical areas for strengthening and streamlining the working of the PRIs. These are taxation, planning and e-governance.

TAXATION

Even though the Panchayati Raj Acts in the states have given taxation powers to the village panchayats, the revenue domain of the intermediate and zila panchayats (tax as well as non-tax) has been kept much smaller and remains confined to secondary areas like ferry services, markets, water and conservancy services, registration of vehicles, cess on stamp duty and so on.

Surely, the political empowerment of panchayats will be meaningless without their financial empowerment. Often, the PRIs are delegated agency functions with funds devolved from the Centre and the states along with detailed guidelines on how these funds should be spent. The lack of adequate sources of revenue and limited discretion on expenditure severely limit the PRIs autonomy.

The PRIs' taxation powers differ from state to state. In Orissa, all taxation powers lie exclusively with the Village Panchayats. In Rajasthan, the Panchayat Samitis enjoy some taxation powers. But these are limited to a few select items such as land rent, *vikas* tax and education cess. In Madhya Pradesh, while the Panchayat Samitis levy business tax and entertainment tax. However, the Zila Parishads don't have taxation powers. In Bihar, the Zila Parishads can levy fees on registration of boats/vehicles, sanitary arrangements in fairs, public street lighting, etc., but the Panchayat Samitis hold concurrent powers in the same areas of taxation.

There is a strong case for transferring the power to tax agriculture to the Panchayats which has constitutionally been in the state domain (going by the division of taxation powers).

Dr. Indira Rajaraman, a noted economist and Member, Thirteenth Finance Commission, suggests an agricultural levy by Panchayats. In her book, *Fiscal Domain of the Panchayats,* she says that the Panchayats should be allowed to retain the entire revenue and encouraged to spend it on productivity augmenting infrastructure in agriculture.

The scheme suggested for agricultural levy by Dr Rajaraman is simple. It requires only minimum information inputs. It is a crop-specific levy principally on high value commercial crops. The proposed levy will not replace the land revenue but will supplement it.

In any case, there is a need to widen the PRI's tax base. They will have to explore additional sources of revenue. The classical items of taxes to be collected by them are imposition of profession tax, cattle registration fee and vehicle registration fee. Why can not they be empowered to take innovative taxation measures in areas like fee on tourist vehicles, special amenities, restaurants, theatres, cyber café, etc.? They could also be encouraged to manage utilities such as transport, water supply and power distribution.

The Government of India's Second Administrative Reforms Commission headed by M. Veerappa Moily, former Karnataka Chief Minister, in its report on *Local Governance*, has rightly stressed the need for the PRIs to become more imaginative and assertive in tapping resources. In this context, the state governments, too, will have to extend their unstinted help and assistance to the PRIs.

PLANNING

Decentralised planning at the level of Panchayats has not yet been institutionalised in all the states. Many State Acts don't contain provisions for preparing development plans at all levels of Panchayats as envisaged under Article 243G of the Constitution.

Haryana has stolen a march over other states in having decided to set up District Planning Committees (DPCs) in all the districts. However, this decision is rather belated. Though the State Government had notified rules for the constitution of these panels on March 12, 1997, successive governments did not pursue it to its logical conclusion. The Bhupinder Singh Hooda Government took a formal decision only on December 4, 2007.

Unfortunately, many states have not taken this role seriously, implying that realistic devolution of powers and responsibilities has not yet taken place. Three reasons can be attributed to the Panchayats' apathetic attitude towards planning. One, they don't have the authority, expertise or infrastructure to implement what they plan.

Two, the lack of untied funds at the disposal of Panchayats. What can these bodies do if they only have the schematic funds to use? They do need untied funds to finance projects that cannot be covered by the tied funds.

And three, the Planning Commission, Government of India, and the State Planning Boards have not taken adequate interest on local level planning. The former has not taken measures for integrating the local plans with the state plans. And the latter have not prepared viable frameworks for preparing local plans.

There is also confusion regarding the nature of district plans (Is it a collection of the Panchayat and Municipal plans?) and the domain of planning (Should district plans focus on those functions devolved to local bodies?). Veerappa Moily's Second Administrative Reforms Commission Report says that the district plan should try to ensure integrated planning for the rural and urban areas in the district.

Surprisingly, many states have not yet constituted the DPCs, an important institution created following the Constitution 74th Amendment. In some states, these are also riddled by other problems. One-fifth of the total members in the DPC can be nominated. A nominated member can also become its chairman. Consequently, these have become tools of political patronage in the ruling party's hands.

In some states, the DPCs have emerged as power centres challenging the authority of the Panchayat-Municipal system. The DPCs are neither accountable directly to the people nor to the Panchayat-Municipal system. There is yet another problem. Separate district plans will have to be prepared for each of the major Centrally-sponsored schemes.

For the metropolitan areas, it has become a challenge for the authorities concerned how to establish an effective interface between the DPC and the Metropolitan Planning Committee (MPC). In Delhi, for instance, the metropolitan area consists of seven revenue districts. Some of these are still in rural areas which may be urbanised after some time. In some cases, the urbanised area could extend to more than one district. The setting up of DPCs and MPCs without delineating their respective jurisdictions will lead to confusion.

In some states like Haryana, the Deputy Commissioner (DC) has been made the Chairperson of the DPC. It is being argued that this overworked functionary has little time for the challenging task of district planning. On the other hand it has been argued that being a neutral functionary, the DC alone can do justice and give equitable treatment to both rural and urban segments of the districts. Therefore ways should be evolved in these states to help the DCs spare reasonable time for district planning.

Indeed, the task of formulating the district plan is daunting. It calls for effective coordination between the elected representatives and official functionaries of the PRIs, on the one hand, and the district heads of the line departments on the other. As the DC has the administrative control over all these functionaries, she/he alone can help achieve coordination in this regard.

Moreover, being the connecting link between the district, the state and the centre, the DC is on a firm footing. She/he is also aware of the objectives of the Five-Year Plan, policies and programmes of the centre and the state. In sharp contrast, if the Presidents or Chairmen of Zila Parishads head the district planning apparatus, they may look at things from a narrow prism and have a altogether different agenda.

E-GOVERNANCE

Undoubtedly, information technology and e-governance have revolutionized the Panchayati Raj system. E-governance is a big boon for the PRIs. The Information Communications Technology (ICT), in particular, is a feather in their cap. It is a leap forward towards empowering them. Information technology has become an important decision-making tool for transparency, Right to Information, social audit, capacity building and e-procurement in the PRIs. Some states have taken encouraging initiatives in this regard, these include Karnataka, Andhra Pradesh, Haryana, Punjab, Orissa, Gujarat, Rajasthan, Kerala and Tamil Nadu.

The national Panchayat portal, launched by the National Informatics Centre (NIT) is, indeed, a dynamic website for all the PRIs. It is local language-enabled wherein the Panchayat representatives can interact with their counterparts across rural areas. This portal provides a framework for individual PRIs to log in and publish their contents on the web. Gram Pradhans seem to be excited about it.

Plan Plus, the NIT-designed software solution assists and guides the process of grassroot planning. It is designed in accordance with the guidelines of the Planning Commission on District Planning. Kerala, Karnataka, Gujarat, Andhra Pradesh, West Bengal and Chhattisgarh have made considerable progress in this field. It brings upfront the total availability of resources and their optimal allocation to demand-led proposals being advocated by the people.

Of all e-governance projects aimed at strengthening the PRIs in the country, Gujarat's *e-Gram* project is the most commendable. Encouraged by the success of a pilot project in the Valukad village of Bhavnagar district, the government has equipped all 13,753 village panchayats with *e-Gram* facility.

This entailed computerisation of the entire village for instant processing of birth and death registration and issuance of certificates such as agriculture, caste, income, electricity and tax. The State Government extends technical and training support to *e-Gram* computer centres.

Under this scheme it has devised a three-phase plan: first put up the infrastructure like chairs, tables and electricity in the Panchayats, followed by computers, then connectivity and then a system to maintain it.

Of course, the Government of India provided a lot of capacity-building funds including technical support for the success of this scheme.

The government was keen not to leave anything incomplete. The officials realised the fact that after providing computers to the Panchayats, they need to make foolproof arrangements for their regular maintenance. Accordingly, they made groups each of which consisted of 30 Panchayats. Five major companies were outsourced to maintain computers with a three-year contract. An IT professional visits every village to check the machines. If there is a problem, there is the call centre mechanism: the taluk-level executive takes care of the taluk's computers, the district-level entrepreneur liaisons with the district officials who maintain the system. There is also a state-level executive.

Equally daunting was how to achieve the connectivity. The problem before the government was not technology but governance. It created the e-Gram society at the state level with the Chief Minister as the head of the governing body. This society has now plans to set-up offices in the USA and the UK for the Gujaratis.

Subsequently, the State Government integrated the Government of India's Common Services Centre (CSC) with the e-Gram society. It aimed at total integration when the CSC scheme sanctions 3,000 computers, the state will match the number.

Significantly, yet another innovation of the Gujarat Government is the concept of Village Computer Entrepreneur (VCE) under which a computer is given to a village operator. The State Government lists out six or seven services that the operator is supposed to provide to the people at a cost. The

IT-savvy Sarpanches were also been involved in the exercise. They are superimposing the CSC in a manner that it gets integrated with the VCE.

It may be concluded that the 73rd and the 74th Constitutional Amendment Acts have given a fillip to democratic decentralisation by strengthening the PRIs. These have also improved the prospects of good governance by making PRIs inclusive through the empowerment of women. But much more needs to be done by removing the bottlenecks. Financial empowerment of the PRIs is urgently needed. The decentralised planning mechanism will have to be strengthened through the capacity-building of the elected representatives of the PRIs and the Members of the DPCs. e-Governance will also have to be promoted by emulating the Gujarat model for ensuring good governance through the institutions of decentralised rural governance.

13

Democratic Decentralisation and Good Governance in India : Promises and Perils

D. SUNDAR RAM

At present, as many as 70 countries are implementing political reforms aimed at the enhancement of role of local self-governments in delivering good governance because democratic decentralisation brings government closer to the people. It refers to the principle that public decisions should be made, when possible, at the level of authority closest to the people. When power is brought closer to the citizens, the political process becomes more transparent and more people can become involved in it.

Devolution of powers, responsibilities and resources to the local self-government institutions also promotes good governance through better service delivery. It deepens democracy and enhances the legitimacy of political system. However, the attainment of good governance depends on the development of the capacity of the local self-government. Devolution is considered to be the most effective form of decentralisation and involves transfer of functions or decision-making authority to legally incorporated local self-government institutions. The issue of decentralised governance has been assuming greater significance because a lot depends on the efficacy of local governance in implementing the targeted poverty alleviation programmes and in managing the economic development.

Local governance, as a matter of fact, is the level of democracy at which the citizen has the most effective opportunity to participate actively and directly in decision-making. At the start of the twenty-first century, there has been a dramatic revival in the emphasis on local democracy. This renewed interest in the principles and procedures of democratic governance at the level closest to the people is in some ways a return 'to the very foundations of democratic theory and practice. If sufficient powers and finances are devolved, the grassroots democratic institutions would get strength to become effective instruments of socio-economic change in contemporary India.

The issue to be examined here is whether the 73rd Constitution Amendment Act makes the Panchayati Raj Institutions constitutional bodies? Will these be able to reflect the aspirations and expectations of the people at the grassroots? What are the factors contributing to the disempowerment of Panchayati Raj Institutions, even 16 years after the enactment of the 73rd Constitution Amendment Act? Therefore, it is time to reflect on the experiences gained in the strategy of devolution of powers and if necessary, for their transformation.

The main objective of the paper is to explore the initiatives of the successive governments at the Centre towards democratic decentralisation through Panchayati Raj Institutions in general and to analyse the emerging problems and challenges in delivering good governance at the grassroots in particular. It is divided into four parts. Part-I examines the concepts of democratic decentralisation and good governance. Part-II maps the sincere efforts of the successive governments at the Centre in the process of administrative decentralisation to the local bodies. Part-III presents the emerging problems and challenges in the working of grassroots democratic institutions and Part-IV suggests some reforms in PRI's governance.

I

CONCEPT OF DEMOCRATIC DECENTRALISATION AND GOOD GOVERNANCE

The significance of decentralised governance was realised after Mahatma Gandhi's insistence on the establishment of Village Panchayats at the grassroots level, as units of local self-government. Since Independence, lots of efforts have been made to decentralise governance both in rural and urban sectors. While introducing the Draft Constitution, a large number of members, including Shibban Lal Saxena, H.V. Kamath, P.S. Deshmukh, A.C. Guha, T. Prakasam, Alladi Krishna Swami Ayyar, M. Anantha Sayanam Ayyangar and N.G. Ranga strongly argued in favour of Panchayat system. As a result, an amendment proposing to insert an Article in the Chapter on Directive Principles of State Policy was moved by K. Santhanam. Thus, the democratic decentralisation became very important after Independence from the point of view of twin objective of democracy and development in the Indian polity.

This is how India moved from big government approach to small government approach and created Panchayats. The first Prime Minister of

India, Pandit Jawaharlal Nehru, described these as the "foundations of democracy" in Independent India. Speaking on the occasion of the Inauguration of Panchayati Raj at Nagaur in Rajasthan on 2nd October, 1959, he expressed his faith in the capability of the people in managing their affairs in the manner considered best by them.

As a result of the enactment of 73rd Constitution Amendment Act of 1992, there has been decentralisation and democratisation of local administration. The Panchayats have been given a constitutional status. Now they are widely recognised as effective political instruments for the realisation of balanced and equitable development in Indian society.

Pranab Bardhan writes that decentralisation is a rage in today's world, and the important reasons suggested by him in this context are loss of legitimacy of the Centre and the States and a corresponding belief that decentralisation can bring a range of benefits directly to the local people.[1] Mohit Bhattacharya feels that decentralisation takes the heavy load of governance off the shoulder of the central and state governments, brings government to the door-step of the people, empowers and makes them active participants in the governance of their local area and in the process deepens democracy.[2] As James Manor opines, the decentralisation improves government responsiveness, draws society into creative partnership with states institutions, makes different types of policies more sustainable and reduces the suspicious and cynicism that the ordinary people have towards government.[3] Rajni Kothari holds that the decentralisation has no meaning unless the institutional framework of both the political system and the socio-economic and cultural systems, through which it reaches out to the people, is transformed towards a functioning democracy in a holistic sense.[4] Prabhat Datta opines that the decentralisation ensure more efficient allocation and utilisation of resources, enhances local resource mobilisation, facilitates participation of the people, ensures target group orientation in the planning and implementation of development programmes, makes monitoring and supervision over the implementation of the development programme more effective and improves local governance.[5] L.C. Jain underlines that, apart from being the prime instrument of decentralisation and development at the grassroots level, the Panchayats assume further importance because of two factors: one, the need to contain the relentless demographic pressures in India, and two, to optimise the use of scarce resources for development.[6] Rajesh Tandon visualises that the decentralised democracy requires nurture and growth of civil society, citizen participation and citizen's associations in order to provide a fertile basis for the practice of collective human enterprise in common public good.[7] E.M.S. Namboodiripad, a major theorist of the decentralisation of the political process and administration in Independent India, views it as a tool to moderate the exploitation of the poor by the landed class in a society with uneven development of capitalism and remnants of feudalism, thus protecting and expanding democracy itself. In the absence of a political action to emancipate the poor, he argues, no programme to assist the 'weaker sections' would be fully effective.

However, in the fight of the exploited against the exploiters, parliamentary democracy is a valuable tool for the former. The extension of parliamentary democracy to the village level would help the rural poor to use this tool more ably in their day-to-day struggles.[8] N.C. Saxena is of the view that recent trends suggest that the Panchyati Raj System in India has not been able to enhance participation and empowerment so far because the Panchayati Raj Institutions operate as an extension of government's line departments rather than as local governance institutions.[9] The Second Administrative Reforms Commission, headed by Shri Veerappa Moily, in its Sixth Report on Local Governance, has argued that only an effective and empowered local governance can be the positive power to promote public goods to curb the negative impulse to abuse authority. The ordinary citizens can hold public servants accountable only when such citizens who are directly affected by their actions are empowered to exercise oversight functions.[10]

The use of the term *'good governance'* was initially articulated in a 1989 World Bank publication.[11] The concept of good governance was identified as a structural necessity for market reform. Thus, good governance is envisaged as a multi-level continuum of national policy-making and cross-cutting international regulatory frameworks. In recent years, considerable attention has been devoted by the academia to the problem of realising good governance. Both in developed and developing parts of the world, there has been a welcome shift of focus from traditional concept of government to the concept of good governance. It is an umbrella concept that refers simultaneously to most of the things that the governments do through the institutions and bureaucracy to the common people in their daily lives.

In general, good governance is perceived as a normative principle of administrative law, which obliges the State to perform its functions in a manner that promotes the values of efficiency, non-corruptibility, and responsiveness to civil society.[12] Traditionally, governance refers to forms of political system and the manner in which power is exercised in utilising country's economic and social resources for development.[13] It also deals with the capacity of government to design, formulate and implement policies and, in general, to discharge government functions. Good governance is associated with efficient and effective administration in a democratic framework.[14] Thus, it is clear that good governance is not simply something that government can achieve or do by itself. It depends on the co-operation and involvement of a large number of citizens and organisations. These requirements are considered not only essential for good governance but are also important for sustainable human development.[15] Hence, the essential pre-requisites to quality for good governance are that the system should be suited to the needs, aspirations, background and ethos of the people concerned and that those selected for operating the system should be endowed with character and competence and motivated by the spirit of public service.[16] Therefore, before we have good governance, we need a good government which is both capable and willing to chalk out the direction of growth on all fronts and is at the same time able to translate its policies into action through productive and accountable administration.

II

GOVERNMENT INITIATIVES AND EFFORTS FOR DEMOCRATIC DECENTRALISATION

After Independence, there have been several attempts to make Panchayats more viable grassroots democratic institutions and to crystallise certain practices which are necessary for rural development.[17] Unfortunately, Panchayat as an institution failed to make its own identity. This prompted the young and dynamic Prime Minister of India, late Rajiv Gandhi, to find out the exact reasons for the failure of the efforts of the Government at the centre towards democratic decentralisation over a period of 25 years or so. To restore the image of Panchayati Raj Institutions in contemporary India, he constituted many Committees, Working Groups and Sub-Committees with Panchayati Raj experts and specialists to identify the loopholes and drawbacks in the working of the Panchayati Raj System. C.H. Hanumantha Rao Committee (1984), G.V.K. Rao Committee (1985); L.M. Singhvi Committee (1986); Sarkaria Commission (1988) and P.K. Thungan Committee (1988) are notable among those.

Rajiv Gandhi was driven by a vision to provide the people with 'representative administration', he repeatedly emphasised it in his address to Nation in January 1985 and included it in the Revised Twenty-point Programme of 1986. To this end, he convened five Regional Workshops[18] of District Collectors/Magistrates in various regions of the country over a period of seven-month in 1988 and concluded that the way forward lay in amending the Constitution to give constitutional sanction and constitutional sanctity to Panchayati Raj. Rajiv Gandhi had direct interaction with the officers responsible for the implementation of the development schemes in the districts in the five regional workshops unmindful of the criticism of this event by Chief Ministers who harped on the theme of 'State Autonomy'.[19] The North-Eastern Regional Workshop held at Imphal in April, 1988 recommended that 'Democratic Decentralisation' was essential for the successful implementation of the Poverty Alleviation Programmes and Rural Development Programmes.[20]

Change in the direction of democratic decentralisation brought into sharp focus the need for the power to the people during his regime. In May 1989, Rajiv Gandhi himself introduced the Constitution (64th Amendment) Bill in the Lok Sabha, saying:

> "Our Bill will ensure that Panchayati Raj has a democratic character similar to the Lok Sabha and the State Assemblies and Constitutional Protection for their functioning as representative institutions of the people".

Speaking on the occasion, he highlighted his vision towards the devolution of powers to PRI's:

> "The single greatest danger we have to guard against is the devolution of powers to the panchayats being followed by the transfer of these powers out of the Panchayati Raj System into other bodies constituted outside the system... It is the purpose of our Bill to ensure that powers delegated to the panchayats remain with the panchayats and are not channeled outside the system. By the same token, our Bill is designed to ensure that all developmental agencies are brought within the framework of the Panchayati Raj Institutions and made responsive to the elected authority".[22]

Although the Bill received the required two-thirds majority in the Lok Sabha, on 13th October 1989, it failed by a handful votes to muster the required constitutional majority in the Rajya Sabha.[23]

V.P. Singh-led National Front Government made another futile attempt to amend the Constitution in this regard. It introduced the Constitution (74th Amendment) Bill in September 1990 but before this was taken up for discussion, there was a change of government at the centre.[24]

Being committed to revitalisation of Panchayati Raj Institutions, the P.V. Narasimha Rao Government introduced the 72nd (Panchayats) Constitutional Amendment Bills, based substantially on the Bill moved in the Eighth Lok Sabha by Rajiv Gandhi but also incorporating some of the changes made in it by the National Front Government. The bill was referred to a Joint Select Committee of the Parliament, which effected some further changes but conformed in very considerable measure to the earlier 1989 initiative. The Lok Sabha and Rajya Sabha passed the bill on the 22nd December, 1992 respectively. By the time, the Parliament passed this bill with sequence changed to 73rd Constitution Amendment.[25] Following its ratification by more than half the State Assemblies as required under the Constitution, the President of India gave his assent, the Constitution (Seventy-third Amendment) Act, 1992 came into force on 24th April, 1993 and the Constitution (Seventy-fourth Amendment) Act, 1992 on 1 June 1993, adding a new part to the Constitution, namely Part IX titled 'The Panchayats'. Thus democracy and devolution of powers to Panchayats have now become part of the Constitution of India. In the Eleventh Schedule, 29 subjects have been listed under Article 243G which stipulates that states may by law endow the Panchayats with such powers and authority as may be required to enable them to function as Institutions of self-government.

In pursuance of its election manifesto, called the National Agenda for Governance, the National Democratic Alliance (NDA) Government headed by A.B. Vajpayee appointed a 13-member National Commission to Review the Working of the Constitution (NCRWC) under the chairmanship of the former Chief Justice of India, M.N. Venkatachaliah on 1st February,[26] 2000. After considering the various viewpoints a comprehensive report submitted by it to the Government of India on 31st March, 2002 for reconstruction of the executive, legislative and judicial aspects of the Constitutional provisions of Governance. There were 38 recommendations on the decentralisation and devolution besides empowerment and strengthening of Panchayati Raj Institutions alone.[27] In addition, the NDA Government took keen interest in organising the All India Panchayat Adhyakshas Sammelan in New Delhi during 5-6 April, 2002 for formulating National Declaration for Local Self-governance, a text consisting of 15 point recommendations.[28] This resolution was at the centre of the recommendations made by the 1,600 elected heads representing 3,40,000 Panchayats of India.

The United Progressive Alliance Government headed by Manmohan Singh, which came to power in 2004, placed its pro-poor strategy of the devolution of powers to Panchayats at the core of its National Common Minimum Programme (NCMP) in the following words:

> "The UPA Government will ensure that all funds given to States for implementation of poverty alleviation and rural development scheme by Panchayats are neither delayed nor diverted. Monitoring will be strict. In addition, after consultations with states, the UPA Government will consider crediting elected panchayats with funds directly. Devolution of funds will be accompanied by similar devolution of functions and functionaries as well. Regular elections to Panchayat bodies will be ensured and the amended act in respect of the Fifth and Sixth Schedule Areas will be implemented. The UPA Government will ensure that the Gram Sabha is empowered to emerge as the foundation of Panchayati Raj".[29]

In keeping with this commitment one of the first acts of the UPA Government after assuming office was the creation of the Union Ministry of Panchayati Raj on 27th May, 2004. The first step in defining the scope of the Ministry's work was taken when the Ministry, jointly with the Union Ministry of Rural Development, organised the Conference of Chief Ministers on Rural Poverty Alleviation and Prosperity through Panchayati Raj, at New Delhi on 29 and 30th June, 2004.[30]

While inaugurating it, the Prime Minister, Manmohan Singh said:

> "The key instrument for integrating economic reforms with institutional reforms in the country-side is Gandhiji's farsighted goal of Purna Swaraj through Gram Swaraj. This was given constitutional shape and sanction by late Shri Rajiv Gandhi vision of empowering Panchayati Raj Institutions to function as 'institutions of self-government', to plan and implement programmes of economic development and social justice. . . . The key issue (here) is action on transfer of functions, functionaries and funds. Transfer of functions are to be based on the principle of subsidiarity and any task that can be

done by a lower level should not move to a higher level. Effective Panchayati Raj requires that functionaries of government work under elected leadership. As far as funds are concerned, the awards of the State Finance Commissions should be fully honoured".[31]

In pursuance of the decisions of the Conference, the Ministry of Panchayati Raj organised a series of Seven Round Tables of State Ministers of Panchayati Raj at Kolkata, Mysore, Raipur, Chandigarh, Srinagar, Guwahati and Jaipur, for detailed deliberation on the blue print for future action. Within a period of 150 days, from 23 July, 2004 to 19 December, 2004, consensus was achieved among all States/Union Territories on a Compendium of Action Points covering 18 jointly identified dimensions of Panchayati Raj and comprising 150 key steps on what remained to be done.[32] The Kolkata Round Table resolved that the States should work towards devolving powers and responsibilities in respect of all matters listed in the Eleventh Schedule in the letter and spirit of Article 243 G of the Constitution. It was also agreed that the devolution of functionaries to Panchayats would be based on the mapping of activities related to the devolved functions by 1 April, 2005. Within three months it was clear that it encompassed a time bound Action Plan and Agenda for devolution of functions, funds and functionaries to Panchayati Raj Institutions.

Following the acceptance of the Compendium Document by all State Chief Ministers, the Union Minister for Panchayati Raj made a series of visits to States and Union Territories to interact with Panchayats and to review the progress in implementing the recommendations of the Seven Round Tables. In this direction, the Union Minister for Panchayati Raj Mani Shankar Aiyar visited 18 States and 3 Union Territories during the period 2005 April to 2007 March.[33]

At the end of each visit, joint statements of conclusions were signed between the Union Minister of Panchayati Raj and the Chief Minister of the State or the appropriate authority in Union Territories. With persistent efforts of the Union Ministry of Panchayati Raj, some states have passed legislation devolving 29 subjects listed in the Eleventh Schedule, while others have devolved 6 and 18 subjects, for undertaking development programmes.

Unfortunately, Panchayats have not been able to become effective instruments of economic development and social justice in many States as the devolution of functions, funds and functionaries has remained largely on paper. Nevertheless, in spite of many deficiencies, it has been found that considerable progress has been made towards evolving a national consensus on the nature, direction and pace of devolution of powers to the Panchayati Raj Institutions.

Details of the devolution of powers to PRI's by various State Governments by the end of October, 2006 may be seen in the following table:

TABLE 1
Devolution of Powers to PRI's

Sl. No.	*State*	*Transfer of Subjects through Legislation*	*Subjects covered under Activity Mapping*
1.	Andhra Pradesh	17 subjects	9 subjects
2.	Assam	29 subjects	29 subjects
3.	Arunachal Pradesh	—	3 subjects
4.	Bihar	25 subjects	25 subjects
5.	Chhattisgarh	29 subjects	27 subjects
6.	Goa	6 subjects	18 subjects
7.	Gujarat	15 subjects	14 subjects
8.	Haryana	29 subjects	10 subjects
9.	Himachal Pradesh	26 subjects	—
10.	Karnataka	29 subjects	29 subjects
11.	Madhya Pradesh	23 subjects	23 subjects
12.	Maharashtra	18 subjects	—
13.	Manipur	22 subjects	22 subjects
14.	Orissa	25 subjects	7 subjects
15.	Punjab	7 subjects	—
16.	Rajasthan	29 subjects	12 subjects
17.	Sikkim	28 subjects	—
18.	Tamil Nadu	29 subjects	—
19.	Tripura	29 subjects	21 subjects
20.	Uttar Pradesh	12 subjects	—
21.	Uttaranchal	14 subjects	9 subjects
22.	West Bengal	29 subjects	15 subjects
Union Territory			
23.	Dadra and Nagar Haveli	29 subjects	29 subjects
24.	Daman and Diu	18 subjects	18 subjects
25.	Andaman & Nicobar Islands	8 subjects	8 subjects
26.	Lakshadweep Islands	25 subjects	25 subjects

Source : *The State of the Panchayats—A Mid-term Review and Appraisal*, 22 November 2006, New Delhi, Ministry of Panchayati Raj, Government of India, 2006.

In this process the Ministry of Panchayati Raj on the eve of the 15th Anniversary of the 73rd Constitution Amendment convened the National Convention of Chairpersons of all Zilla Parishads and Intermediate Panchayats in New Delhi during 22-24 April, 2008. At this historic event, nearly 10,000 delegates adopted a National Charter, which was earlier prepared by the Core Committee of District and Intermediate Panchayats in March 2008 after considering the various view points through responses elicited and received.[34] It was presented to the Prime Minister, Manmohan Singh on 24th April, 2008 at New Delhi.

III

GRASSROOTS INSTITUTIONS AND GOOD GOVERNANCE : EMERGING CHALLENGES

In a democracy, people elect representatives for ensuring a responsive and responsible administration. It is said that they are accountable to the people because they have to get their mandate renewed every five years and it is through the ballot that they are made accountable. According to Yogendra Narain, former Secretary-General of Rajya Sabha, the concept of accountability in public governance is nebulous for three reasons:[35] *First,* in a system of hierarchical administration there are no well-defined areas of individual responsibility and accountability. *Secondly,* administration is a continuous process and the result of an action might be evident only years late. *Thirdly,* public governance is no more governance by a single institution, the government. N. Vittal, the former Chief Vigilance Commissioner of India, while exploring the dynamics of accountability in administration, stated that it depends on individual public servant's sense of duty and commitment to work which in turn depends on his background, education and upbringing, acceptance of certain social values and norms and organisational framework in which the public servant works.[36]

As the basic unit of local self-governance, the effective functioning of Village Panchayat is vital for good governance. When we use the expression local self-government, we limit it to two purposes: The *first,* preparations of plans for economic development and social justice, and the *second,* the implementation of these programmes.[37] The issue of good governance may be seen at two planes[38] at the operational level, where it is described in terms of efficiency, absence of corruption in public life, accountability and transparency and at the institutional plane, where it is perceived in the forms it takes: democratic, decentralised participatory and operated by political incentives or its obverse, disincentives. However, in the opinion of Vinod Vyasulu,[39] "a necessary condition is to engage with elected representatives. There is great need for their capacity building in accounting, budgeting and monitoring. It is only when elected representatives have the full responsibility of not only deciding upon what work to undertake, but also to raise the finances for it, by taxes or otherwise in a hard budget constraint situation, that changes become possible".

Nevertheless, it is clear that rural development experiments in India have gone through a considerable amount of metamorphosis and there were several socio-political and economic forces, which helped shaping and directing them. Joydeep Baruah and Indranee Dutta have identified four general and common characteristics in this context.[40] *Firstly,* economic development is an essential precondition to the social transformation, which is considered as the main objective of rural development strategy. *Secondly,* it seeks to increase efficiency and productivity of the agricultural sector for ensuring food security and commercialisation. *Thirdly,* its emphasis is on the issues of equity, social security and justice. *Fourthly,* it aims at enhancing rural citizen's participation in evolving locally appropriate planning. Therefore, for a future model of high quality good governance at the grassroots, it is necessary to educate the citizens of their rights and duties. If we have to strengthen the grassroots democratic institutions in India, we must let the citizens become aware of their rights. It is only when a person knows his rights that he can fight for them and thus ensure that the government becomes responsive and transparent at the grassroots level. The progress of devolution of function, functionaries and finances in respect of 29 subjects listed in the Eleventh Schedule is, however, not uniform among the states, despite sincere efforts and initiatives taken by the Union Ministry of Panchayati Raj, Government of India, for the past four years.

To give effect to the 73rd Constitutional Amendment in letter and spirit, we have to bring the Second Generation of Reforms for the empowerment of Panchayati Raj Institutions in India. There is a strong and urgent need for removing the loopholes and obstacles. Its functioning can be made effective only by giving sufficient powers, functions and funds. There are three areas of the Indian Constitution that require change to empower the Panchayati Raj Institutions. *First,* removal of contradictions within the Constitution itself, such as in the Directive Principles (Article 40) which promises to promote only Village Panchayats and does not include Panchayats at the higher level and to replace the existing definition of 'local government' under the Seventh Schedule (List II, Item 5) to include Panchayats. *Secondly,* to insert a separate Article which ensures autonomy to the Panchayats in managing their own functions, taxes, staff and organisation with constitutional guarantee of local government autonomy. *Thirdly,* to insert a local list of functions and taxes, by making corresponding adjustments in the State and Concurrent Lists under the Seventh Schedule.

IV

REFORMATORY CHANGES

What we now need in the sixteenth anniversary year of constitutionally obligated Panchayati Raj, is a stock-taking of the experience of all the states which will enable us to review the time-bound implementation of the devolution of 3F's—Functions, Finances and Functionaries to the PRI's. We hope that the past experiences shall guide the policy-makers at the helm of affairs in framing the design of empowered Panchayati Raj Institutions for good governance at the grassroot level in the days to come. This would require renewed interest in changing the structure of the grassroots institutions administration from 'imposed development' approach to 'self-determined development' approach.

It may be further necessary to incorporate the following changes for delivering good governance at the grassroots level:

1. To introduce the Indian Panchayati Raj Service (IPRS) at all India level and minimise the supremacy of the Collector's Raj in the decision-making of local self-government institutions;
2. To strengthen the decentralised planning at the grassroots and to provide an opportunity for more and more people to be involved in formulation of their own developmental plans through Gram Sabhas and other statutory bodies;
3. To re-define the role and responsibilities of MP's/MLA's in Panchayati Raj administration and to distribute work between the three-tiers of the governance;
4. To identify the real beneficiaries and the disadvantaged sections of the society while implementing various welfare and development schemes in a transparen way through Gram Sabha and to immediately display and publish the list of beneficiaries on the notice boards of the Gram Panchayats and vernacular papers;
5. To provide adequate training to the elected representatives of PRI's, governmental agencies and the NGOs for their capacity building in a regular manner throughout their tenure;
6. To give incentives and awards to those grassroots democratic institutions at the District, Taluka and Gram Panchayat levels which strengthen good governance in all respects every year;
7. To make effective use of Information Technology in Panchayati Raj administration (e-Panchayat) for quick and efficient delivery of public services at the grassroots level; and
8. To create "Panchayati Raj Consolidated Fund" in each and every Village Panchayat through public donations and contributions, and inculcate a participatory development approach in the minds of elected representatives of Panchayati Raj Institutions as well as citizens at the grassroots.

Notes and References

1. Pranab Bardhan, *Decentralisation of Governance and Development*, Berkerley, University of California, 2000.
2. Mohit Bhattacharya, "Decentralisation:Trends and Debates", *Administrative Change*, Vol. XXXI, No. 2 and Vol. XXXII, No. 1, January-December, 2004, p. 31.
3. James Manor, *Directions in Development: The Political Economy of Democratic Decentralisation*, Washington D.C., the World Bank, 1999, p. 35.
4. Rajni Kothari, "Decentralisation: The Real Issue", *Seminar*, No. 360, August 1989, p. 17.
5. Prabhat Datta, "Local Politics, Decentralisation and Poverty Reduction: Analytical and Methodological Issues", *Socialist Perspective*, Vol. 32, Nos. 3 and 4, December 2004 to March 2005, p. 167.
6. L.C. Jain, "Strengthening the Foundations", *Seminar*, No. 451, March, 1997, p. 29.
7. Rajesh Tandon, "Grassroots Democracy", *Seminar*, No. 451, March, 1997, p. 39.

8. E.M.S. Namboodiripad, "Democratic Decentralisation in Kerala Today", *ISDA Journal*, Vol. 2, No. 4, October-December, 1992, pp. 263-65.
9. N.C. Saxena, "Democratic Decentralisation through Panchayati Raj Institutions : The Indian Experiences", in D. Sundar Ram (Ed.), *Role of Panchayati Raj Institutions in 60 Years of Independent India: Vision of the Future*, New Delhi, Academy of Grassroots Studies and Research of India and Kanishka Publishers, Distributors, 2008, p. 35.
10. *Report* on Local Governance: *An Inspiring Journey into the Future*, New Delhi, Second Administrative Reforms Commission (Sixth Report), Government of India, October 2007, p. 16.
11. *World Bank*, Sub-Saharan Africa: From Crisis to Sustainable Growth, *Washington D.C., World Bank, 1989. In 1989, the concept of "governance" was for the first time highlighted in a World Bank document on Sub-Saharan Africa. By good governance was meant, at that time, sound development management. Four key dimensions identified in this context were: (a) public sector management; (b) accountability; (c) legal framework for development; and (d) information and transparency.*
12. J.N. Rosenau Compare, *Along the Domestic-Foreign Frontier: Exploring Governance in a Turbulent World*, Cambridge, Cambridge University Press, 1997.
13. Mick Moore, "Declining to Learn from the East: The World Bank on Governance and Development", *IDS Bulletin*, Vol. 24, No. 1, 1993, p. 39.
14. H.K. Asmerom, K. Borgman and R. Hoppe, "Good Governance, Decentralisation and Democratisation in Post-Colonial State", *The Indian Journal of Public Administration*, Vo. 41, No. 4, October-December, 1995, p. 736.
15. Peter Blunt, "Cultural Relativism, Good Governance and Sustainable Human Development", *Public Administration and Development*, Vol. 15, No. 1, January-March, 1995, pp. 5-7.
16. Subash C. Kashyap, "Good Governance and the Constitution", *Politics India*, Vol. 1, No. 3, September, 1996, p. 22.
17. The story of Panchayati Raj in Independent India has been a story of ups and downs. According to Shri Ashok Mehta Committee, it seems to have passed through 3 phases: the phase of ascendancy (1959-64); the phase of stagnation (1965-69); and the phase of decline (1969-77). Subsequent events have unequivocally shown that the phase of decline was coming to an end and a new phase started about 1978 which may be called "Panchayati Raj Reforms Phase". Following the enactment of 73rd Constitution Amendment Act, the Panchayati Raj Institutions have revived its glory and considered as "Constitutional bodies". For a penetrating analyses, See. (i) D. Sundar Ram (Ed.), *Dynamics of Grassroots Governance in India: Dreams and Realities*, 2 Volumes, New Delhi, Academy of Grassroots Studies and Research of India and Kanishka Publishers, Distributors, 2007; (ii) George Mathew (Ed.), *Panchayati Raj: From Legislation to Movement*, New Delhi, Concept Publishing Company, 1994; (iii) S.N. Jha and P.C. Mathur (Eds.), *Decentralisation and Local Politics*, New Delhi, Sage Publications, 1999; (iv) M. Wadhwani and S.N. Mishra (Eds.), *Dreams and Realities: Expectations from Panchayati Raj*, New Delhi, Concept Publishing Company, 2004; (v) *The State of the Panchayats: A Mid-term Review and Appraisal*, 3 Volumes, New Delhi, Ministry of, Panchayati Raj, Government of India, 2006; and (vi) D. Sundar Ram (Ed.), *Role of Panchayati Raj Institutions in 60 Years of Independent India: Vision of the Future*, New Delhi, Academy of Grassroots Studies and Research of India and Kanishka Publishers, Distributors, 2008.
18. The Five Regional Workshops of the District Collectors/Magistrate were held in Bhopal (December, 1987); Hyderabad (February, 1988); Imphal and Jaipur (April, 1988) and Coimbatore (June, 1988). After the completion of the five regional workshops, the youthful bureaucrats opted for renunciation of power by strongly recommending '*Democratic Decentralisation*' at the district with emphasis on '*District Planning*'.
19. While introducing the 73rd Constitutional Amendment Bill, the CPM Lok Sabha Members *Shri Chitta Basu* and *Shri Somnath Chatterjee* opposed the Bill, contrary to the violation of the devolution of power between the States and the Centre as determined by the Constitution of India. Participating in the debate on the Bill, Shri *Chitta Basu* said: "..... But may I know whether this kind of legislation should be sponsored in this

House? I am going into the merits of the case. I would like to say that it falls within the purview of State List in item No. 5. It is violative of the basic principles of federalism and undermines the basic structure of the Constitution. The Sarkaria Commission is also contrary to that. I, therefore, oppose for leave to introduce the Bill". Another CPM Senior leader *Shri Somnath Chatterjee* said : "Sir, the trouble is that all the States are not having appropriate panchayat laws. The concept behind a Constitution Amendment is that all the states are either not making laws or are not implementing the laws. But in the name, if you try to encroach into the powers of the State Governments, we object to that. We objected last time also. We have to see whether still mischief is there or not. But at this stage, let it come". For more discussion, See, *Lok Sabha Debates*, September 16, 1991.

20. V.A. Vasudevaraju, "Panchayati Raj Democracy *vs.* Parliamentary Democracy", in G. Palanithurai (Ed.), *Empowering People—Issues and Solutions*, New Delhi, Kanishka Publishers, Distributors, 1996, p. 75.
21. The 73rd Constitutional Amendment Act, 1992 provided Constitutional Status to the Panchayati Raj Institutions. The Amendment also institutionalised a three-tier system of panchayats (except for states with a population of less than 2 million), with panchayats at the village, block and district levels, but what is revolutionary in this Act is "political empowerment of women". See. *The Constitution (Seventy-third Amendment) Act, 1992*, Gazette of India Extraordinary, Part-II, Section-I, New Delhi, Government of India, April 20, 1993.
22. For the Text of the Prime Minister Shri Rajiv Gandhi's Statement on 64th Constitution Amendment Bill, See, "Power to the People", *Rajiv Gandhi's Speeches*, Vol. V, New Delhi, Ministry of Information & Broadcasting, Government of India, 1989.
23. It is interesting to note that the 64th & 65th Constitution Amendment Bills were lost in the Rajya Sabha by 3 votes only.
24. See. N.R. Inamdar, "Panchayati Raj Leadership : Emerging Dimensions", *Journal of Rural Development*, Vol. 10, No. 3, September, 1991.
25. See. (i) S.S. Singh and S.N. Mishra, *Legislature Framework of Panchayati Raj in India*, New Delhi, Intellectual Publishing House, 1993, (ii) Swetha Mishra, *Democratic Decentralisation in India: Study in Retrospect and Prospect*, New Delhi, Mittal Publications, 1994.
26. *The Hindu*, February 2, 2000, p. 1 and *Times of India*, February 2, 2000.
27. For more details, See, *Report of the National Commission to Review the Working of the Constitution* (Chairman: Shri Justice M.N. Venkatachaliah), New Delhi, Government of India, 2002.
28. For full text of the 15 Resolutions, See, The National Declaration for Local Self-Governance: Recommendation, *Kurukshetra*, April, 2002.
29. See, *The National Common Minimum Programme (NCMP)—A Document*, May 2004, New Delhi, Government of India, 2004.
30. For the first time in Independent India, the Ministry of Panchayati Raj at the Centre came into existence on 27 May 2004, under the headship of Shri Mani Shankar Aiyar. No previous Government has had a separate Ministry or even Department of Panchayati Raj. The Ministry is a unique, first ever innovation of the UPA Government led by Dr. Manmohan Singh.
31. For a full Text of the Speech, See. *Chief Minister's Conference on Rural Prosperity and Poverty Eradication through Panchayati Raj*, Inaugural Address by Dr. Manmohan Singh, New Delhi, 29th June, 2004.
32. For a full Text of Compendium of Resolutions of the Seven Round-Tables of Ministers, In-Charge of Panchayati Raj in the State Government (July-December, 2004), See, *The State of the Panchayats—A Mid-term Review and Appraisal*, 22 November 2006, Volume III, New Delhi, Ministry of Panchayati Raj, Government of India, 2006, pp. 170-99.
33. As part of the State Visits, the Union Minister for Panchayati Raj, Shri Mani Shankar Aiyar visited the following states during 2005 April to 2007 March and reached the Memorandum of Understandings (MoUs) with the respective State Governments and Union Territories: (1) Karnataka (29-30 April and 1 May, 2005); (2) West Bengal (13-15 May, 2005); (3) Uttaranchal (24 June, 2005); (4) Haryana (17-22, August, 2005);

Chhattisgarh (28 August, 2005); (6) Orissa (23-26 October, 2005); (7) Arunachal Pradesh (7-9 November, 2005); (8) Rajasthan (2-4 December, 2005); (9) Lakshadweep (23 January, 2006); (10) Sikkim (30 March, 1 & 2 April, 2006); (11) Goa (11-12 April, 2006); (12) Andhra Pradesh (19-22 April, 2006); (13) Punjab (25-26 April, 2006); (14) Himachal Pradesh (27-30 May, 2006); (15) Kerala (19-22 July, 2006); (16) Assam (9-12 September, 2006); (17) Manipur (4-5 October, 2006); (18) Madhya Pradesh (17 December, 2006); (19) Puducherry (11 January, 2007); (20) Tripura (11 February, 2007); (21) Andaman & Nicobar Islands (19 March, 2007).

34. For the full text of Fifteenth Anniversary Charter on Panchayati Raj, "*Inclusive Growth through Inclusive Governance*", New Delhi, Ministry of Panchayati Raj, Government of India, 24 April, 2008.
35. For an interesting thesis, See, Yogendra Narain, "Transparency and Accountability in Public Governance", *Mainstream*, Vol. XLIII, No. 6, January 29, 2005 (Republic Day Special), pp. 21-25 and 50.
36. For an elaborate discussion, See, N. Vittal, "Probity in Public Life in 21st Century", in D. Sundar Ram (Ed.) *Transforming Indian Politics in the New Millennium: Agenda for Institutional Reforms*, Jaipur, Academy of Grassroots Studies and Research of India and National Publishing House, 2009.
37. Mani Shankar Aiyar, "Panchayati Raj in India: An Institution of Grassroots Development", in D. Sundar Ram (Ed.), *Panchayati Raj Reforms in India: Power to the People at the Grassroots*, New Delhi, Academy of Grassroots Studies and Research of India and Kanishka Publishers, Distributors, 2007, pp. 13-33.
38. D. Bandyopadhyay and Amitava Mukherjee, "Introduction", in D. Bandyopadhyay and Amitava Mukherjee (Eds.) *New Issues in Panchayati Raj*, New Delhi, Concept Publishing Company, 2004, p. 11.
39. Vinod Vyasulu, "Transformation in Governance since 1990's—Some Reflections", *Economic and Political Weekly*, Vol. IXL, No. 24, June 5, 2005, pp. 2383-4.
40. Joydeep Baruah and Indranee Dutta, "Competitive Villages, Rural Enterprises and Rural Development: The Indian Experiments and Experiences", *Political Economy Journal of India*, Vol. 13, No. 1, January-June 2004, p. 64.

14

Impact of Globalisation on Good Governance and the Need for Democratic Decentralisation

PREM R. BHARDWAJ

The world community has been facing contradiction of economic development and social exclusion of large section of people across the world ever since the collapse of Soviet Union and end of socialism in Eastern Europe in 1989. It was only after the end of cold war that the free market economy was projected as an ultimate tool of human development and all the excesses committed against humanity by the western world during the cold war were given 'reflexive justification' on the pretext of defence against, what J.F. Kennedy called, 'the monolithic and ruthless conspiracy' of Kremlin. So any sort of alternative to market-centred approach of development was rejected out-rightly by the developed West even before the end of cold war.

The end of cold war witnessed an "impressive flow of rhetoric assuring that the West would now be free to pursue its traditional dedication to freedom, democracy, justice and human rights unhampered by super power rivalry' (Chomsky, 2008, 20) and new policy perceptions such as 'humanitarian intervention' and 'responsibility to protect', were framed to intervene and control the outer world, especially the South. It was simply a tactic of the dominating west to confirm its self-image by providing to the world community its biased analyses of the historical developments of early 1990s. The sphere of intervention was not merely political or military, it was also well designed. It was a strong invasion over the economy, society and culture of developing or under-developed regions. The current swing of globalisation advocated by the market forces is necessarily a part of this big design of superimposition and dominance.

Despite being the most debated issue of our times, there is no comprehensive theory that could provide a precise definition of globalisation, probably because of its multiple implications for various facets of human lives. The whole debate that is related to interconnectivity of nations and human societies all across the world pinpoints the fact that the idea of globalisation includes everything from cultural fusion to integration of global financial market. But it is the economic aspect of globalisation supplemented with exercise of power that is particularly full of contradictions and counter arguments. It is probably because of misinterpretation of historical developments, on the one hand, and the unquestioned march of neo-liberal strategies, on the other hand, that, the debate about globalisation is not around stopping or trying to stop it in any way at present stage. It is perhaps, being assumed that it has become the part of history that moves forward. The main question that has emerged in the form of debate is how can it be managed and controlled and how can its fruits be distributed through humanitarian intervention.

In spite of all these limitations at theoretical level, it is amply evident that there are groups of people who are excluded from the process of global integration all over the world mainly in the poor and backward regions where extra inputs are needed to bring the people to a respectable level. And, at the same time, there are other groups of the people who fall in the category of gainers by grabbing better opportunities. The most debated part of globalisation discourse is motivated by the neo-liberal analysis which pertains to economic interrelationships among different communities or societies. In fact the collapse of state socialism in former Soviet Union and Eastern Europe paved the way for the reorientation of social order based on the global market system and motivated by the principles of free trade and global competition and amidst the prevailing unequal global settings the process of social exclusion of large sections of people in almost all societies of the world. It is only one part of world i.e., the West that has come closer in terms of culture as well as economy and, at the same time, it is also associated with the interconnectedness of market class elsewhere. Thus, globalisation is very often characterised as 'truncated globalisation' or 'Triadisation' concentrated in the triad of Western Europe, North America and Japan (Pieterse, from Net), however its reach has extended to outer world also.

Though it is beyond the scope of this paper to investigate various dimensions of the implications of processes of globalisation, yet it can be stated that there may be the cultural fusion (or de-culturisation of developing societies under the up-thrust of Americanisation of global society) at broader sphere, but in terms of opportunities for development, the prevailing social hierarchies are responding differently according to their positions in economic settings. In this context, the dichotomised notion of 'inclusion' and 'exclusion' is becoming increasingly relevant not only at international level but also at the national or regional levels.

In fact, the recent technological and economic changes have enforced a paradigm shift both in strategies and practices of development. In simplest way, development should be comprehensive and necessarily inclusive. The notion of inclusive development implies that, at present stage, the development is exclusionary in practice as well as in strategy. As argued by Castles (from Net), development is a 'continual process of internal' (referring to economic growth, industrialisation, improved administration, etc. In short, it is a development of modern capitalist state) and 'external' (referring to European Colonisation of rest of the world with the accompanying differences of western values, institutions and technologies) growth based on the values of rationality, secularity and efficiency. The ongoing transformations in economy and politics decipher that the uncontrolled market is set to eliminate all alternatives that claim to be the right paths for the mission of modern civilisation. In fact, the theorisation of market as the only means of development and progress is nothing but imposition of *laissez-faire* economics and free market of the West on the Non-Western world. If we look into the nature of contradictions between globalisation and development, the notion of development became problematic from late 1980s due to the changes enforced by the process of globalisation. It is also clear from the emerging trends that it is strongly associated with the intensification of social inequalities which are reflected in the form of unequal accessibility of different sections of societies to humane values and opportunities. Consequently, rich are becoming more rich and poor are becoming more poor, leading them to the state of exclusion from the processes of economic development and political decision making.

Therefore, the most important question, with which the academics as well as policy-makers have to confront is: How can the objective of good governance be achieved particularly in a society, where, besides historical settings, the processes of globalisation have been accentuating the social exclusions by adding the new groups to the list of excluded? Answer to this question is imbedded in the other related questions that need serious analysis. For instance, can we take Indian society to participatory equity with the help of market-centred approach of development? Then there are some other questions related to diagnostic strategies that would help in developing futuristic vision for modern human societies. For example, how to counter the invasion of market over social democracy and democratic institutions mainly in developing countries? How can the goal of comprehensive development be achieved in an environment where the process of exclusion of larger sections has been intensified as a consequence of ruthless march of capital and market? How can modern society achieve the goal of good governance at a stage when large numbers of people are being increasingly dragged out of the domain of political decision making?

To find out the answer to such questions, meticulous analyses of facts is needed.

This paper is a modest attempt to investigate various interrelated phenomena that are influencing the emerging scenario of Indian politics at this critical stage. It is clear that, as a consequence of globalisation, the socially excluded sections of people in India lack in terms of participatory and inclusive governance. The present paper is also an attempt to discuss the ongoing discourse about the implications of globalisation for good governance. Surely the humanity cannot progress forward if the new diagnostics in the form of market-centred approach does not address the issues related to common people and if the whole process takes forward only a few resourceful sections of society.

The argument in this paper begins with the assumption that the political processes, even in the so called modern democracies, cannot achieve the objective of good governance through globalisation or, to be more precise, with the help of market-oriented strategies. The emerging trends indicate that instead of bringing the historically excluded sections of people under the domain of development, the current swing of modernity through market governance has dragged quite a sizeable number of people out of the framework of modernisation and development. This process of exclusion has been posing a serious challenge for the instrumentation of good governance. Keeping this background in mind, the following assumptions would provide bases for the understanding of ongoing antagonism of economic globalisation and process of social exclusion.

First, the economic dimension of globalisation has clearly led to 'demise of social democracy and the modern welfare state' (Beall, from Net) simply because neo-liberalistic thrust of market governance is absolutely contrary to the spirit of democracy. The forces of market, working on principle of global competitiveness, specifically in developing and backward countries, have pressurised the governments to reduce state spending and interventions. So much so that state institutions are being hijacked by these forces to ensure the security of market economy at the cost of social democracy.

Second, it is true that the social exclusion is a historical phenomenon having multi-dimensional facets but process of globalisation has added new vigour to it. Because of absence of a just mechanism for value distribution, the poor and weaker sections have been left with no choice but to be the part of this unfair game in which their defeat is inevitable. The dream of inclusive development is absolutely contrary to the process of globalisation because 'terms of inclusion' vary in accordance with the accessibility of people to the new values and opportunities available in the new environment.

Third, the experiences in India make it very clear that instead of bringing the excluded people within the framework of development and modernisation—as the dream was shown by the forces of globalisation in early 1990s—the market institutions have not only dragged them away but have also added to their number by excluding even those sections of society that were earlier controlling the reasonable sources of sustenance. For instance, the market allured the small farmers in India with the promise of high profit but marginalised them pathetically. The farmers' suicides in Andhra Pradesh, Maharashtra and Punjab are clearly associated with this phenomenon.

Fourth, the governance connotes 'command mechanism' working within a political society that is supposed to provide 'security, prosperity coherence, order and continuity of the system' (Rosenau, 2000, from Net). But all these parameters of governance have become the prerogatives of a particular section of society. The governance can be called 'good' if the state institutions are really sensitive and democratic and are capable of achieving the goal of inclusive development especially by distributing the benefits of modernisation judiciously. It is evident that the integration of global economic processes under the market regulations is clearly related to the increasing social differentiation in India and other developing countries. Thus, market governance can never provide good governance simply because it is 'governance without government' (Bhardwaj, 2002).

Fifth, at this juncture of history the whole debate of inclusive development is polarised between democracy and social exclusion. Democracy is the legitimate mode of governance as it is based on people's participation in political decision-making and economic development. Whereas the 'exclusion' of people from means of production and distribution is a dynamic feature of economic globalisation. So, the dichotomy of 'exclusion' and 'inclusion' is polarised in the binary of globalisation and democracy. This binary becomes critically prominent because of the fact that the globalisation has various forms and there are various modes of regulations among these different forms varying according to historical antecedents and economic settings, whereas the quest for democracy is governed by universal principles. Thus, goal of inclusive development through market dominance is unrealistic.

Sixth, it is true that social exclusion is associated with poverty but the story of market oriented economic reforms reveals that inequalities have been multiplied intensively by the working of economic system during last two decades in India. Impoverishment is not simply the denial of economic resources and opportunities, it is also the denial of full citizenship i.e., exclusion from the norms of civilisation. It is rightly stated by Atkinson (cited in Beall) that "social exclusion is invariably a cause of poverty and inequality not necessarily consequence of them". Since the market-centred development multiplies inequality and widens the gap between the rich and the poor, the inclusive development is unconceivable without state intervention.

Seventh, the Indian political system is at crossroads at present stage. The democratisation of civil society has ignited the aspirations of political class as well as common people at political front. Instances of human rights movements, environment awareness campaigns and, above all, movements for political power, indicate that democracy in India has led to inclusion of groups of people of different origin at different levels, especially those who were not earlier the part of political decision-making over a period of time. But, the process of economic globalisation over past two decades has led to systematic exclusion of various groups of people. This has consequently vitiated the working of Indian democracy. It is only the minority living in urban centres already enjoying better opportunities that has been included in the process of economic development, obviously through market.

Finally, it is clear that social exclusion is a product of this unhealthy competition. The reactions to these discriminatory practices are appearing in the form of communal clustering of people not only in India but all across the world. It is reflected in terms of group behaviour which is exhibited in the form of aggression against other groups. So, this exclusion is emerging as main cause of inter-community conflicts that are becoming increasingly unmanageable.

The meticulous analysis of the emerging trends related to prevailing contradictions between search for egalitarian society, on the one hand, and adverse implications of market reforms, on the other, establish that the economic globalisation has multiplied the forms of exclusion of people. It is clear that the ability of people to take advantage of globalisation depends on their not being excluded from the opportunities. It means that with the concentration of resources in the hands of those few who fall in the list of gainers, the majority has been denied the opportunity to integrate within the market system. Various forms of exclusion that are surely the consequences of globalisation include—*exclusion from employment and opportunity; exclusion from traditional economic activities without any alternative and security mechanisms (e.g., farmers, women and children); exclusion from skills, capabilities and assets; exclusion from protection and security network; exclusion from the list of claimants of right of inclusion; exclusion from the institutions of political decision-making and above all the adverse inclusion of weaker sections (mainly women and children) and their entry into unsafe and immoral activities as a consequence of social exclusion.*

All these forms of exclusion are the result of 'pulling up ladder' policy of market which implies that once the heights have been achieved, the others are debarred to ride to the level. In one way or the other, such policy appears as continuity of the colonial strategy of exploitation. The poor and weak people are the ultimate victims of this exclusion drive. It has been rightly pointed by Castles (from Net) that "globalisation and industrial restructuring led to marginalisation, impoverishment and social exclusion for large number of people in both—the old industrial countries and rest of the world". But here it is also important to mention that the process of globalisation has affected the developing countries much more badly simply because of the vast disparities prevailing in them.

The displacement of Indian farmers from the economically sustainable productive system to market-centred agricultural production system has made them vulnerable simply because market never comes to their protection at the time of failure of crops or unviable prices. Failure of Bt. Cotton seeds in Andhra Pradesh and Maharashtra exposed this vulnerability of farmers to the excesses of market. Similar is the story related to the working conditions in the industries where the petty labourers are forced to work in literally inhumane conditions and there are no safety networks for the unorganised migratory labourers.

In fact, the market mechanism in India has incorporated minority of rich into such a process of development as imposes serious constraints on the excluded majority groups of the poor. All these excluded groups have limited social and economic mobility because of institutionalised inequalities that are being created by the forces of globalisation. As suggested by Narayan and Kapoor, "without (state) organisation that is representative and accountable, the economic and societal interests of marginalised groups will not be met". The evidences show that the marginalisation of socially and economically excluded sections is characterised by the failure of state and civil society to control the excesses of market or at least to sensitise the market forces to own the social responsibility. Governance of civil society is the prerogative of state but how can the state institutions working under the dictates of market forces provide good governance? The market is governed by the principle of maximisation of profit and it represents the market players.

This leads us to the question: What are the alternative strategies available before the statesmen and policy-makers in the given circumstances? Right at the outset, in the above context, it is clear that the market is so harsh and rash that it hardly leaves any scope for the search of alternatives. However, it can be stated that the State is the only institution which can be re-activated in the interest of social democracy. It cannot be, therefore, allowed to be hijacked by the forces of market. The most important aspect of any diagnostic measure lies necessarily in the proper understanding of the nature of problem itself. "The response to exclusion is inclusion" (Louis, from Net). This can be done only in the form of policy measures by the State for inclusion of groups that have been marginalised by the market forces.

Firstly, the decision-makers have to devise coherent policies for economic and social inclusion at both the levels—communities and nation. Secondly, while framing the policies there must be a visible shift from the market priority to the social priority. Thirdly, the labour market institutions need to be strengthened to provide capabilities and credentials for the access to the opportunities to those who have excluded by the process of globalisation.

In sum, the need of the hour is to ensure protection of the basic rights of marginalised people, especially by preventing the adverse inclusion. This can be achieved only by strengthening the local democracy through democratic decentralisation. The enactment and implementation of the 73rd Constitutional Amendment Act (1992) has gone a long way in this direction. The one-third reservations for women and the reservations for the

Scheduled Castes and the Scheduled Tribes in proportion to their share in population is a step in the direction of ensuring basic rights of these disadvantaged sections of Indian Society. Besides, the change in the role of the Panchayati Raj Institutions from the performance of civic and developmental functions to making the plans of economic development and social justice on the subjects of the 11th Schedule devolved on them by the state legislatures has to be seen in the same perspective. What we really need now is the genuine devolution of functions, functionaries and funds on the Panchayati Raj Institutions. Only then the local democracy can be strengthened for meeting the challenges that have emerged in the Indian Polity due to the impact of globalization. This not only requires political will on the part the state government but also the building of strong pressure at the grassroots level for forcing them to do functional and financial empowerment of Panchayati Raj Institutions for making them Institutions of Self-Government in the real sense of the word.

REFERENCES

Atkinson, A.B., (1998) "Social Exclusion, Poverty and Unemployment", in A.B. Atkinson and J. Hills (eds.), *Exclusion, Employment and Opportunity*, CASE papers, Centre for Analysis of Social Exclusion, London School of Economics, London.

Beall, Jo, "Globalisation and Social Exclusion in Cities: Framing the Debate with Lessons from Africa and Asia", available at http://www.lse.ac.uk/collections/DESTIN/pdf/WP27.pdf

Bhardwaj, Prem R., (2002) "Globalisation: Governance without Government—An Indian Experience", *Punjab Journal of Politics*, Vol. XXXVI, No. 2, 29-45.

Carr, Mrilyn and Martha Chen, (2004) "Globalisation, Social Exclusion and Work", Working paper, Policy Integration Department, World Commission on Social Dimension of Globalisation, International Labour Office, Geneva, available at, http://www.ilo.org/dyn/dwresources/docs/625/F1146925582/gender%20and%20globlisation.pdf

Castles, Stephen, "Development, Social Transformation and Globalisation", available at http://www.materialien.org/worldwide/pga/castles.pdf

Chomsky, Noam, (2008) "Humanitarian Imperialism", *Analytical Monthly Review*, Vol. 6, No. 6, September 2008, 20-46.

Louis, Prakash, "Social Exclusion—A Conceptual and Theoretical Framework", available at http://www.empowerpoor.org/download/Social_Exclusion_PACS_final.pdf

Louis, Prakash, "Social Exclusion—A Conceptual and Theoretical Framework", available at http //emmpowerpoor.org/downloads/Social_Exclusion_PACS_final.pdf

Mishra, S.K. and P. Nayak, (2006) "Socio-economic Dimensions of Globalisation in India", (working paper) available at http://www.freewebs.com/nehu_economics/secoglob_india.pdf

Narayan, Deepa and Soumya Kapoor, (2005) "Beyond Ideologies: Creating Wealth for the Poor", Arusha Conference, "New Frontiers of Social Policy", Dec. 12-15, 2005, also available at internet.

Pieterse, Jan Nederveen, "Globalisation North South—Representations of Uneven Development and the Interaction of Modernities", available at https://netfilesuiuc.edu/jnp/www/pdf/Glob%20North%20South%20J.pdf

Rosenau, Jasmes, (2002) "The First Global Revolution: A report of the Council of Rome", in David Held and Anthony McGrew (eds.), *The Global Transformations Reader*, Polity Press.

15

Democratic Decentralisation, Good Governance and Human Governance : A Conceptual Analysis

VINAY KUMAR MALHOTRA

I

One may ask at the out set, out of the two concepts—'democratic decentralisation' and 'good governance' that are in vogue these days, which comes first. Democratic decentralisation, as the prerequisite of good governance, has reinforced the very old concept of decentralisation since the 1990s. No doubt, the concept of decentralisation is an old one that grew with the growth of democracy. But the concept of good governance came only in the early 1990s from the developed donor countries and the international financial institutions such as the World Bank (WB) and the International Monetary Fund (IMF). But it infused a new lease of life in the old concept of decentralisation especially in the developing countries of Asia, Africa and South America with India being no exception. Emphasis on good governance by the international financial institutions and the developed donor countries gave a big boost to implementation of the concept of democratic decentralisation in developing countries.

In India, the then Prime Minister, Rajiv Gandhi, acted as a crusader for democratic decentralisation in late 1980s, i.e. even before insistence by international financial institutions and developed countries on the good governance. He introduced the 64th Amendment Bill on 15th May 1989 for this purpose. But it failed to get the required 2/3 majority in the Rajya

Sabha. The 73rd Amendment Act of 1992 which was passed after the demise of Rajiv Gandhi clearly shows his democratic vision based on the ancient values and the ideas of Mahatma Gandhi and Jawaharlal Nehru (Kapoor, 2006: 63-69).

II. GOOD GOVERNANCE : A POST-MODERN AND NEO-LIBERAL CONCEPT

It was from the 1960s that the post-modernism became prominent globally owing to the writings of French intellectuals and American literary critics. In addition, the gaining of momentum by civil liberty, counter culture, environmental movements, feminism, anti-war, anti-nuclear campaigns, alternative development perspectives and the rapidity of decolonization also gave a fillip to this trend. The term 'modern' was actually used in the nineteenth century to distinguish the 'present' times from the 'past'. The modern era, however, started with the Enlightenment, which began during the eighteenth century, though some would trace it from the Renaissance. The major elements of modernity were reason, rationality, science, positivism, democracy, secularism, rule of law and capitalist mode of enterprise and development.

By the middle of the twentieth century, the 'crisis/failure/end of modernity' became a hot topic of discussion and debate. Habermas says that post-modernism represented a 'conservative response to the limits and inadequacies of the scheme of modernity'. (Habermas, 1987: 4). Lyotard wrote that the status of knowledge has changed with entry of societies into post-industrial age and entry of cultures into post-modernism (1986:3). Similar was Bell's (1973) notion of post-industrial society manifested by the transformation in the political economy of the western societies owing to advances in information and telecommunication technologies and consequent changes in culture and society. While industrial society revolved around the coordination of workers and machines for production of goods, post-industrial society has been working around knowledge, for the sake of social control and showing the way for innovation and change (Bell, 1973: 20).

Thus, post-industrial society suggests the possibility of decentralisation of work and industrial structures. It gives further boost to decentralisation in political systems. Thus, the post-modern slogan of politics, 'think globally, act locally'—is an essential meeting point of neo-liberalism and post-modernism.

Neo-Liberalism, the leading ideology of the present global political and economic order, is noticeable in the policies and programmes across a broad spectrum of countries, institutions and political forces. In the post-Second World War era, many countries embraced the Keynesian welfare formula to solve economic problems. The justification for state intervention was avoidance of class struggle, maintenance of full employment, reduction of social inequality, promotion of social equity and security and solution of other problems of capitalist mode of production. This welfare formula with 'big government', 'state intervention' started fading away in late 1970s and 1980s owing to the fiscal crisis and lower rates of growth, shifts in tax structure, cuts on public spending, wage and price controls and anti-inflation monetary policies (Seethi, 2001: 314). The Keynesian formula, consequently, became highly questionable and a new package of economic measures and new 'national management' techniques came to the fore in the West. After the collapse of Communism in the early 1990s, all developed and developing countries adopted and executed neo-liberal policies with a minimal role for the state in economic affairs. The state in neo-liberal model insists on 'efficiency', 'productivity' and 'development', and the issues of 'welfare' and 'social justice' have consequently been relegated. Thus neo-liberalism ideology sustains a questionable claim that the development needs of post-modern societies can be achieved through an unregulated market (Teeple, 1995: 82). The IMF, W.B. and the WTO publicised neo-liberal tenets through out the world.

As a result, the neo-liberal agenda of 'participatory development', 'empowerment' and decentralisation became prevalent in the world. In most of the developing countries, it was first introduced in the name of Structural Adjustment Programme (SAP) accompanied by packages of decentralisation/community participation development strategies. All kinds of states, including the United States, Britain, South Africa, India, Brazil and Bolivia, have undergone such experiments of decentralisation and local level development. There has been downsizing of 'big governments' across the world and power being relocated to local governments and non-state actors (Cusimano, 2000: 323). The W.B., IMF and WTO are propagating 'local development/decentralisation' programmes in order to encourage new social forces in the development process such as Non-Governmental Organisation (NGOs), voluntary/community active groups, etc. This way decentralisation is upheld and maintained by liberalisation, privatisation, deregulation, delegation and devolution.

Thus the new concept of 'local development and decentralisation' is an off-shoot of neo-liberalism. The international financial institutions usually promote this as it sustains 'local' as a functional for a smooth capital accumulation. With this another new concept 'civil society' has been launched by the developed countries and international financial institutions. In due course, it became a funding package of Western agencies along with good governance and decentralisation. Neo-liberals maintain that civil society, while retaining autonomy and identity, can overcome the overbearing and authoritarian state and thereby strengthen democratisation and good governance (Seethi, 2001: 315). The NGOs themselves have felt that civil society can be highly 'productive'. It not only helps in getting Northern funding but also provides legitimacy to their activities and interventions. When the state rolls back, civil society intervenes to offer 'efficient service delivery and targeted poverty eradication programmes' (World Bank, 1999).

A large number of definitions have been given and roughly eighty definitions have been deliberated over a period of less than two decades and it is pity that the direction came for such discussion from the donor agencies who have lent and aided in plenty for development works in the developing countries but these have not been used properly by the receiving countries. Good governance (efficient, effective, responsive, corruption-free and citizen friendly) is vital to the administration for ensuring people's trust in and promoting social harmony, political stability and economic development (Putnam, 2000: World Bank, 1977).

III. GOOD GOVERNANCE IN DIFFERENT COUNTRIES

Good Governance in Developed Countries

Good governance is associated in developed countries with the market and new public management models to reduce costs and enhance the accountability of administrators and satisfaction of the citizens. Privatisation, corporatisation and contracting of public activities, competition, entrepreneurial ability and managerial autonomy to the managers are the guiding principles for administrative reforms and governance. It focused on the production of more goods and services to the satisfaction of citizens with low budget, less bureaucracy and few rules (Johnston and Calumech, 1999).

Good Governance in Developing Countries

Good governance has been related in developing countries to political (pluralism, participation, decentralisation, human rights and consensus); economic (economic liberalisation, private ownership, investment, growth, poverty alleviation); social (civil society and NGOs and social capital or social cohesion), legal (rule of law and independent judiciary); and administrative (accountability, transparency, less corruption, efficiency, effectiveness and responsiveness) reforms by the international development and donor agencies (Kaul, 1999; Konig, 1999; World Bank, 1999). In other words, good governance is strictly connected with institutionalised values such as democracy, observance of human rights and rule of law and greater efficiency within the public sector. Their main stress is on the removal of corruption and strengthening of civil society, people's participation, transparency, administrative efficiency and accountability (Bhatta and Gonzales III, 1999).

Most of the countries have endeavored to restrict the role of the state, including downsizing the bureaucracy, devolution of authority, cost reduction, contracting out some of the operative functions of the government, developing and designing result-oriented appraisal systems, and commercialisation as well as market orientation of the governmental activities. This has been supported by effective accountability through an open reporting system. The administration is clearly shifting from rule to result orientation, from systems to enterprise, from obedience to reward, from inaction to action, from centralisation to decentralisation and from duties of administrators to the rights of citizens (Palanithurai, 2005: 290; World Bank, 1994).

Good Governance in India

Good governance is identified in India with probity in public life and responsive and people friendly administration. It is an important agenda for all major political parties. Removal of corruption through anti-corruption institutions like Lokpal, electoral reforms, Right to Information, transparency in administration (procurement and tendering), depoliticisation of appointments and transfers of administrators and e-governance are the guiding principles for administrative reforms. Participatory democracy and accountability of administration are also visualised by strengthening decentralised self-governing institutions like Panchayati Raj Institutions (PRIs) (particularly the Gram Sabha, social auditing, monitoring, *Jansunwai*, people's planning and so on) and stakeholders' organizations (water, forest, educational, health and other such committees), apart from other reforms (privatisation of services, down-sizing, right-sizing and so on) (Sangita, 2002: 327).

Nehruian model of governance was earlier tried in India from 1947 to 1991. This model of governance relied on secularism, democratic participation, decentralisation of powers on the basis of federalism, command, regulated and planned economy. Governance was directed towards socialistic pattern of society, economic development and assertion of national independence in international affairs. To achieve that goal, a complex network of governmental institutions, organisations, and agencies was set-up for promoters of planned development of the country. But by the late 1980s, it was realised that this model of governance has not produced the desired results. Moreover, the dys-functionality of many bureaucratic and quasi-bureaucratic governing institutions was exposed.

"The minority government, led by Prime Minister, Narsimha Rao, recognized the weaknesses and limitations of Indian economy and governance. It abandoned the cautions and hesitations of former governments, and embraced the philosophy of liberal economic reforms in 1991. Since then, India has launched a new model of development," writes Kumar (2008: 18). No doubt, like elsewhere, Western donor countries and international financial institutions like the IMF, W.B. and later on the WTO also played their role through their conditionality in bringing the concept of good governance and decentralisation to India. Thus new institutions were created to achieve rapid economic growth and immunity against earlier governmentalisation of the whole society. The old democratic structural pattern, style of leadership, bureaucratic structure and mechanical centralised development model was considered incapable and inadequate of handling changes occurring at global and domestic levels. Therefore, it was appropriate to devise systems and style of governance to meet the challenges to fulfil people's needs and aspiration. Globalisation, liberalisation and privatization became new policy framework of governance in India as well as in world at large. Foreign technology, foreign capital and foreign investments have been encouraged, market freed and powers devolved. A new scenario has emerged on Indian horizon, which demanded a shift in the style, context, direction and emphasis of governance as in many other countries (Ghosh, 1992: 23).

IV. GOOD GOVERNANCE AND DECENTRALISATION AT GRASSROOTS IN INDIA

Palanithurai rightly says, "Good governance has to start from the grassroots as it works closely with the community and the society" (2005: 291). Decentralised democratic governance creates new incentives that can induce efficiency, effectiveness and responsiveness. In other words, decentralised governance creates incentives such as: increased competition among levels of government, increased local control over resources, increased decision-making authority, increased targeting of services to local needs and desires, and increased transparency or improving efficiency (Brinkerhoff, 2000: 601). Democratic decentralisation and participative management also contribute to better compliance and enforcement with low cost, since decisions regarding selection of schemes and design of projects are taken in consultation with various stakeholders in the organization (Sangita, 2002: 339).

The Article 40 in the Chapter on Directive Principles of State Policy of the Indian Constitution has very well stipulated for the organization of Village Panchayats. Although, it is an advisory provision yet it provided the opportunity to make PRIs as the institutions of local self-governance and to discharge the civic functions. But as the subject of local government is in the State List, respective state legislatures enacted laws to set-up these bodies, naturally, as per their own convenience and suitability. This resulted in structural and functional variability in the local governance system established by various states in the country before the 73rd Constitutional Amendment Act was passed by the Parliament in 1992.

This Amendment institutionalized periodical elections to the rural local bodies, provided for reservation to the women and weaker sections in the representative local bodies, and mandated the State Governments to devolve functions, functionaries and funds (popularly and briefly known as 3-Fs) to the PRIs. It has raised hopes that this new measure would further strengthen the twin processes of good governance and decentralisation.

The PRIs created under new system are surely empowered, not only because of certain responsibilities that are entrusted to them but because of certain other provisions also. These are: (i) provision for establishing an adequately represented electoral base with a fixed tenure of five years; (ii) a clearly stated provision for holding regular elections and within six months in the event of premature dissolution of Gram Panchayat or vacancy in the office-bearers and members; (iii) provisions for establishing institutions and evolving mechanisms for consolidating and coordinating, planning and development initiatives and actions of the Panchayats, expecting it might ensure enhanced people's participation; and (iv) crystal clear efforts to expand their role/functions and to strengthen their fiscal jurisdiction, power and authority (Malik, 2005: 773).

V. SHORTCOMINGS AND CONSTRAINTS

Thus, the Amendment has also paved the way for greater democratisation and decentralisation of Indian polity at micro-level. It has not only boosted the process of democratisation and decentralisation but has also converted the PRIs into the harbingers of rural development at grassroot level. But at the same time, the process of good governance and decentralisation in India suffers from the following problems:

Lack of Awareness and Training amongst the Elected Representatives and Corruption

Major shortcomings are: lack of awareness of their own responsibilities amongst the elected representatives, lack of proper training for programme implementation, dearth of proper publicity of the different development-oriented schemes, the problem of language and comprehension amongst the leadership, irregularity of the meetings, prevalence of corruption, etc. in all the States and especially in Haryana (Mishra and Dhaka, 2004).

Male Domination, Caste and Class Characteristic Unchanged

The Bihar Government brought a Panchayat Raj Act in 1993, based on the stipulations in the Constitutional Amendment. But the elections to the local bodies could be held only after 7 years of the Act coming into force. "The leadership of the Panchayats became liberal and broad based, but its caste and class characteristic remain unchanged," says Misra (1999). Sumita Misra's work examined the dynamics of local politics in the backward State of Bihar. She observes that the participation of women has been pathetically low even after the introduction of Statutory Panchayats. The leadership has been male dominant. Reservation of seats has increased the lower caste participation and representation. However, in the open category, the upper castes, especially the Bhumihars, are dominant. The landowning communities dominate the block level politics, whereas at the Panchayat level leaders come from the landless and poor peasant groups. Family status, income, education and occupation play an important role in the emergence of informal leadership (Misra, 1999: 150).

Absence of Commitment and Competent Leaders

Democratic decentralisation and participative management model suffer from some other constraints. Absence of commitment and competent leaders, and politicisation of administration are the main constraints for promoting good governance in India. Many local level leaders are yet to be familiarised with statecraft. Elite control and domination over democratic institutions hurt the interests of the poor, despite the increase of their representation.

Decentralisation vs. State Control

The excessive state control has reduced the PRIs to the status of subordinate agencies of the State Government and their autonomy has been completely disappeared. These have been so much circumscribed by internal checks and external controls that they have now failed to bear the strain of the development activities. The techniques used by the State Government to control PRIs include power to cancel resolutions, access to record, inspections, grants-in-aid, reports and enquiries, hearing of appeals, supervision and removal, dissolutions, appointing administrators, auditing of accounts, amending statute, prior approval and issuing of direction. It should not make PRIs dancing dolls, (Singh, 2005: 221).

Inadequate Devolution of "3 Fs"

Even sixteen years after the 73rd Amendment to Indian Constitution, devolution of 3 Fs—Functions, Functionaries and Funds—to local bodies is neither adequate nor complete. One can find a wide deviation in the matter of devolution of functions and functionaries to the different levels of panchayats in the country. It is also clear that the states like Karnataka, Kerala, Madhya Pradesh, Maharashtra, Rajasthan, West Bengal and Sikkim fair well in terms of devolution of functions and to some extent, funds. This way, functional responsibilities have been devolved only in those states which had good traditions of local governance even during pre-73rd Amendment period. The devolution of functions had not taken place even by 2001 in six states—Assam, Chhattisgarh, Kerala, Karnataka, UP and West Bengal. In brief, the devolution of functions remains a far cry in many States.

It has also been found that expenditure responsibilities of local bodies have increased greatly but there is no corresponding increase in funds to complement the additional responsibilities given to these institutions. The authority for devolving financial resources (taxes, duties, tolls and fees, grants-in-aid) to local governments and the resources which should be shared by the state with local bodies, continue to be with state legislatures (Article 243-G, The Constitutional (Seventy-third Amendment) Act, 1992). Further, the State Finance Commissions have been constituted to recommend financial support from the state to these institutions and for determination of taxes, tolls and fees that could be assigned to or appropriated by the local bodies (Article 243-I, *ibid.*). But the acceptance of their recommendations depends upon the sweet will of the State Government. Even then, it is correct that a large part of financial resources of these institutions are drawn largely from the grants-in-aid from the state and centre while share of own tax and non-tax revenue is very meager.

VI. CONCLUSION
FROM GOOD GOVERNANCE TO HUMAN GOVERNANCE

Like elsewhere, the concept of good governance is confined in India to western perspective, especially to the perspective of multi-lateral and international financial institutions whereas endeavor should have been made to incorporate visions of Mahatma Gandhi, Rabindra Nath Tagore, and Ambedkar in the Indian facet of good governance. The concept of good governance as tool of democratic government, which is 'reinventing' itself, should become in Indian context a weapon of social transformation, not the tool of 'surveillance' and 'policy interventions' and for private sector activities in context of 'rolling back of the state', 'minimal state' and the 'retreat of state' (Barthwal, 2005).

Only enacting legislations and establishing representative institutions in a disengaged manner cannot be enough to ensure good governance. The regime has to actively encourage civil societal engagement of actors with their institutions. In most of the countries, there is 'Retreat of the State' and the 'emergence of civil society', similarly there is going on a transition from 'state intervention' to 'civil society intervention'. India cannot totally escape itself this world-wide trend. But at the same time, India along with other developing countries should reinvent its governing system and process. In this situation, Mahbub ul Haq's attempt to reconceptualise development in 'human development' terms deserves special attention. From 'human development' to 'human governance' (not good governance as propounded by the World Bank) as aptly conceptualised by Haq, it has been a major methodological and epistemological leap in our understanding of governance-development nexus (Bhattacharya, 2001: 356). The main tenets of human development model are to improve the capability and expand the opportunities of all people, irrespective of caste, class, gender and ethnicity. The concept of human governance further stresses that governance, if it is to promote human development, has to be not just pro-people or people centered, but it has to be owned by people (Haq, 1999).

The concept of good governance has thus been enlarged, widened and redefined. The three interconnecting aspects of 'human governance' have been identified as (i) *good political governance* in terms of law, accountability and transparency, constitutionalism and decentralisation; (ii) *good economic governance* that relates to securing macro-economic stability, guaranteeing property rights, removing market distortions, and along with investing in people's development, assuring environmental protection and promoting economic growth with justice; and, (iii) *good civic governance* marked by the free interplay of broader civil society groups and securing fundamental human, political and economic rights for those usually excluded from the formal structures of power (e.g. the women, the poor, the ethnic and religious minorities).

The concept of 'human governance' is a bold attempt to invent what is now widely known as the Human Governance Index (HGI) that watches a country's governance from some quantitative and qualitative data. Methodologically, there are many questions involved in the process of formation of the HGI; yet one has now a useful working tool with which to evaluate governmental performance.

If human governance is achieved in India, the issue of decentralisation will automatically settle down. What to talk about human governance, even good governance remains far cry in India especially at local level. Decentralisation has so far taken place only with an array of barriers and obstacles.

References

Barthwal, C.P. (Ed.) (2005). *Good Governance in India,* New Delhi: Deep and Deep Publications, pp. 302.

Bell, Daniel (1973). *The Coming of Post-Industrial Society,* New York: Basic Books.

Bhatta, Gambhir and Joaquin, L. Gonazalez III (1999). "Of Governance and Milking Cows" in Joan Corkery (ed.). *Governance: Concepts and Applications,* Brussels: International Institute of Administrative Sciences (IIAS), pp. 221-42.

Bhattacharya, Mohit (2001). "Globalisation, Governance and Development," *The Indian Journal of Political Science* (Guntur), Vol. 62, No. 3, Sept. 2001, pp. 349-57.

Cusimano, Maryann K. (2000). "Sovereignty's Future," in Maryann K. Cusimano, (ed.) *Beyond Sovereignty: Issues for a Global Agenda,* Boston: Bedford/St. Martin"s.

Ghosh, Arun (1992). "Federalism, Democracy and Decentralisation," *Economic and Political Weekly,* November 14, 1992, p. 23.

Habermas, (1987). *The Philosophical Discourse of Modernity.* Cambridge: Polity Press.

Haq, Mahbub ul (1999). *Human Development in South Asia: The Crisis of Governance,* Oxford: Oxford University Press.

Kapoor, Usha (2006). "Democracy at Grassroots—Rajiv Gandhi's Vision", *Journal of Political Science,* Vol. II, No. 2, Nov. 2006, pp. 63-69.

Kaul, Mohan (1999). "Issues in Governance: A Common Wealth Perspective" in Joan Corkery (ed.), *Governance: Concepts and Applications,* Brussels: International Institute of Administrative Sciences (IIAS).

Konig, Klaus (1999). "Good Governance—as Steering and Value Concept for the Modern Administrative State", in Joan Corkery (ed.), *Governance: Concepts and Applications,* Brussels: International Institute of Administrative Sciences (IIAS).

Kumar, S.B. (2008). "Overview of Good Governance in India," *Third Concept,* Vol. 22, No. 258, August 2008, pp. 17-21.

Lyotard, J.F. (1986). *The Postmodern Condition: A Report of Knowledge.* Manchester: Manchester University Press.

Malik, A.S. (2005). "Local Self-Government at Village Level—An Assessment," *The Indian Journal of Political Science,* LXVI, No. 4, Oct.-Dec. 2005, pp. 773-92.

Mishra, Suresh and Rajvir S. Dhaka (2004). *Grassroot Democracy in Action,* New Delhi: Concept Publishing Company, p. 180.

Misra, Sumita (1999). *Grassroots Politics in India,* New Delhi: Mittal Publications, p. 150.

Palanithurai, G. (2005). "Good Governance at Grassroots," *The Indian Journal of Political Science* (Meerut), Vol. LXVI, No. 2, April-June, 2005, pp. 289-312.

Putnam, Robert (2000). *Bowling Alone: The Collapse and Revival of American Community,* NY: Simon and Schuster.

Sangita, S.N. (2002). "Administrative Reforms for Good Governance," in *The Indian Journal of Political Science,* Vol. 63, No. 4, Dec. 2002, pp. 325-50.

Seethi, K.M. (2001). "Postmodernism, Neo-Liberalism and Civil Society: A Critique of the Development Strategies in the Era of Globalisation", *The Indian Journal of Political Science,* Vol. 62, No. 3, September 2001, pp. 308-20.

Singh, Mohinder and Kumar, Vijay (2005). "State Control over Panchayat Raj Institutions," *The Indian Journal of Political Science*, Vol. LXVI, No. 2, April-June, 2005, pp. 221-32.

World Bank (1997). "What can Developing Countries Learn from East Asia's Economic Growth", Takatoshi, Ito, *Annual World Bank Conferences on Development Economics/The World Bank*, 213-15.

Teeple, Gray (1995). *Globalization and the Decline of Social Reform*, New Jersey: Humanities Press.

Takatoshi, Ito (1997) "What can Developing Countries Learn from East Asia's Economic Growth" in *Annual World Bank Conferences on Development Economics*, The World Bank, pp. 213-15.

World Bank (1994). *Governance: The World Bank's Exercise*, Washington: World Bank.

World Bank (1999). "Fostering Institutions to Contain Corruption," *The World Bank* (24).

World Bank (1999). *Non-governmental Organizations in World Bank Supported Projects: A Review.* Washington, D.C.: World Bank.

16

The RTI and Good Governance at Local Level

MOHINDER SINGH

Accountability, openness and accessibility of information to people about the functioning of governments at the central, state and local levels are the vital components of good governance. The Right to Information Act, 2005 has certainly prompted these. It has enthused the public even during the short period in which it has been in force. The Act has, therefore, created a lot of hope about the emergence of good governance. It is expected to galvanise administrative processes and build a healthy relationship between the citizen and the government through necessary corrections, reforms and improvements. However, it would require a reasonable time for becoming effective.[1]

The present paper discusses and examines as to how far the Right to Information can be helpful in the process of good governance at the local level with special reference to Panchayati Raj. It also seeks to suggest suitable measures for this purpose.

The importance of the RTI for achieving good governance has rightly been emphasised by the Second Administrative Reforms Commission as follows:

> "Without good governance, no amount of developmental schemes can bring improvements in the quality of life of the citizens. Good governance has four elements—transparency, accountability, predictability and participation. Transparency refers to availability of information to the general public and clarity about functioning of

governmental institutions. Right to Information opens up government's records to public scrutiny, thereby arming citizens with a vital tool to inform them about what the government does and how effectively, thus making the government more accountable. Transparency in government organisations makes them function more objectively thereby enhancing predictability. Information about functioning of government also enables citizens to participate in the governance process effectively. In a fundamental sense, right to information is a basic necessity of good governance".[2]

The Right to Information, has indeed helped in empowering people to combat state corruption; to prevent administrative high handedness and arbitrariness; to bridge the gap between the provider and recipient of public services; to make the citizen a part of the decision-making process in the government; to provide responsive administration; to strength the foundations of grassroots democracy through people's participation in local governance and development activities; and to have access to other righs.[3]

Active participation of both women and men in the governance is a must. In its absence, the basic goals of good governance can not be achieved. That governance is good which provides opportunities to the people in deciding future courses of action, monitoring and evaluation. There are various delivery points where the incidence of corruption, delay, harassment and rude behaviour towards public has increased. As a result, public officials are viewed as unresponsive and lukewarm. This has happened as no worthwhile political leaders have been left to guide, advise, control and supervise them. It has been observed that quality of governance has gone down, particularly, at the grassroots or the cutting edge level where it comes in direct contact with the common man.[4]

It has been aptly pointed out that the elected representatives at the local level are not accountable to the local communities because they receive their funds in the form of grants directly from the central government. According to a rough estimate, there are as many as 154 centrally sponsored schemes dealing with the subjects devolved upon PRIs. A nexus has developed over the years between the block level officials and the elected representatives of the PRIs and the latter only undertake such projects as involve constructions, contractors and commissions. It is a fact that central funding of state sector activities is problematic due to one or the other reasons. Thus, the central funding has led to an erosion of accountability.[5]

A study conducted in the Village Panchayats of Sanager Block of Jaipur district of Rajasthan has reached the broad conclusion that most of the respondents recognise the Gram Sabha as a basic unit in the framework of rural local self-government. However, the participation in its meetings is low as most of them believe that programmes are, by and large, confined only to the papers. These are not properly implemented. Whenever decisions are taken, even those are not implemented. Participation in the Gram Sabha meetings is also low due to lack of faith in their representatives among the villagers. And, the politicians, bureaucrats and local level leaders show indifference in ensuring effective functioning of Gram Sabha fearing that this may threaten their power.[6]

It has also been observed that secrecy and lack of openness in the transactions are among the root causes of corruption in the Gram Panchayats. Transparency is required because, in most of the cases, the meetings of Gram Sabha are not convened periodically despite the provision for it in the PR Act of the state. In some other cases, bogus signatures of the members are obtained to meet the requirement of quorum. The elected women representatives of Panchayats generally do not attend the meetings their relatives attend these on their part or their signatures/thumb impressions are obtained by sending the proceedings register to their houses.

It too has been observed that some of the Sarpanches even do not circulate the agenda of the meeting of the Gram Panchayats among all the Panches and important decisions are taken by them in secret meetings. Besides, neither the proceedings of the meetings are made available to all the members nor the documents relating to the financial transactions are kept open for the scrutiny by the Panches and the Gram Sabha members. As a result, the nexus between the rural bureaucracy and the heads of Panchayats is able to manipulate the funds.[7]

Moreover, elections are expected, under the prescribed rules, to be fair and free from any type of corruption, but ignorance of the Election Code of Conduct results in vitiating the electoral atmosphere. The use of alcohol and violence is widespread. The candidates, infact, use all type of means to win election by hook or crook and money flows like water. After having won the election, they indulge in corrupt practices to recover the amount spent by them. They freely misuse and embezzle resources of Panchayats for this purpose.

One of the most important pre-requisites for good governance, it may be mentioned, is the rule of law. No progress or development can be achieved in a society, unless the people comply with the rules. Unfortunately, these are frequently violated to favour the supporters. As a result, the democratic values get ignored on the one pretext or the other. Our study on Rajasthan has found that ineffective functioning of Gram Sabha is due to the lack of awareness among the rural masses about its role. Even most of the Panches do not know as to what decisions have been taken and how have these been implemented.

SUGGESTIONS

Awareness Generation

The concerned persons are also not aware of various aspects of RTI Act. Therefore, it is suggested that a general awareness programme should be launched to educate not only the elected representatives but also the masses on the RTI Act so that good governance can be ensured in the working of Gram Panchayats.

Action to be taken

By the Government

- Formulating and implementing of a policy on RTI at local level.
- Providing sufficient funds.

By the NGOs/Civil Society/Training Institutes/Universities

- Developing easily understandable literature on RTI in local language.
- Organising the public meetings to disseminate awareness and knowledge among the masses.
- Motivating the locally available youth for this purpose.
- Organising the street plays, community-based workshops and role plays.
- Educating the rural masses about the procedure of seeking information and other requisite provisions of the RTI, Act.

By the Mass Media

- Bringing out regular features on the role of PRIs under RTI.
- Highlighting the role of Panchayats in providing the information on demand.
- Publishing reports on the status of accountability, transparency, efficiency and effectiveness in the Panchayats.
- Attracting the attention of government and people towards concealment of facts by them while giving information under RTI.

Capacity Building

As most of the elected representatives and the officials of the Gram Panchayats, as reported earlier, do not have adequate knowledge of various aspects of RTI, necessary training on the same should be imparted to them.

Action to be taken by the Government

- Providing sufficient funds to governmental and non-governmental institutions including training institutes and other educational institutions for imparting need-based training.
- Ensuring periodic monitoring and evaluation of the training imparted.
- Taking appropriate steps for regular feedback to make the training more effective and useful.

Action to be taken by NGOs/Civil Society/Training Institutes/Universities

- Identifying dedicated, sincere and enthusiastic trainers.
- Arranging suitable training of trainers programmes covering the pertinent issues regarding RTI and good governance.
- Involving experts on the RTI in training and interactions.
- Developing training manuals, modules and guidelines.
- Using the latest methods and techniques of training to make it interesting.
- Ensuring that the trainers have been fully motivated.
- Dividing them into groups for sending them to impart further training to the elected representatives of PRIs.
- Imparting cluster-wise training at regular intervals as per the convenience of the participants.

Regular Monitoring and Evaluation

Regular monitoring and evaluation of every programmes is also needed to assess their impact on bringing improvement in RTI regime. This job should be assigned to an independent professional agency. The monitoring and evaluation of their impact on the masses in general and weaker sections in particular is particularly needed in this context.

Action to be taken by Government

- Preparing guidelines and instructions to be followed in the monitoring and evaluation of the impact of RTI Act.
- Involving government agencies/organisations, NGOs, Civil Society and other institutions for the fair conduct of monitoring and evaluation.
- Providing sufficient time for the completion of monitoring and valuation of implementation of RTI Act.
- Taking prompt action to overcome the identified problems and weaknesses.

By NGOs/Civil Society/Institutes

- Preparing a team of independent functionaries for ensuring effective monitoring and evaluation.
- Developing most suitable and comprehensive schedules for this work.
- Getting the monitoring and evaluation work completed within a specified period.
- Disseminating the findings and results by sharing the same.
- Building pressure to get the required changes incorporated in the Training Module.

By Media

- Giving wide publicity to the weaknesses and the problems encountered.
- Pressurising the concerned agencies/institutions to take immediate action.
- Bringing the deficiencies and improvement in the capacity-building to the notice of all the stakeholders.

Creation of Conducive Atmosphere

For effective implementation of RTI Act, there is a dire need for providing conducive atmosphere so that every person gets the needed information on demand without any delay. Therefore, strict action-oriented approach should be adopted.

Action to be taken by the Government

- Ensuring that bureaucratic hurdles do not interrupt the smooth implementation of RTI Act.
- Instructing all officials to extend all possible support to the person seeking information under the Act.
- Arranging special lectures to motivate both the officials and non-officials to discharge their duties and responsibilities under the RTI in an honest, dedicated and sincere manner.
- Making it sure that their indifferent attitude is changed.

Action to be taken by NGOs/Civil Society

- Extending whole-hearted support in developing conducive atmosphere for the expeditious disposal of RTI cases.
- Interacting with the concerned officials/non-officials through informal interactions.
- Honouring the role of those who are really devoted to the RTI regime and perform their duties without delay and in an unbiased approach.

If the above suggestions are implemented sincerely, the RTI regime shall be strengthened in the Gram Panchayats. This in turn will lead to good governance by facilitating transparency, enhancing accountability and checking corruption and misuse of powers and funds.

Notes and References

1. S.L. Goel, *Right to Information and Good Governance*, Deep & Deep Publications Pvt. Ltd., New Delhi, 2007.

2. Government of India, Second Administrative Reforms Commission, New Delhi, *First Report on Right to Information: Master Key to Good Governance,* June 2006, para 1.1.1.
3. Jaytilk Guha Roy, "Right to Information: A Key to Accountable and Transparent Administration", in Dhameja Alka (ed.), *Contemporary Debates in Public Administration,* Printice-Hall of India Pvt. Ltd., 2003.
4. U.C. Aggarwal, "Good Governance: Cutting Edge of Administration", *Indian Journal of Public Administration,* Vol. XLIV, No. 3, July-September 1998.
5. Administrative Staff College of India, "Governance Challenges in Resurgent India: Enhancing Policy Implementation and Outcomes", *ASTI, Journal of Training & Development,* Vol. IX, No. 1, January to June 2008.
6. Mohinder Singh, "Transparency in Functions: Vital for Gram Panchayats," *Indian Journal of Public Administration,* Vol. XLIX, No. 4, October-December, 2003.

PART III

The Conceptual and Operational Dimensions

17

The Concept of Democratic Decentralisation

S. BHATNAGAR

This brief write up seeks to demystify the concept of democratic decentralisation and to discuss its genesis and development in India. The objective behind this exercise is to put the Panchayati Raj Institutions in a proper conceptual and historical perspective. This has become essential because there continues to prevail a great deal of ambivalence, ambiguity, confusion and lack of clarity on the concept of democratic decentralisation and the nature of the institutions of decentralised governance among the political leaders, administrators and the social scientists.

I

At the outset let us try to understand the term decentralisation. For comprehending the term, we must know that it involves devolution. And, the devolution must be differentiated from de-concentration which connotes an administrative arrangement under which a superior officer, actuated by the desire to make his department function more effectively and efficiently, delegates to his subordinate field officials 'the capacity to act' in his name, without, however, transferring to them the authority he enjoys. He, however, allows them a considerable degree of discretion so that they may be able to dispose of the matter on the spot and do not bother him about trivial details by making repeated reference to him. But that does not imply that the officials to whom power is delegated come to possess an unfettered authority in their jurisdictional sphere. Their authority remains drastically limited to those few matters in regard to which the transfer has been specifically made. Moreover, they always remain dependent on the overall authority of their superior. It can very well be illustrated by the example of the administrative system that the British had built up in India in which the District Collector or the Deputy Commissioner, being 'man on the spot', was delegated certain responsibilities. He had to perform these on behalf of the provincial government.

Devolution, on the other hand is a process wherein power is transferred from one organ of government to another or from central level to state level or from state level to local level or from the central level to local level. A certain sphere of jurisdiction, either functional or territorial, is clearly or distinctly set apart for the care of a constitutionally or legally set-up body, which while administering its authority, also enjoys, what MacMahon calls, 'some power of self-direction'. Devolution may be effected either 'constitutionally' or 'statutorily'. The former course is adopted generally in the case of federations where the powers are divided between the federal centre and the federating autonomous units. The division is effected by means of a written and a rigid constitution so that the division once made may not be frequently tampered with by the powers that be. This arrangement is territorial in character.

Authority may also be devolved by the centre to the subordinate units by means of a parliamentary statute. This transfer of authority can be both territorial and functional in character. The central government of a unitary state and the provincial (state) government of a federation and the central government of a federal polity often transfer the administration of such affairs through the constitutional amendment to the local government institutions which can conveniently be disposed of locally. In the same manner, the modern welfare states also part with the managerial aspects of a certain function and vest it in a legally constituted body.

To sum up, decentralisation is undoubtedly a very complex term. It indicates a situation wherein authority is dispersed from a single centre to a number of centres. It could be either administrative or democratic. While, the administrative decentralisation, means administrative deconcentration, the democratic decentralisation means the devolution of power by means of parliamentary statutes or constitutional amendment to the democratically elected bodies of the people at the various levels.

The prefixing of the word 'democratic' implies that the transfer of powers is only to those bodies which are not only democratically elected by the people but also function democratically. In other words, they are responsible to the people at every stage of their working and for every single act of theirs. They (people) who, in turn, possess the power of censuring the conduct of the elected representatives whenever they want to do so. The latter aspect of responsibility is perhaps more important than the former, because democracy in constitution is also implied in another concept, namely, 'democratic centralism', which is the very anti-thesis of 'democratic decentralisation'. Democratic centralisation is an innovation that the Communist regime had made in the now disintegrated USSR after the Bolshevik Revolution in 1917. It means democracy in constitution but centralisation in decision-making. Under this system people are free to elect their rulers, but once they have elected them and the broad outlines of their policy are approved, the people cannot question the decisions that they had taken. They must accept them without any questioning or reservations. Democratic decentralisation, on the other hand, confers upon the people full freedom both in regard to election of the leaders and the making of the policies and their execution. They are free to question those decisions, criticise those and demand changes in them.

Bringing out a distinction between the two concepts, Late Prof. Iqbal Narain of the Department of Political Science, Rajasthan University and one of the tallest Political Scientists of India, says, "*Under democratic decentralisation the underlying idea is to widen the area of democracy, (which may exist at the top) by granting both authority and autonomy to the people at the lower levels. One could say that here the attempt is to create democracies within democracies. In contrast to this, unde democratic centralism, the idea is to provide a democratic base to the autocratic top*".

Thus democratic decentralisation seeks to vest effective power in a larger measure in the institutions of local government so that they may be developed into what Bryce describes as 'the tiny fountainheads of democracy'. In other words, the objective behind democratic decentralisation is the establishment of a decentralised and participatory democracy instead of centralised democracy.

II

The concept of democratic decentralisation had been an important element of political discourse in Indian Political thought during the colonial period. The Father of Nation, Mahatma Gandhi, accorded it a pivotal position by formulating the concepts of Panchayati Raj and Gram Swaraj. However, the makers of the Indian Constitution relegated it to insignificance and reluctantly agreed to include Panchayats only in Article 40 of the non-justiciable Directive Principles of State Policy. As a matter of fact, they designed the Constitution for the creation of a polity in which the centre had been made very strong and the states had been made relatively weaker. They did not share the Gandhian view of village communities as autonomous republics and instead wanted a highly centralized system for achieving the objectives of modernisation, economic development and nation-building. The village communities were perceived by them as traditional, backward and apolitical. In other words, they set-up a polity based on the concept of democratic centralisation instead of democratic decentralisation.

But the failure of the Community Development Programme (1952) made the decision-makers at the central level to go in for democratic decentralisation. This programme was a bureaucratic way of dealing with the pressing problem of all-round backwardness in the rural society. All the development departments, such as, agriculture, animal husbandry, social and general education, public health, etc., were equipped with the necessary field staff and other resources and they were made a part of the Community Development Administration. These specialists, armed with adequate power and authority, were to go out to the countryside, establish a close contact with the villagers, study their individual social and economic problems, and suggest possible solutions, thereby infusing in them fresh thinking for a new way of life. As a result of persistent efforts, the villagers were supposed to develop the will to change and improve their lot.

But the Community Development Programme, however, failed to arouse the enthusiasm of the people owing its bureaucratic implementation. Consequently, people's co-operation and initiative could not be stimulated. The district and the block level development/advisory committees comprising of the nominated representatives could not make it a peoples' programme. The problem was made further complex by the tendency of the BDOs to bypass the elected representatives of the Gram Panchayats and to rely on the rural rich and the traditional leaders for implementing various programmes. The lack of development orientation among the Deputy Commissioners on the one hand, and their inadequate understanding of the rural problems, on the other hand, also created hurdles. Therefore, the programme could not be made people-friendly. As a result, the development programme began to fade. It was, therefore, felt essential that new centres of initiative be created for the people. It was hoped that once such centres are created, development will tend to become a self-propelling process. It will no longer need any prodding from the bureaucracy.

The only suitable and congenial place where centres for such local initiative can be build up, it was realized, are the villages and towns. These being generally small in size, people here are connected with one another by a variety of relationship. Hence it is comparatively easy to associate them with development activities, particularly when these are explained to them in terms of immediate local benefits. Their association with the local development schemes and mass campaigns could stimulate their interest in the welfare of their localities. In this way, it was felt, local initiative shall grow gradually. But all this was possible only if they are enabled to understand responsibility in the context of local institutions. In other words, a consensus emerged at the national level that the local institutions must be effectively organised on democratic lines and vested with substantial power of action based on local initiative, i.e. power must be delegated to them in good measure and they must not be made merely the administrative agencies of the higher levels of the bureaucracy. If once these institutions of local government are set-up as the centres of local power, acting more or less in their own right, they will it was hoped provide initiative and enthusiasm, thereby making the task of development easier. Local government institutions, it was rightly recognised, must be organised in accordance with the principle of democratic decentralisation as this was the *sine qua non* for the success of a development programme.

The Government of India gradually recognised that local government has a special role to play as a valuable corrective to maladministration and political manoeuvring. Local government, it was felt, provides a forum for the whole village to participate in the dual process of making and implementing decisions. It was argued that when the people begin to do things themselves, they shall begin to consider the decisions as their own. The psychological impact of participation shall make them realise that their responsibilities as citizens extend beyond merely participating in a poll after every three years or five years. It shall also make them to realise that their representatives will work effectively only if they themselves maintain an interest in public affairs and express their views. Beginning with small things, people will gradually develop an interest in the bigger affairs of the nation.

The institutions of local government, it was perceived, can further help neutralise the influence of bureaucracy which, unfortunately, is corroding the effectiveness of Indian democracy. The bureaucrats are anti-democratic both, it was aptly felt, by nature and upbringing. As a matter of fact their continued association with office routine and files makes them stereotype in character, conservative in outlook and rigid in behaviour. Being the votaries of the official routine and procedure, they tend to become impervious to popular feelings. They have a natural propensity of getting immune to public criticism. The inevitable result has been that whatever democratic spirit has been present at the central and state government levels is diluted in the course of the execution of policies. It goes without saying that when things are done to the people and not in partnership with them as has been happening in India, the democracy loses its meaning as well as its vitality. It logically leads to the loss of people's confidence in themselves, which is the very foundation of a democratic government. In such a state of affairs, institutions, which bring officials in direct contact with their masters and offer the latter an opportunity to directly participate in the affairs of their locality, act as a bulwark against the growing influence of bureaucracy. The local government official, knowing that his master is watching him, would obviously work with a greater sense of responsibility. Consequently, democracy could be ensured at all levels of the Indian polity through the decentralised governance.

It was the above conceptual perception of the inadequacy of the political centralisation and administrative decentralisation that made the ruling elite of India to adopt the path of democratic decentralisation in 1959 for mobilising human and material resources by creating the system of Panchayati Raj, the three-tier scheme of democratic decentralisation, suggested by the Balvantray Mehta Study Team (1957).

Rajasthan was the first state to set-up Panchayati Raj in 1959. It had been established in almost all the states by 1962 due to the strong support that had been extended to it by Jawaharlal Nehru, the first Prime Minister of India. But the demise of Nehru in 1964, however, was as had been rightly apprehended by Nehru himself, followed by the sabotage of this scheme of democratic decentralisation by the ruling class which instead believed in political and administrative centralisation. Even Asoka Mehta Committee Report (1978) failed to revive it.

This reversion to the administrative decentralisation from democratic decentralisation in the post-Nehru era led to the ineffective implementation of the rural development programme The District Rural Development Agencies that had been set-up in the 1980s for implementing the poverty alleviation and the employment generation programmes failed to deliver. It was the recognition of the above fact that made Rajiv Gandhi, the then Prime Minister of India, to revive the agenda for democratic decentralisation by moving the 64th Constitutional Amendment Bill in the Lok Sabha in 1989. However, the Bill could not become an Act as it failed to muster the requisite two-third majority in the Rajya Sabha. This unfinished task was accomplished by P.V. Narasimha Rao by evolving a consensus in favour of the 73rd Constitutional Amendment Act (1992) despite the fact that he was heading a Minority Government. An added reason for its enactment was the emphasis of the World Bank on democratic decentralisation as a condition for financial aid because it was perceived by the Bank as the basic pre-requisite for good governance.

III

The above discussion leads us to the conclusion that the concept of democratic decentralisation implies genuine devolution of powers to the institutions of grassroots democracy by the central and the state governments and the quest for the democratic decentralisation may be traced from the colonial period. But its institutionalisation has been possible only after the implementation of the recommendations of the Balvantray Mehta Study Team in 1959. It got a further impetus by the 73rd Constitutional Amendment Act (1992) which constitutionalized the Panchayati Raj Institutions. However, the experience of the working of Panchayati Raj Institutions, since the enactment of conformity legislations by various states in 1994 shows that it has remained a mirage so far due to the reluctance of political leaders and bureaucracy to share power with the representatives of people in the institutions of decentralised rural governance. Therefore, a mass movement will have to be launched by all those interested in making the ideal of democratic decentralisation a reality. The elected representatives of the Panchayati Raj Institutions, the NGOs, the Media and the Academia will have to join hands for launching this new struggle for liberating the people from the strangle hold of the vested interests opposed to the transfer of power to people.

REFERENCES

S. Bhatnagar, *Panchayati Raj in Kangra*, Orient Longman, Delhi, 1967.

Surat Singh, *Decentralised Rural Governance, Myth & Reality*, Concept Publishing Company, New Delhi, 2004.

S.C. Jain, *Community Development and Panchayati Raj*, Allied Publishers, Bombay, 1967.

Buddhadeb Ghosh, "Panchayati Raj: Evolution of the Concept", *ISS Occasional Paper Series-25*, Institute of Social Sciences, New Delhi, 2000.

Partha Nath Mukherji, "Participatory Decentralisation: Panchayati Raj and Deepening Indian Democracy", *ISS Occasional Paper Series-34*, Institute of Social Sciences, New Delhi, 2006.

18

The Evolution of Concept of Panchayati Raj, from Democratic Decentralisation to Good Governance

SAROJ MALIK AND SHAMIM QURESHI

The genesis of the concept of Panchayati Raj is often erroneously traced from the institution of the Traditional Panchayats of the village communities which had come into existence in the ancient period for performing the functions of conflict-resolution and system-maintenance soon after the conversion of pastrol societies into the agrarian ones following the emergence of agriculture as the main mode of production. It is also fallaciously linked with the caste (Jati)/sub-caste/(up-Jati), *gotra* (clan) and cluster (*Khap*). Panchayats which had come into being during the medieval era for the resolution of intra and inter-caste/clan disputes and for providing defense against external aggression. It is also wrongly associated with the institutions of the Statutory Panchayats that had been created in the colonial period on the recommendations of the Royal Commission on decentralisation (1907) for discharging the civic functions by mobilising their own resources and for reducing the financial burden of the provincial governments. Likewise, it has been romantically linked with, without the least justification, with the Gandhian ideas of Gram Swaraj and decentralisation which envisaged free India as a commonwealth of economically self-sufficient and politically independent villages. Another perspective in this context is to view Panchayati Raj as an extension of the institution of the Village Panchayats and as rural local-self-government bodies that had been promised by the makers of the Indian Constitution in the non-justiciable Directive Principles of State Policy to accommodate and pacify the Gandhians who were appalled and annoyed over the non-inclusion of Panchayats in what they perceived as a Non-Gandhian/Anti-Gandhian Constitution framed by the Drafting Committee of the Constituent Assembly of India. Here, it will not be out of place to reproduce Article 40 of the Indian Constitution on the organisation of Panchayats, "The State shall take steps to organise village Panchayats and endow them with such powers and authority as may be necessary to enable them to function as units of self-government".

Another widely prevalent misperception is to see the Panchayati Raj as a logical step for the creation of the Gram Panchayats by various State Governments after the First General Elections in 1952 to fulfil the promise that had been made by the Congress Party, which had come to power in almost all the states of the Indian Union, during its election campaign. The enactment of the Gram Panchayat Acts by various states after these elections has to be seen in this perspective.

The fact of the matter is that the Panchayati Raj is the name of the scheme of democratic decentralisation suggested by Balvantray Mehta Study Team (1957) for streamlining the process of rural development after it found that bureaucratically operated Community Development Programme (1952), that had been launched for awakening the dormant forces of progress in rural society and to bring about a silent revolution in it had failed due to lack of popular support. It was the realization of the hard truth by the Study Team that neither the Collector/Deputy Commissioner, District Development Officer, Block Development Officer and his Extension Officers and the Village Level Workers (the Gram Sewaks) nor the nominated District Advisory and Block Advisory Committees can bring about transformation in rural society. The Team rightly believed that the nominated Block Development Councils and the District Development Councils too cannot perform the role of decentralised planning in an effective manner and this task will have to be assigned to the democratically elected block level bodies. It aptly felt that the existing institutions like the District Boards, School Boards and the Gram Panchayats are not fit instruments for designing and implementing rural development programme. That is why it suggested a scheme of democratic decentralisation which envisaged the creation of a democratically elected and organically linked three-tier structure of democratic decentralisation with Gram Panchayats at the village level at the base, Panchayat Samiti at the block level in the middle and the district level Zila Parishad at the top.

For insulating this development mechanism from partisan politics and for keeping the political parties out of these, they suggested an indirect system of elections. The members of the Gram Sabha were to elect the Panches and Sarpanches, they in turn were to elect the members of the Panchayat Samitis who were later on to elect the members of the Zila Parishad. The Cooperative Societies and the Market Committees were also to be associated with Panchayat Samitis by giving them a representation so there could be cooperation and coordination between them in the pursuit of the goal of rural development. The Mahila Mandals, Youth Clubs, the Bharat Sevak Samaj and other voluntary organizations and the Community-based Organizations too were to be linked with the Panchayati Raj Institutions for mobilising popular support.

The Collector/Deputy Commissioner was to be Chairperson of the Zila Parishad for ensuring coordination and cooperation between the District Administration and Panchayati Raj Institutions and for giving guidance to the elected representatives in the task of planning and implementing the rural development programmes and for ensuring the assistance of the district level officers of various line departments to the Panchayati Raj Institutions.

The MPs, MLAs and the MLCs were also to be associated with the Panchayati Raj Institutions for linking the Gram Sabha, the Gram Panchayat, the Panchayat Samiti and the Zila Parishad with the state legislatures and the Union Parliament. They were also supposed to act as the friends, philosophers and the guides of the elected representatives of these bodies.

The key role in planning and implementation of the rural development programmes was to be played by the block level institution, the Panchayat Samiti, because the block, according to Balvantray Mehta Study Team is neither as small as a village to lack leadership and resources nor as large as the district which is too distant from people. Moreover, it is not only associated in the rural psyche with the phenomenon of rural development but also has the rural administrative and technical infrastructure consisting of the BDO, the Extension Officers of various departments like agriculture, cooperation, health, education, industries, veterinary and engineering as well as the village level extension workers (VLWs), the Gram Sewaks.

While the Gram Panchayat was not only to perform the function of implementing its own rural development plans but also those of the Panchayat Samiti. The Panchayat Samiti was to coordinate the functions of the Gram Panchayats, prepare and implement its own plans and implement these with the assistance of the Gram Panchayats and also to perform the agency functions for implementing the plans and programmes of the Zila Parishad, State Government and the Government of India. The Zila Parishad was to be mainly a supervisory and coordinating body.

This scheme of democratic decentralisation suggested by Balvantrai Mehta Study Team (1957) was approved by the National Development Council and the Conference of the Ministers of Local Self Government. However, a consensus emerged at these that in view of the significance of the experiment, on the one hand, and the diversities in the environments of various states, on the other hand, there should be no rigidity in the implementation of this scheme and every state should be free to evolve its own model of democratic decentralisation on Panchayati Raj.

That is why there emerged in due course of time, two broad models of Panchayati Raj in various states. The first is known as the Rajasthan Model.

This was almost completely based on the scheme of democratic decentralisation suggested by Balvantray Mehta Study Team. It made the block level body, the Panchayat Samiti, as the key unit for the decentralisation of the powers of planning and its implementation, provided for indirect elections, made provisions for the association of the MPs and the MLAs with the Panchayati Raj Institutions, gave a key role to the District Collector in it and laid emphasis on close relationship between the PRIs and the Cooperative Institutions.

The second, the Maharashtra Model, made the district level body, the Zila Parishad as the unit for the decentralisation of the powers of planning and implementation, provided for the direct elections, excluded MLAs and MPs from the PRIs and kept the District Collector outside the sphere of the Panchayat Raj. Instead, it created the institution of the Chief Executive Officer of the Zila Parishad as the head of the Development Administration in the district and put all the Line Departments under its control. The Panchayat Samiti was virtually reduced to the status of a Committee of Zila Parishad under this system.

But out of these two models of democratic decentralisation, the Maharastra model was found to be more functional for decentralised rural development than Rajasthan model. That is why the Study Teams on Panchayati Raj set-up by the Government of Karnataka and the Government of Punjab in the 1960s recommended the adoption of Maharastra model for strengthening Panchayati Raj Institutions in their states. Even S.K. Dey, Nehru's conscience keeper, had also expressed the view that Panchayati Raj has struck deep roots in Maharashtra and Gujarat which had adopted this model and has failed to do so in the northern states which had gone in for the Rajasthan model.

Be that as it may, Nehru's apprehension about the future of democratic decentralisation or Panchayati Raj proved true and gradually the Panchayati Raj System that had been arduously created by him was wrecked by his successors who did not share his passionate commitment for democratic decentralisation.

The Janata Party, which came to power at the centre in the 1977 parliamentary elections, failed to fulfil its promise of revitalising this scheme of democratic decentralisation because of the instability during its rule owing to the struggle for power in the fractions of the Janata Party—the Congress (O), Jana Sangh, BJP, Socialist Party and the CFD.

The Report of the High Powered Committee on Panchayati Raj headed by Asoka Mehta (1978) recommended introduction of direct elections, creation of a two tier structure consisting of Zila Parishad and Mandal Panchayats and assignment of a dynamic role to them in rural development through their empowerment for the revitalisation of Panchayati Raj Institution. It, however, suggested the abolition of the Panchayat Samitis and Gram Panchayats. But these recommendations could not be implemented as Janata Government was voted out in 1979 and the Congress (I) Government which was opposed to democratic decentralisation was voted to power in 1980 parliamentary elections. However, the Non-Congress Governments of West-Bengal, Karnataka and Andhra Pradesh did take concrete steps for strengthening Panchayati Raj Institutions in their states in the post-election period (1980-83). But in the rest of the country, the Panchayati Raj Institutions remained virtually paralysed due to gradual erosion in their powers and depletion of their resources. The creation of the District Rural Development Agencies in 1980 for the implementation of the rural development programmes of the Government of India proved to be the proverbial last straw to break camel's back.

But the poor governance of the Rural Development Programme by the government agencies led to the siphoning off of virtually 85 paisa out of every rupee spent on these, and those for whom these poverty alleviation and employment generation programmes were meant could receive only the remaining 15 paisa. It was the realisation of this dismal state of affairs that made the late Rajiv Gandhi to think of constitutionalising the Panchayati Raj Institutions and of empowering them to become institutions of self-government so that these could make and implement plans for economic development and social justice.

For ensuring inclusive rural development, he suggested adequate reservations for women and weaker sections. But his initiative for the institutionalisation of the above objectives in 1989 could not be implemented as the 64th Amendment Bill failed to get the requisite two-third majority support in the Rajya Sabha because it was perceived by the Non-Congress parties as a disguised attempt to erode the limited autonomy that the states possessed in Indian federal polity with a strong centre.

However, P.V. Narasimha Rao, who became Prime Minister of India in 1991, was able to get Rajiv's vision constitutionalised in 1992 through the enactment of the 73rd Constitutional Amendment by building a consensus in its favour. This Amendment became an Act in 1993.

The 73rd Constitutional Amendment inserted Part-IX and Article 243 in the Indian Constitution in which the following provisions have been made:

1. *Article. 243A—Gram Sabha*: A Gram Sabha may exercise such powers and functions at village level as the legislature of a State may, by law, provide.
2. *Article 243B—Constitution of Panchayats*: There shall be constituted in every state, Panchayats at the village, intermediate and district levels in accordance with the provisions of this part.
3. *243C—Composition of Panchayats*: All the seats in a Panchayat shall be filled by persons chosen by direct election from the territorial constituencies in the Panchayat Area.
4. *243D—Reservation of Seats*: Seats shall be reserved for the Scheduled Castes and the Scheduled Tribes in proportion to their share in the total population but not less than one-third (including to the Scheduled Castes and Scheduled Tribes) of the total number of seats shall be reserved for the women of these categories.

5. *243G—Powers, Authority and Responsibilities of Panchayats*: Subject to the provisions of this Constitution, the legislature of a state may, by law, endow the Panchayats with such powers and authority as may be necessary to enable them to function as institutions of self-government and such law may contain provisions for the devolution of powers and responsibilities upon Panchayats at the appropriate level, subject to such conditions as may be specified therein, with respect to:
   (a) the preparation of plans for economic development and social justice; and
   (b) the implementation of schemes of economic development and social justice as may be entrusted to them including those in relations to the matters listed in the Eleventh Schedule.

All the states enacted conformity legislations in 1994 and operationalised the new system of Panchayati Raj. This system contained in-built provisions for the good governance. It not only gave a constitutional status to the Gram Sabha but also made the Gram Panchayats responsible to it. Besides, it provided for a mechanism for transparency in the working of Gram Panchayat through the social audit by the Gram Sabha. Moreover, the Acts of various states provided to people the right to get a copy of any decisions of the Gram Panchayat by making the nominal payment for it.

It was hoped that the Panchayati Raj System in general and the institution of the Gram Sabha in particular will ensure that the rural development programmes are implemented in an honest and efficient manner and the fruit of rural development programmes are able to reach the poor for whom these were meant. But these hopes were belied and it was found that the corruption has been magnified because of the increase in the number of the stakeholders in it. Earlier the funds were embezzled by the development bureaucracy and technocracy, now elected representatives also became claimants in this loot.

It was to counter this that Aruana Roy led MKSS, a well known NGO, launched the programme of *Jan Sunwai* in Rajasthan in 1995 and later on began a campaign for the Right to Information. This campaign gradually became a nationwide phenomenon and the Right to Information Acts were enacted by some of the states and by the Government of India in 2002 in the form of Freedom of Information Act. But despite these, the good governance remained elusive in the rural development administration and the Panchayati Raj Institution.

It was in this background that the Right to Information Act, 2005 has been enacted and operationalised by setting up Central Information Commission, State Information Commissions and by the appointment of Assistant State Public Information Officers, State Public Information Officers and the First Appellate Authorities in all the departments of the Union Government, State Governments and all the Public Undertakings included in the PRIs and the Urban Local Bodies. Besides, the provision has been made in the National Rural Employment Guarantee Scheme for the Right to Information, Social Audit and Social Audit Forum.

The primary aim of the RTI regime is to ensure good governance by making the decision-making transparent and by ensuring accountability through this device. But the goal of good governance remains elusive due to the lack of awareness among the masses and the persistence of the colonial mindset in the bureaucracy.

But that as it may, the rural development programmes, the Community Development Programme and the NES Schemes, led to democratic decentralisation or Panchayati Raj in 1959 and the New Panchayati Raj System has led to the establishment of the RTI regime which sooner or later, is bound to ensure good governance. But a mass campaign in a mission mode is needed for this purpose.

19

S.K. Dey's Paradigm of Democratic Decentralisation

RANBIR SINGH AND B.K. KAUSHIK

Born on September 13, 1906 at Laxmi Basa Village in Medinipur Taluka of Slyhat district in Bengal province (now a part of Bangla Desh), S.K. Dey could be legitimately ranked amongst the top most Indians of the 20th Century.[1] This person with a multi-faceted personality was an organic intellectual in the sense in which Gramsci has used this term.[2] Despite getting higher education in the USA and his success in achieving a top position in a multi-national company, he remained steadfast to his rural roots and peasant background. That is why he gave priority to the uplift of the rural masses and amelioration of peasantry over his lucrative career in a subsidiary of the General Electric Company. Dey was a true nationalist with a burning desire of serving his country. This is what prompted him to give up a top executive position in that reputed concern and undertake the responsibility of the rehabilitation of Refugees from Pakistan who had to migrate to India from Pakistan after leaving their homes and hearth in the wake of the communal riots that preceded and followed the Partition of India on August 15, 1947. In this context, his innovative and dedicated role has been aptly acknowledged by Pandit Jawahar Lal Nehru, the first Prime Minister of India.

Trained as an electrical engineer at the prestigious American universities of Purdue and Michigan, Dey proved himself an accomplished social engineer while working as the Honorary Technical Advisor to the Ministry of Rehabilitation in the Government of India in 1948-51. He was also recognised as an efficient administrator on account of his successful role as the Community Project Administrator, in the Ministry of Community Development, Cooperation and Panchayati Raj, and as a Minister for Mining in the Union Cabinet. Dey also deserves recognition as one of the pioneers in the field of development journalism on account of his role in launching *Kurukshetra*, now a monthly organ of the Ministry of Rural Development, Government of India. He was indeed a rare blend of a philosopher and a practitioner who played an important role in the nation-building process for more than four decades after the liberation of India from the colonial rule in 1947 till his death on September 24, 1989. But far more important than all these roles, was his contribution as a social scientist in the field of Social, Economic and Political Thought in India. His brilliant paradigm of democratic decentralisation merits special attention of the social scientists, administrators, political leaders and other stakeholders in the decentralised rural governance.

S.K. Dey viewed Panchayati Raj not merely as democratic decentralisation of development administration but also as an essential component of the political democracy without which it remains incomplete and limited only to the central and state levels and does not percolate to the local level. Moreover, according to Dey, when the Community Development Programme was confined to a very small number of projects, the staff could be trained with special attention and work could be supervised from the centre down to the ground. When expansion took place, the old attention was no longer possible either for the training or for the supervision. Besides, it brought in its wake fantastically rising curves of the demand for facilities from the government. Moreover, the dominant sections of the rural society began to get the lion's share in its benefits. Even the cooperatives were captured by them. Furthermore, instead of becoming 'peoples programme', it became a *government's programme*. The introduction of the scheme of democratic decentralisation, popularly known as the Panchayati Raj on October 2, 1959 on the recommendation of the Balvantray Mehta Study Team has to be seen in this perspective.

S.K. Dey, who institutionalised Panchayati Raj as the Union Minister for Community Development, Cooperation and Panchayati Raj, had the deep insight to identify the following issues that came to the fore after its introduction in 1959:

The Need for Strengthening the Gram Sabha

Dey rightly felt that the Gram Sabha, the general assembly of the Panchayat area, needs to be activated for ensuring the direct participation of the people in the decision-making process. It can be made to act as a deterrent to the arbitrary actions of its executive, the Gram Panchayat. In other words, he recognised that both representative democracy (the Gram Sabha) and participatory democracy (the Gram Sabha) have to be strengthened simultaneously. He perceptively posed the question: Can the two systems co-exist in a manner that they nourish each other?

The Linking of the Gram Sabha to Lok Sabha

Dey was of the view that it is essential to link the representative institutions of people at the local, state and national levels. That is why he favoured the association of the members of parliament and legislatures with the Panchayati Raj Institutions in which the Gram Panchayat, the Panchayat Samiti and the Zila Parishad are organically linked with each other through a system of indirect elections. In this context, he aptly raised the question: Would it be desirable to extend the system of indirect election from district level to the state level and from the state level to the centre?

Direct versus Indirect Elections

According to Dey, the indirect elections have the advantage of organically linking the lower tier institutions with the higher tier bodies. But at the same time, he recognised that indirect elections could give rise to the emergence of the hegemony of the entrenched castes and classes in these institutions. The direct elections, on the other hand, ensure their representative and democratic character. But these may retard the growth of an effective link between successive tiers in the federal system. Therefore, Dey rightly raised the question: What is the balance of advantages of the direct and the indirect election systems?

Combination of Civic and Development Functions

He had the deep insight to recognise that the combination of civic and development functions in the Panchayat Raj Institutions may be problematic as the local government institutions have a tendency to confine themselves to civic functions. Assignment of the development functions to these may also not be deemed appropriate in view of the lack of development orientation in their representatives. Therefore, Dey raised the issue: Would it be desirable to combine these two functions which are different in nature?

Mixing Centralized Planning and Local Planning

He also recognised the need for balancing the centralised planning through the Planning Commission with the decentralised planning through the Panchayati Raj Institutions. While centralised planning, Dey felt, was needed for reflecting the national priorities, the decentralised planning was essential for reflecting the local needs and aspirations. That is why he posed the question: How to coordinate the two types of planning?

Participation of Political Parties in Panchayati Raj

Dey apprehended that the participation of political parties in the elections to Panchayati Raj Institutions could tend to aggravate caste based factionalism in them. It may also help the vested interests in acquiring control over these bodies. On the other hand, the participation of the political parties is essential for the much needed political education of the rural masses that is required for the success of the democracy at the grassroots. It was on account of the above paradox that he raised the poser:

Is it desirable for the political parties to keep away from the elections of the Panchayati Raj Institutions?

Training and Education

Dey aptly recognised that the elected representatives of Panchayati Raj Institutions needed training to comprehend their powers and responsibilities. For this, it was essential that they be given short-term training after their election in the Panchayati Raj Training Centres. At the same time he felt that the practical experience while working in the Panchayati Raj Institutions will be of greater help for the capacity-building of elected representatives. Hence he raised the issue: Which is the superior way viz. their capacity-building-training or practical experience?

Involvement of Voluntary Organisations in the Panchayati Raj Institutions

Dey also recognised the need for the involvement of NGOs in the working of the Panchayati Raj Institutions. He felt that it will be functional for social and economic development through the institution of grassroots governance. But at the same time, perhaps, he feared, if excessive, it could be counter productive. Therefore, he raised the question: What should be the extent of the involvement of NGOs in the Panchayati Raj Institutions?

Emerging Pattern of Leadership in Panchayati Raj Institutions

Dey recognised that at the initial stage of the Panchayati Raj elections, traditional leadership based on caste and power groups may become deeply entrenched in these. But he was also optimistic that representatives from the backward sections and the younger age groups of the community shall begin to come forward after the first elections. This, according to him, promises the emergence of progressive leadership in the Panchayati Raj Institutions. Hence he put forth the poser: How to expedite the emergence of progressive leadership?

Outlook for the Future

Dey also examined the issue of the modernisation and industrialisation of the traditional and agricultural economy of India through democratic governance instead of a totalitarian regime. Therefore, he wanted the Panchayati Raj Institutions to become the instruments of development. It is in this context that he raised the issue: How can a poor country modernise and industrialise itself, as rapidly as a totalitarian state, through the democratic method?

S.K. Dey was also perceptive enough to foresee that the Panchayati Raj may not be rolled back in most of the states except in Maharashtra and Gujarat where genuine decentralisation of powers had already taken place. This is evident from his dialogue with Nehru in 1964.[2] Dey's prophesy proved true as Nehru's successors did not share his enthusiasm for

Panchayati Raj because they believed in the centralisation and de-politicisation instead of decentralisation and politicisation. Dey was not only eased out of the Ministry of Community Development, Cooperation and Panchayati Raj in 1966 but was also forced to quit politics in 1967.

But this did not dampen his enthusiasm for Panchayati Raj. He joined hands with Jayaprakash Narayan in 1973 for strengthening the institutions of decentralised rural governance by advocating an amendment in the Indian Constitution for according a constitutional status to the Panchayati Raj Institutions so that these could be saved from the caprice and malice of the state governments which were not favourably disposed towards them.

S.K. Dey also played an important role in the re-invigoration of Panchayati Raj in the post–Asoka Mehta Committee Report (1978) phase. He guided and inspired Rama Krishna Hegde, the then Chief Minister of Karnataka, and Abdul Nazeer Sab, a Minister in his government, for taking lead in the revival of Panchayati Raj in their state in 1983.[3] It has also been claimed that Dey was one of the persons who influenced Rajiv Gandhi to take initiative for the constitutionalization of Panchayati Raj through the 64th Amendment Bill in 1989.[4] However, Dey died on May 24, 1989 much before his dream could be realised through the enactment of the 73rd Amendment in 1992. It needs to be explored as to how far this Amendment converges or diverges from Dey's paradigm of Panchayati Raj.

In the above context, it is important to scrutinise whether this paradigm developed by him in the cold-war phase when India had adopted the path of self-reliance under the leadership of Jawaharlal Nehru remains relevant more than a decade and a half after the adoption of the path of liberalisation, privatisation and globalisation in 1991 due to the compulsions created by the changes in the national milieu and the international context. It must also be examined as to how far Dey's paradigm could help us in ushering in development with a humans face in general and in tackling the problems and availing the opportunities created by the WHO regime in particular. It too needs to be scrutinised as to how far it could be instrumental in promoting good governance by ensuring transparency, responsiveness, accountability in the decentralised rural governance, which has remained a mirage even after more than 15 years of the implementation of the 73rd Constitutional Amendment. Last but not the least, there is a dire need for a critical examination of the hypothesis that S.K. Dey's paradigm of democratic decentralisation has become a *sine qua non* for good governance in this era of globalisation.[5]

Notes and References

1. For a biographical note, refer to Nikhil Kolpe, *'Power to the People from Gram Sabha'*, National Symposium in Commensuration of L11 S.K. Dey Birth Centenary (1906-2006), ANSSIRD, Mysore, September 13, 2005.
2. S.K. Dey, *Destination Man: Towards a New World* (1982, p. 88) cited by S.R. Mehrotra, "Jawaharlal Nehru: A Reassessment" in Suneera Kapoor (ed.) *Thought and Vision of Jawaharlal Nehru*, Anamika Publishers & Distributors, New Delhi, 2005, p. 26.

3. R. Sudarshan, *Community Development and Panchayati Raj, Report of a Seminar,* 11C, Monograph 13, India International Centre, New Delhi, 1990, pp. 8-10.
4. Union Minister for Panchayati Raj, Mani Shankar Aiyar's Message for National Symposium on the eve of S.K. Dey's Birth Centenary at ANSSIRD, Mysore on September 13, 2005.
5. For the concept of Globalization refer to, B. Ramesh Babu, "Future is Federal, Local Governance in the Era of Globalization", *The Grassroots Governance of Journal,* Vol. IV, No. 2, December, 2006, pp. 318-23.

20

The Paradox of Political Decentralisation and Economic Centralisation

SUNITA DHAKA AND YOGMAYA

The Father of Nation, Mahatma Gandhi, had rightly realised that a continental sized polity marked with social pluralities, cultural diversities and linguistic heterogeneities could not be governed through a centralised political system. That is why he strongly argued for the creation of a political arrangement based on the concept of democratic decentralisation instead of administrative centralisation that had been imposed on India by the colonial administration for enabling the British empire to keep it under subjugation for its economic exploitation.

Therefore, he pleaded for the creation of a decentralised polity with the Gram Panchayat at its base. He wanted to make India a commonwealth of politically independent and economically self-sufficient village republics. Gandhi had the vision of an Independent India based on Gram Swaraj. He wanted maximum powers at the base (with the Gram Panchayats) and minimum powers at the top (with the central government). Thus he had designed a grand theory of democratic decentralisation which was bi-dimensional. On the one side, he favoured creation of the super-structure of the political decentralisation through Panchyati Raj, on the other hand, he argued for the strengthening of its base through economic decentralisation. His plea for village self-sufficiency, his opposition to the use of machines, his theory of bread labour, his advocacy of Khadi and Charkha economy and his theory of trusteeship of property were basic ingredients of his scheme of economic decentralisation. The Mahatma had the imagination to foresee that political decentralisation would not be sustainable without economic decentralisation. In other words, the democratic decentralisation needed the both. Perhaps, he had the wisdom to perceive that in the absence of political decentralisation, there can be no economic decentralisation and in the absence of economic decentralisation, there can be no political decentralisation. He viewed them as inseparable components of his concept of democratic decentralisation.

But the quest for modernisation, challenge of simultaneous development and the hurry to achieve instantly what had been made possible in Europe in many centuries, on one hand, and the trauma of partition and internal as well as the external threats to the unity, integrity and sovereignty of India, on the other hand, made the Constitution-makers to ignore the wisdom of the Father of Nation and they decided to set up a highly centralised parliamentary system borrowed from a small-sized and homogeneous nation, Great Britain, having a unitary system. They did feel compelled to graft a federal system on it on account of the ungovernability of our huge polity in terms of the size of its population and area, on the one hand, and the logical consequence of the process of federalisation that had been initiated during the colonial period by the Government of India Act, 1935, on the other hand. But the federal system that they had super-imposed on the parliamentary system was having more of unitarian features than the federal ones.

The Constitution-makers ignored the Mahatma to such a gross extent that the word 'Panchayat' was conspicuous by its absence in the Draft Constitution of India. The Chairman of the Drafting Committee, B.R. Ambedkar, had so much contempt for this institution, which had been hailed as a Village Republic by Charles Matcalfe, the Provisional Governor General of India (1835-36), that he declared, "They were nothing but a stink of localism and den of ignorance and communalism". He went to the extent of concluding, "I am glad that the Draft Constitution has discarded the village and made the individual as its unit". And, Pandit Jawaharlal Nehru, the then Prime Minister of India, and the most powerful face behind making of the Indian Constitution, decided to keep quite inspite of being the political heir of Mahatma Gandhi. It is a different matter that powerful protest of a Gandhian like Rajendra Prasad, the President of the Constituted Assembly, forced Ambedkar to incorporate the goal of creation of Gram Panchayat in the non-justiciable Directive Principles of State Policy, Article 40, which, *inter alia* laid down:

> "The State shall take steps to organise village panchayats and endow them with such power and authority as may be necessary to enable, them to function as units of self-government". It was in the above scenario that the salience of Gram Panchayats was indirectly conceded in the First Five Year Plan in the context of the Community Development Programme; in these words "the actual programmes in

localities should be determined by local needs"; unless the people have a sense of ownership of the programme, 'no substantial results will be gained'; 'people's participation must be not only in project execution, but also in project planning'; 'if the people are to be trained to be builders of the future, the works have to be entrusted even at a certain risk to the people themselves through their representative agencies, the government organisation furnishing them technical assistance and essential finance.'

The recommendations of the sub-committee of the All India Congress Committee headed by HD Malviya for the strengthening of the Gram Panchayats and inclusion of the promise to create these institutions in the Manifesto of the Congress party released on the eve of the First General Elections (1952) has to be seen in this perspective. The enactment of the Gram Panchayat Acts by various states in the first half of the 1950s too should be viewed from this very angle.

The introduction of Panchayati Raj, the scheme for democratic decentralisation, designed by Balvantray Mehta Study Team (1957), which aimed at the devolution of powers from the district administration to the democratically elected and organically linked three-tier structure comprising of Gram Panchayats at the base, Panchayat Samitis at the intermediate level and the Zila Parishads at the top, for mobilising human and material resources for the Community Development Programme and also for acting as the Institutions of Rural Local Self-Government at the village, block and district levels, was no doubt an initiative in the direction of political decentralisation.

The 73rd Constitutional Amendment Act (1992) which sought to strengthen the Panchayati Raj Institutions by according them a constitutional status, by providing for them a uniform three tier structure of decentralised rural governance in all the states except in those with a population of less than 20 lacs, reservations of one-third membership and offices for women and the reservations for the scheduled castes/scheduled tribes in proportion to their share in population at all the levels, uniform five year term and holding of fresh elections within six months of the dissolution of a PRI, State Election Commission for ensuring free, fair and regular elections, State Finance Commission for dividing resources between the State Government and the local government bodies and the inclusion of 11th Schedule in the Constitution for the devolution of 29 items by the state legislatures on the Panchayati Raj Institutions to enable them to make and implement plans for economic development and social justice too aimed at political decentralisation.

The provision for the District Planning Committee (DPC) consisting of the representatives of Panchayati Raj Institutions and the Urban Local Bodies for making the district plan by consolidating the plans of Gram Panchayats, Panchayat Samitis and Zila Parishad and the Urban Local Bodies by the 74th Constitutional Amendment Act (1993) too had the objective of further political decentralisation through the institutionalisation of decentralised planning. The recommendations of the Expert Group on Grassroots Planning (2006) that the State Plans under the 11th Five Year Plan should be based on the District Plans prepared by the DPCs too have to be perceived as a step in that very direction.

But paradoxically since the Second Five Year Plan, there took place a paradigm shift towards the economic centralisation by giving priority to heavy industries over the Khadi and Village Industries (KVIs). The same trend persisted in the Third Five Year Plan, the Annual Plans, the Fourth Five Year Plan and the Fifth Five Year Plan. The Sixth Five Year Plan designed by the Janata Government in 1978 did change the priority from the heavy industries to KVIs. But it could not be implemented due to the fall of this government in 1979 as a result of split in the party. The Revised Sixth Five Year Plan designed during the Congress-I regime and the subsequent Five Year Plans up to the Tenth Five Year Plan have been giving priority to heavy industries instead of KVIs.

This is clearly evident from the data given in the following table:

Public Sector Outlay and Five Year Plan Provisions for KVI Sector

Plan Period	*Public Sector Outlays (Rs.)*	*Plan Allocation on for KVI (Rs.)*	*Funds made available for KVI (Rs.)*	*Column 3 as % of Column 2*
First Plan	1,960.00	15.00	11.58	0.77
Second Plan	4,672.00	83.78	78.71	1.79
Third Plan	8,577.00	92.40	86.90	1.08
Annual Plan (1966-67 to 1968-69)	6,757.00	53.05	53.05	0.79
Fourth Plan	16,160.00	111.00	97.73	0.07
Fifth Plan	37,250.00	180.00	118.26	0.48
Annual Plan (1978-79 to 1979-80)	24,192.00	154.20	154.20	0.64
Sixth Plan	97,500.00	480.00	521.72	0.49
Seventh Plan	1,80,000.00	540.00	611.21	0.30
Eighth Plan	4,34,100.00	900.00	1,251.20	0.21
Ninth Plan	8,59,200.00	1,993.00	1,604.42	0.23
Tenth Plan	15,25,639.00	3,649.00	2,608.12	0.24

Source : Compiled from various Reports of the Working Group on KVI, Planning Commission, Government of India, New Delhi.

The data in the table show that the share of KVI sector in the public sector outlay has been on the decline and gone down from 1.79 per cent in Second Five Year Plan to 0.24 per cent in the Tenth Five Year Plan. It is also clear from the Table that the funds allocated to KVI during the Five Year Plans have not been fully provided to the KVI sector.

These also show that the outlay for KVIs needs to be increased beyond the present provisions in the Five Year Plan. The provisions of funds made in the Five Year Plans can be a vital source for the revival of khadi and village industries in India by providing them a number of facilities like power, water, raw materials, transport, training, etc. at one place.

The Tenth Five Year Plan has identified five mission projects for the KVIs to sharpen their focus and to concentrate resources in selected areas of its core competence. It had invested Rs. 7,500 crores in biotechnology related processing industries. But, despite this the growth of the KVIs has remained retarded so far.

The net result of this paradox of political decentralisation and economic centralisation has been the sabotage of the design of democratic decentralisation. This leads us to the question: What should be done in this context? The simple answer is that the KVIs should be promoted. But this alone would be no guarantee to ensure economic decentralisation; cooperative movement should also be strengthened. As suggested by S.K. Dey (*Three Pillars of Democracy*, Ministry of Community Development and Cooperation, Govt. of India, New Delhi, 1963), the cooperatives should be created in Urban Areas as well. Besides, there should be industrial cooperatives and cooperatives for the weaker sections of the community. Last but not the least, federal cooperative organizations too should be created. Otherwise, all the efforts for political decentralisation will be defeated and the democratic decentralisation shall remain a mirage.

21

Decentralisation and Good Governance : Some Issues and Challenges at the Third Tier of Governance

O.P. Bohra

The World Bank has defined governance as 'the manner in which power is exercised in the management of a country's economic and social resources for development'. The good governance has been characterised by it as 'predictable, open and enlightened policy-making; a bureaucracy imbued with a professional ethos; an executive arm of government accountable for its actions and a strong civil society participating in public affairs; and all behaving under the rule of law'.

INDIA'S NEW STRATEGY FOR GOOD GOVERNANCE

The new strategy of good governance has been adopted by the Government of India in response to the challenges of the processes of globalisation, privatisation, and liberalisation in the last decade of the 20th Century. It includes:

(i) improved people's participation by way of effective decentralisation through local self governments;
(ii) involving civil society and voluntary organisations to accelerate socio-economic development;

(iii) ensuring right to information for transparency;
(iv) reforming civil service to improve accountability and efficiency;
(v) administrative procedural reforms for a hassle-free public-government interface;
(vi) improving the fiscal health of government by improving the resource mobilisation through a transparent and equitable tax administration and by correcting the subsidy and pricing system of various public services;
(vii) reforming the judicial system for a speedy delivery of justice;
(viii) improving the co-ordination between different public agencies and departments involved in development for a better synergy and efficiency;
(ix) systematic and professional programme/project formulation, implementation and monitoring;
(x) empowering the marginalised and the excluded to equip them to act as pressure groups to resist bad governance and exploitation by vested interests; and
(xi) using information technology for a transparent and efficient administration.

GOVERNMENT'S ROLE IN NEW PARADIGM OF GOVERNANCE

The World Bank[1] is of the view that the need for government intervention in economic development arises due to various reasons. Only government is powerful enough to establish the legal and institutional system which can facilitate production and exchange. Ensuring macro-economic stability through appropriate fiscal and monetary policy is another important area for government intervention.

At the time of failure of market economy, it is government's responsibility to intervene and provide basic services like health, road, and education. It also helps in bringing about equitable distribution of wealth through redistributive measures. In the provision of sustainable development for the future generation also, its role is very important. Some of these arguments have, however, been contradicted by many scholars.[2] Their major objections are:

(i) individuals may know more about their preferences and circumstances than the government;
(ii) government may make bigger mistakes than markets;
(iii) it may be incapable of administering planning;
(iv) government control may prevent private sector's initiatives;
(v) incentives, rewards and discipline of the market cannot be easily replicated within public organisations and systems;

(vi) regulation and controls may create lobbying and corruption often called rent seeking, to influence controls; and

(vii) vested interests and privileged groups may dominate the government and secure their interests and positions.

A few experts (Dreze and Sen 2002) have argued that the role of government is neither positive nor negative in achieving the development goals. However, in some cases it was observed that government led policy made a significant impact on economic development. On the other hand, there are instances where the state approach has been unable to overcome even the basic problems of poverty and misery. It is argued that the government can neither have a minimalist role nor an entirely proactive role; an analysis of the emerging role or model of the state in India in recent years reveals that there are multiple and contradictory kind of models that are emerging.[3] In the new paradigm, state is compelled to change its role. The state has to facilitate market institutions through suitable legal and institutional mechanisms as well as to put in place appropriate regulatory mechanisms to prevent market abuse or manipulation.

CIVIL SOCIETY—SIGNIFICANCE AND ROLE

In the alternative model of development, the civil society has assumed great significance. In the wider sense, it includes not only the household but local community as well as other social organisations, and the NGOs.[4] In the new paradigm of governance, the civil society organizations with their institutional plurality, autonomy, and voluntary participation have been recognised as its contribution. It has also been recognized as 'third sector'.[5] The rationale for the current participatory approach to development also comes from the arguments seeking greater role for civil society. In the new governance paradigm, civil society institutions are expected to play a key role along with the state and market in the delivery of development. The past experience with the civil society institutions, especially the NGOs, for poverty alleviation gives a mixed picture. NGOs have shown much strength for poverty alleviation as well as in the provision of basic services to the poor. They work in the close proximity of the poor and understand their needs better. For implementing the programmes it ensures effective participation. Their involvement is innovative and cost effective in efficient delivery of services. In Bangladesh, the NGOs have entered in the arena of micro-finance service also.[6] But there are limitations to their coverage. They also have limited role to play in bringing about equality.[7] Again, when the NGOs depend too much on outside donors, they are more like to be driven by the donors' agenda in all their activities rather than deciding their priorities in an autonomous way. It raises the question of their accountability. Despite these limitations, many see a major role for civil society in addressing the future challenges of development.

CHALLENGING ISSUES OF GOVERNANCE

1. Corruption and Growth—A Causal Relationship

In the literature it has been well established that inefficiency is a result of corruption. It directly affects growth by low level of investment in economy. The hypothesis of accelerated growth and improvement in social welfare and its relationship with strong leadership and proper functioning of bureaucracy is well established (See Krueger, 1993). Mauro (1995) has also suggested that there is a two-way causal relationship between corruption and growth. Corruption results in low growth and low incomes lead to higher propensity to be corrupt. But the dearth of literature on corruption in Asian countries has also been pointed out by Myrdal (1998).

2. Public-Private Sector

The size of public and private sectors affects the level of governance in a big way. For efficient, effective and good governance, it is required to differentiate the areas for the public and private provision of goods and services. Some of the public goods such as solid waste management can be managed more efficiently by private service-providers. Similarly, the police and military should be the responsibilities of public sector (government).

CONCLUSION

The new paradigm appears to be emerging as a result of the changing role of state both in the developed and developing countries. For the developing countries like India, it has assumed the form of good governance through decentralised rural governance.

It is posing a major challenge for poverty eradication. Pluralisation of state for development is its major feature. Development is no longer the sole responsibility of state. The challenges of development are to be addressed jointly by state along with market and civil society. All the three agencies are to act in unison for attaining development and change. A key requirement for the new governance is the harmonisation of the relationship between different actors so that the common goals could be attained smoothly without any conflict of interests.

While the new paradigm is yet to emerge in its fullest form, there is both skepticism and optimism about its possible outcomes for the issues like poverty alleviation and equality. There is a fear that the new paradigm is serving as an instrument or facade for thrusting upon the capitalist and neo-liberal order on developing countries. It may reverse the past achievements of the state-led developmental regime. The other view is that the new (good) governance paradigm is the need of the hour for making amends in the past failures of the state-led development. It is needed for achieving higher economic and human development.

Be that as it may, the new paradigm of good governance has certainly raised significant issues and challenges at the third tier of governance, which has emerged after the 73rd Amendment in the rural areas and the Municipalities in the Urban Areas after the 74th Amendment, as a significant factor in governance. Two major problems in this context, however, are those of demarcating the role of civil society in local governance and of ensuring healthy interface between the institutions of decentralised governance and the NGOs.

Box 1

Good Governance—Characteristics

Participation

All men and women should have a voice in decision-making, either directly or through legitimate intermediate institutions that represent their interests. Such broad participation is built on freedom of association and speech, as well as capacities to participate constructively

Rule of Law

Legal frameworks should be fair and enforced impartially, particularly the laws on human rights

Transparency

Transparency is built on the free flow of information. Processes, institutions and information are directly accessible to those concerned with them, and enough information is provided to understand and monitor them.

Responsiveness

Institutions and processes try to serve all stakeholders

Consensus Orientation

Good governance mediates differing interests to reach a broad consensus on what is in the best interests of the group and, where possible, on policies and procedures.

Equity

All men and women have opportunities to improve or maintain their well-being

Effectiveness and Efficiency

Processes and institutions produce results that meet needs while making the best use of resources.

Accountability

Decision-makers in government, the private sector and civil society organizations are accountable to the public, as well as to institutional stakeholders. This accountability differs depending on the organization and whether the decision is internal or external to an organization.

Strategic Vision

Leaders and the public have a broad and long-term perspective on good governance and human development, along with a sense of what is needed for such development. There is also an understanding of the historical, cultural and social complexities in which that perspective is grounded

Notes and References

1. See, The World Bank (1997).
2. Some of the problems of state intervention as identified by Nicholas Stern are (Meier and Rauch, 2000).
   Stern (Meier and Rauch, 2000).
3. See, Jayal 2001.
4. See, Abebe (2000).
5. Dantwala *et. al.* 2001.
6. Uphoff *et. al.* 1998.
7. Chandhoke (2003).

References

Banerjee, Ajit M. and Chandrasekaran (1996). *Reviweing Governance—Issues and Options*, New Delhi, Tata McGraw Hill.

Chandhoke, Neera (2003) "Governance and the Pluralisation of the State: Implications for Democratic Citizenship", *Economic and Political Weekly*, Vol. 38(28), pp. 2957-68.

Chopra, S.K. (1997), "*Towards Good Governance*", New Delhi, Konark.

Dreze, Jean and Amartya Sen (2002) *India: Development and Participation*. New Delhi, Oxford University Press.

Edwards, Michael and David Hulme (1998), *Non-Governmental Organisations: Performance and Accountability*, London: Earthscan Publications.

Gairola, B.K. (2008), "An e-Governance for Panchayats", in Kochar Sameer ed. *Infrastructure and Governance*, New Delhi, Academic Foundation.

Iyer, Mani Shankar (2008), "State of Panchayats: The Journey thus Far", in Kochar Sameer ed. *Infrastructure and Governance*, New Delhi, Academic Foundation.

Jayal, Niraja Gopal (2001) "Reinventing the State: The Emergence of Alternative Models of Governance in India in the 1990s" in Jayal and Pai (eds.).

Kashyap, S.C. (2000), Institutions of Governance in South Asia, New Delhi, Konark Publishers Pvt. Ltd.

Kochar, Sameer Deepak, B. Pathak, H. Krishnamurthy and Gursharan Dhanjali (2008), *Infrastructure and Governance*, New Delhi, Academic Foundation.

Martinussen, J. (1997) *Society, State and Market: A Guide to Competing Theories of Development*, London: Zed Books.

Meier, Gerald M. and James, E. Rauch (2000), *Leading Issues in Economic Development*, New York: Oxford University Press.

Oklay, Peter *et. al.* (1991), *Projects with People: The Practice of Participation in Rural Development*, Geneva: International Labour Office.

Patnaik, Utsa and Prabhat Patnaik (2001), "The State, Poverty, and Development in India" in Niraja Gopal, Jayal and Sudha Pai (eds.), *Democratic Governance in India: Challenges of Poverty, Development, and Identity*, New Delhi: Sage Publications.

Prasad, Beni (1968), *"Theory of Government in Ancient India"*, Allahabad, Central Book Depot.

Shah, Anwar (2006), Corruption and Decentralized Public Governance, in Ahmed, E. and Giorgio Brcsio, (2006), in Ahmed Ehtisham and Giorgio Brosio (2006) Hand Book of Fiscal Federalism, EE Massachusetts.

22

Some Steps for Good Governance through Democratic Decentralisation

CHAITALI PAL AND ANUPAMA ARYA

Right from the time of the evolution of state and formation of governments in these, attempts have been consistently made to explore as to how good governance can be ensured. For the realisation of this objective, various suggestions have been advanced from time to time. The centrality of the concepts of *Ram Rajya* and *Raj Dharam* in Ancient Indian Political Thought may be cited by way of illustration. The *Manu Samriti* and Kautilya's *Arthshastra*, which constitute its core, too had provided blue prints for good governance.

In the Modern Indian Political Thought the Father of Nation-Mahatma Gandhi, had expressed the view during the national movement that decentralisation is the basic pre-requisite for good governance. But after independence, the makers of the Indian Constitution established such a parliamentary democracy in which the centre has been made exceptionally strong instead of decentralisation. Although, the states too have been given important powers in it, but the powers have not been decentralised upto the local bodies.

The process of the decentralisation of powers to local level, as a matter of fact began only after the implementation of the recommendations of Balvantrai Mehta Study Team in 1959 despite the fact that Article 40 of the Directive Principles of State Policy laid down that the State shall create Gram Panchayats as institutions of local self-government. The above mentioned Study Team suggested the need for democratic decentralisation for the success of Community Development Programme that had been launched on October 2, 1952 for ensuring efficiency in the working of local government institutions. It suggested the creation of a democratically elected and organically linked three tier structure of Panchayati Raj comprising of the Gram Panchayat at the village level, the Panchayat Samiti at the Community Development Block Level and the Zila Parishad at the district level. It was suggested that the powers of the state government and district administration be decentralised to these bodies. Rajasthan was the first state to set-up Panchayati Raj in 1959 and it had been gradually set-up in almost all the states of the Indian Union by 1962.

Although from the conceptual point of view, democratic decentralisation means devolution of powers by the centre or state governments to the institutions of local self-government, it has become synonym of Panchayati Raj in the Indian context.

But the Panchayati Raj gradually became weak in the post-1964 period due to several reasons including lack of faith in it among the political leaders, the hostility of bureaucracy, apathy of rural masses, factionalism in the rural society, poor quality of rural leadership and the absence of healthy interface between the officials and the non-officials.

The 73rd Constitutional Amendment has been enacted to revitalise the moribund system of Panchayati Raj. It has provided a constitutional status to the scheme of democratic decentralisation. As many as 29 subjects have been listed in the 11th schedule of the Indian Constitution on which the powers of making and implementing plans on economic development and social justice could be devolved by the state legislatures on the Panchayati Raj Institutions (PRIs). It has also been laid down that these institutions of decentralised rural governance shall function as institutions of self-government.

To ensure their inclusive and democratic structure, the women have been given one-third representation in these at all the three levels. Likewise, the schedule castes and the schedule tribes have been given representation in the PRIs in proportion to their strength in the population of a district, a block and a village. Prior to it, there was no provision for the genuine representation of women and weaker sections in these. They were given only nominal or notional representation through cooption. Moreover, earlier there was no provision for the representation of the backward classes, now these too can be given reservations by the state governments.

Furthermore, the 73rd Amendment has not only provided for a uniform three-tier structure of Panchayati Raj in all the states except those having a population of less than 20 lakhs but has also introduced the system of direct elections for ensuring their democratic character. Additionally, the Amendment has not only provided for the creation of State Election Commission to ensure regular and fair elections after every five years but has also made provision for the establishment of State Finance Commission to ensure adequate resources to the PRIs.

Last but not the least, the 74th Amendment to the Indian Constitution has made provision for the establishment of District Planning Committees

(DPCs) comprising of the representatives of PRIs and urban local bodies for consolidating the plans of the rural and urban local bodies. This has been done to ensure decentralised planning. It is also pertinent to mention here that the Planning Commission has made it obligatory for the states to prepare their State Plans under the 11th Five Year Plan on the basis of District Plans prepared by the DPCs. Thus, the 73rd and the 74th Amendments have tried to make Panchayti Raj system democratic and decentralised in the true sense of the word.

In the meantime, significant changes had taken place at the international level. After the disintegration of USSR, the hegemony of USA was established on international politics and the World Bank and International Monitory Fund were able to acquire control over the international economic system. The World Bank started putting the condition of Good Governance for advancing loans to the developing countries. It defined Good Governance as a 'transparent, an accountable and a rule of law-based administration'. Besides, the emergence of WTO regime initiated the processes of liberalisation, privatisation and globalisation. Like, other countries, India too adopted this path.

In the above context, it may be mentioned that, before the enactment of 73rd Amendment, the concept of Good Governance was considered relevant and necessary only for the union government and the state governments. But, after the accordance of constitutional status to the PRIs by the 73rd Amendment, it is now being increasingly recognised that this is also essential and necessary for the institutions of decentralised rural governance.

In the meanwhile, the enactment and implementation of the Right to Information Act, 2005 has added a new dimension to the democratic decentralisation and good governance. It has made it obligatory for the public authorities, including the central government, the state government, the PRIs and the urban local bodies, to create a mechanism for ensuring the access to information to all those citizens of India who seek it. It may be noted here that the genesis of the Right to Information has to be traced from the implementation of the 73rd Amendment Act and the establishment of new Panchayati Raj system in Rajasthan in 1995 (Gopal Reddy, "The Right to Information: An analysis of its Evolution and Socio-Political Implications", *Punjab Journal of Politics*, Vol. XXX, No. 1, 2006). It was the campaign launched by MKSS that led to the creation of powerful movement for the Right to Information in Rajasthan which gradually spread over to other states and ultimately culminated in the enactment of the Right to Information Act, 2005.

Therefore, it becomes necessary to understand the meaning of good governance as well as to suggest ways and means for ensuring it in the working of Panchayati Raj Institutions.

According to O.P. Dwivedi and D.S. Misra ("A Good Governance Model for India : Search from Within", *Indian Journal of Public Administration*, Vol. LI, No. 4, October-December, 2005), good governance implies an administrative system having the following characteristics: Democratic pluralism; legitimacy in the eyes of the public under the law of the land; consensus among competing interests and equity in approach; public participation in decision-making; rule of law to ensure fairness and non-partisanship; responsiveness towards the stakeholders; efficient and effective accountability; transparency in action; moral governance; and a vision for sustainable and long-term human development.

According to them, good governance refers not only to the government but also to all the players involved in the process of governance. Accountability, incorruptibility, sensitivity and ethical conduct are the key factors of good governance. Who is accountable to whom depends on whether decisions or actions taken are internal or external to an organisation or institution. As a fundamental principle, according to Dwivedi & Misra, various instruments of governance are accountable to those who will be directly or indirectly affected by the decisions or actions. Transparency and rule of law are prerequisites for ensuring accountability. Moral or ethical behaviour is essential for the sustainability of dynamic relationship formed during the conduct of the governance.

According to Mohinder Singh & Vijay Kumar ("Economic Reforms and Good Governance in Panchayati Raj", S. Kaushil and Surat Singh (ed.) *Reforms, Rural Development and the Human Face : Perspectives, Perceptions, Prescriptions*, Deep & Deep Publication, New Delhi, 2006) the basic characteristics of good governance are: Efficiency, effectiveness, reasonableness, fairness and people friendliness, openness and transparency, de-bureaucratisation by changing the mindset of functionaries, professionalisation through improved skills, enhanced capability, better performance, freedom from corruption, decentralised management, better budgeting, proper accounting & auditing and accountability.

In the context of Panchayati Raj, we may say that its elected representatives and official functionaries should work in accordance with the wishes of the people and for the welfare of the people. They should work in such a manner that the benefit of rural development programmes is able to reach the weaker sections for whom these had been designed.

For realising the above objectives, it is essential to ensure the following steps in the working of PRIs:

1. The Gram Sabha should be activated and all the decisions for development, planning and administration should be made through this institution.
2. The Gram Panchayat should function as a collective body and the decision should be taken by the Gram Panchayat as a whole instead of being made only by the Sarpanch and the Gram Sachiv.
3. The Mahila Mandals, Youth Clubs and Self-Help Groups be associated with the Gram Sabha and the Gram Panchayat.

4. The Committee System should be strengthened and all the panches should be given role in the decision-making by associating them with the various committees.
5. The Gram Sachiv and other village level functionaries of the line departments should provide assistance to the Gram Panchayat and the Gram Sabha in the performance of their functions. They should be accountable to these bodies.
6. There should be transparency in the decision-making process of the Gram Panchayat.
7. There should be collective decision-making in the Panchayat Samiti. All the members of the Samiti should participate in this process. The role of decision-making should not be limited only to the Chairperson of the Samiti and the BDO—its Executive Officer.
8. The proceedings of the Panchayat Samiti should be recorded in a proper manner and be in accordance with the provisions of the Panchayati Raj Acts.
9. The Committee System be strengthened in the Panchayat Samiti as well, for making the members of the Samiti partners in the decision-making process.
10. The BDO and the officers of the line departments should regard themselves as the servants of people and should help the Gram Panchayats and Panchayat Samitis in performing their roles in an effective manner.
11. There should be cooperation and coordination between the Gram Panchayat and the Panchayat Samiti. The Sarpanches of the Gram Panchayats should not feel that they can bye-pass the Samiti.
12. The Zila Parishads should function in an effective manner and these should ensure coordination in the working of Gram Panchayats and Panchayat Samitis.
13. The DPCs should be constituted as per the spirit of the 73rd and 74th Amendments and should also be activated.
14. The Committee System should be strengthened at the Zila Parishad level too.
15. There should be healthy interface between elected representatives and government officials at all the three levels so that they could work for rural development and public welfare in general and for the welfare of weaker sections in particular.
16. The administration of Panchayati Raj at all the three levels should be made free from discrimination and favouritism by eliminating corruption.
17. The elected representatives and the government officials should work for the empowerment of the Panchayati Raj Institutions by giving due partnership to women and the weaker sections, make proper use of resources for sustainable rural development and by implementing various rural development schemes in such a manner that their fruit are able to reach the target groups.

18. Concerted efforts should be made for the capacity building of elected representatives as well as of the official functionaries through genuinely effective and need-based training programmes.
19. The emphasis in the training programmes should be on changing the mindset of various stakeholders in Panchayati Raj and rural development administration.
20. The Right to Information should be implemented in a sincere manner and for this the requisite mechanism should be put to the place so that the Right to Information regime is established in the true sense of the word. Besides, awareness on RTI be created among the rural masses. Moreover, the capacity-building of the SPIOs, APIOs and the appellate authorities should be done so that they are able to perform their functions in an effective and judicious manner.

It is earnestly hoped that if the above steps are taken by the state governments, good governance can be ensured in the system of democratic decentralisation or Panchayati Raj. These steps could undoubtedly make decentralised rural governance and rural development administration more effective, efficient, transparent, sensitive, accountable, participatory and equality and equity-based. Otherwise, the goal of good governance through democratic decentralisation shall remain elusive and the very purpose of the 73rd Constitutional Amendment shall be defeated.

PART IV

Experiences of Democratic Decentralisation in States

23

Structure and Working of Panchayati Raj in Kerala

P.P. BALAN

INTRODUCTION

Immediately after the State was formed in 1956, Government of Kerala thought of democratic decentralisation. The Administrative Reforms Committee appointed by it made detailed recommendations in 1958. But nothing significant was done in decentralised development for over three decades despite enactment of laws. As in the case of the rest of India, with the formation of a large number of State-level Boards/Corporations/Authorities for almost all areas, even the existing village and urban local bodies got virtually atrophied over the years because many of their functions were taken over by such para statelets. There was, however, a short-lived attempt to form District Councils in 1990, following a comprehensive Report on Decentralisation. But with the passage of the 73rd and 74th amendments to the Constitution of India in 1992, Kerala carried out pioneering reforms and has embarked on a path of comprehensive decentralisation since 1995.

STRATEGY OF DECENTRALISATION IN KERALA

Traditional wisdom calls for capacity building of local governments before giving power to them in degrees to match the improvements in capacity. But real and effective decentralisation probably calls for a big bang approach—functions, powers and resources being transferred in one go. If decentralisation is effected in one blow, the suddenness would stun potential dissenters into silent acceptance. Before they could realize what they have lost, decentralisation would have become a *fait accompli*. The 'reversals' of giving responsibility and then building capacity, of giving powers and then creating procedures and systems, of giving funds and then setting up umpiring systems, however, do help in another way. If the government transfers a lot of responsibilities and funds, considerable pressure would be built on the government from various sides to ensure that the responsibilities are carried out effectively and the funds are utilised properly. It would then become Government's responsibility to ensure that decentralisation really works. Kerala followed the big bang approach and the hindsight shows that strategically it was a sound decision as it would have been impossible to transfer power in small doses.

To operationalise decentralisation, Kerala chose the path of participatory local level planning at the entry point. This succeeded to a considerable extent in harnessing public action in favour of decentralisation. In order to push the system and force the process, a campaign approach known as the 'People's Planning' Campaign was followed for decentralised planning. This Campaign created a powerful demand factor for decentralisation and guided it along the right path. It succeeded, to a large degree, in setting the agenda for decentralisation.

LEGISLATIVE ENTITLEMENTS

The Kerala Panchayat Raj Act 1994 was in itself a path-breaking law. It was thoroughly restructured in 1999 and several innovative features were built in it for laying strong legal foundation to build up genuine institutions of Local Self Government. The salient features of the amended Act are summarized below:

(a) Grama Sabha

Kerala does not have traditional villages which are sociological units marked by a compact spatial cluster of settlements with a social pattern in their lay out. It has made a bold attempt to induce people's participation by creating a fourth-tier in the form of Grama Sabhas equated with the electoral constituency of a Village Panchayat Member. All the electors of the Ward are members of the Grama Sabha. At the most, there are twelve to eighteen of these in every Village Panchayat.

The Grama Sabha has been given clear rights and responsibilities. It has absolute powers for identification of beneficiaries, strong advisory powers for prioritising developmental needs and wide powers of social audit.

(b) Definition of Functional Domains

The 11th Schedule of the Indian Constitution actually does not carve out the functional domains of local governments to demarcate their role in planning for economic development and social justice and in the implementation of such plans. Unlike many other states, Kerala has attempted to define the functional areas of the different tiers of PRIs as precisely as possible. In areas related to infrastructure and management of public institutions, the functional differentiation is sharp and clear, but in productive sectors it is difficult to clearly earmark functions separately for each tier. Only through experience can the natural functional area in such sectors be got marked. There is a clear recognition that the role of local governments ranges from an Agent, Adviser, Manager, Partner and Actor. The objective behind the democratic decentralisation is to reduce the agency role and to expand the autonomous-actor role. The Kerala Act, it may be specified, classifies functions of the PRIs as the mandatory, the general and the sector-wise functions.

(c) Committee System

All Village and Block Panchayats have three Standing Committees and the District Panchayats have five Standing Committees. The Standing Committees are constituted in such a way that every Member of the Panchayat gets a chance to serve on one or the other Standing Committee. Each of these is assigned certain subjects. These are expected to go into the subject areas in great detail both at the planning and implementation stages.

For the purpose of co-ordination among the Standing Committee, a Steering Committee has been constituted. It consists of the President and Vice-President of the Panchayat and the Chairpersons of Standing Committees. In addition, there are Functional Committees for different subjects which can include experts and practitioners. Moreover, the Panchayats are free to constitute Sub Committees to assist the Standing Committees and the Functional Committees. There is also a provision in the Act for the constitution of Joint Committees with neighboring Local Governments.

(d) Control by Government

The amended Kerala Panchayat Raj Act drastically reduced the governmental control over Panchayat Raj Institutions. While the government can issue general guidelines regarding national and State policies, it cannot meddle in the day to day affairs or interfere in the individual decisions. It can cancel resolutions of the Panchayats only through the prescribed process and that too in consultation with the Ombudsman or the Appellate Tribunal according to the subject matter of the resolution. Similarly, a Panchayat can be dissolved directly by the government only if it fails to pass the budget or if the majority of its members resign. In all other cases, a due process has to be followed and the Ombudsman has to be consulted before the dissolution takes place. This is a unique feature which does not exist even in the Center-State relations.

(e) Setting up of Independent Institutions

In order to reduce the governmental control and to foster the growth of self government as envisaged in the Constitution, the Act provides for the creation of independent institutions to deal with various aspects of functioning of the local government. They are listed below:

(a) *The State Election Commission.* The Election Commission has been given powers which go beyond those required for the conduct of elections. It has been empowered to delimit Wards—a task which was earlier performed by the executive. The Commission has also been given the power to disqualify defectors.

(b) *The Finance Commission.* This has been given the mandate required by the Constitution. The first SFC was constituted in 1994 and the second in 1999 and the third in 2004. Almost all the recommendations of the three SFCs have been implemented.

(c) *Ombudsman for Local Governments.* This is a high power institution which has been given vast powers to check malfunctioning in the discharge of developmental functions by the local governments.

(d) *Appellate Tribunals.* These have been constituted at the Regional/District level to take care of the appeals by the citizens against the decisions of the local governments taken in the exercise of their regulatory role like the issue of license and grant of permit.

(e) *State Development Council.* This is headed by the Chief Minister. It consists of the entire Cabinet, the Leader of Opposition, and the Vice-Chairman of the State Planning Board, the Chief Secretary, and all the District Panchayat Presidents who are also the Chairpersons of the District Planning Committees and the representatives of other tiers of local governments. This institution has taken lead in policy formulation and in sorting out operation issues.

(f) Supremacy of the Elected Body

The Presidents of every Panchayat Raj Institution has been declared as the executive authority. The senior most officials of various departments have been brought under the control of the Panchayat Raj Institutions and they have been declared as Ex-Officio Secretaries for that subject. The Panchayats have full administrative control, including the powers of disciplinary action, over its own staff as well as over the staff transferred to it. In order to ensure a healthy relationship between the officials and the elected members, the Act prescribes a code of conduct, which lays down certain directive principles of polite behaviour such as respect for elected authorities and also provides for the protection to the civil servant for rendering free and fearless advice.

OPERATIONALIZING DECENTRALISED PARTICIPATORY PLANNING

The Campaign launched during the Ninth Plan succeeded in providing a concrete methodology for participatory planning for local level development. The salient features of this methodology are described below:

(1) *Need Identification*: Through a meeting of Grama Sabha/Ward Sabha, i.e., the ward or the electoral constituency of a Village Panchayat or Municipality Member, the felt needs of the community are identified. There is a provision for period of environment creation to mobilize maximum participation in Grama Sabha/Ward Sabha meetings. Statistics reveal that about 10-12% of the rural population has been generally participating in these. Their minutes are forwarded to the Local Governments. Each meeting is chaired by the elected member and has an official as its co-ordinator.

(2) *Situation Analysis*: Based on the demands emanating from the first special Grama Sabha/Ward Sabha meeting and based also on both primary and secondary developmental data, exhaustive Development Reports are prepared and printed for every Local Government in the State. These Reports describe the status of each sector of development with reference to available data, analyze the problems and point out the directions for further development. This was a one time exercise for a Plan period and the Reports have been revised before the Tenth Five Year Plan.

(3) *Strategy Setting*: Based on the Gram Sabha/Ward Sabha feedback and the Development Report, a one day seminar is held at the Local Government level in which the participation of experts, elected members, representatives nominated by the Sabhas, practitioners from among the public is ensured. The development seminars suggest the broad priorities and the general strategies for developmental projects to be taken up in a particular year.

(4) *Projectisation*: The ideas thrown up by the above three stages are translated in the form of Projects by the Working Groups at the Local Government level. For each Local Government, there are about eight Working Groups dealing with different sectors of development. Each Working Group is headed by an elected member and is assisted by the concerned government official. The Vice-Chairman of Working Group is normally a non-government expert in the sector. The Projects are prepared in the suggested format. These outline the objectives, describe the benefits, explain the funding and give the details of the mode of execution and phases of the Project.

(5) *Plan Finalization*: From among the Projects, based on the allocation communicated, the concerned Local Government finalises its plan for the year and this plan is submitted to the District Planning Committees (DPCs) through the Technical Advisory Committees. The Panchayat is free to take up any Project, irrespective of its cost, subject, of course, to the resources actually available within the sectoral limits.

(6) *Plan Vetting*: The Block or the District level Technical Advisory Committees consisting of official and non-official experts vet the Projects for their technical viability in conformity with the mandatory government guidelines on planning and costing, and forward them to the DPC. They cannot change priorities of the Projects. They can only ask for rectification.

(7) *Plan Approval*: The DPC gives the formal approval to the plans after which the Local Government can start implementation. It is to be noted that the DPC too cannot change the priority of a Local Government. It can only ensure that the government guidelines are followed. Administrative approval for implementation is given project-wise by the Local Government. Every Local Government has unlimited powers of Administrative sanctions subject only to the limits of its financial resources.

Setting up Accountability Systems

Since substantial responsibilities have been passed on to the local governments. Accountability Systems have come to acquire special importance. Harmony in local government functioning and participatory budgeting too are stressed upon. Therefore, in addition to the traditional systems of checks and balances, new forms of downward accountability to the people have also been structured in these. Their main components are given below:

(1) *Committee System for Decision-making:* All the decisions of local governments are to be taken by the Committees through consensus or by voting. Power has not been concentrated in any individual.

(2) *Right to Information*: All documents of the local governments, except very few ones like health records of patients, contract documents before finalization etc., have been declared as public documents by law. Every citizen has the right to peruse them or ask for their photocopies. In a literate and politically conscious society like that of Kerala, this is a powerful provision against corruption.

(3) *Participatory Budgeting*: The evolution of a budget, particularly for development works, is through comprehensive planning process which allows space for citizen interaction and intervention, expert involvement in final budgeting before the approval by elected

bodies. This provides adequate protection against arbitrary decision-making.

(4) *Due Process in the Selection of Beneficiaries*: This is ensured through the following steps:
   (a) Clear enunciation of eligibility and prioritisation criteria at the time of scheme formulation.
   (b) Assigning weightages to each prioritisation criterion.
   (c) Inserting of applications in writing.
   (d) Enquiry process into the applications by awarding marks to each criterion.
   (e) Opportunity to each applicant to see all the records including the application forms of others.

(5) *Technical Sanction*: The process of giving Technical Sanction has been taken out of the departmental technical hierarchy. Technical Committees consisting of engineering experts, drawn from governmental, academic and non-governmental sources, have been constituted at the Block/Municipal/Corporation/District levels. This gives some protection against the inflation of estimates and the dilution of technical standards.

(6) *Audit System*: The traditional audit system through Local Fund Audit Department has been strengthened with the technical support of the Accountant General. A special Concurrent Audit System has been designed. It is manned by surplus staff from the Panchayat and Urban Affairs Departments and headed by an Officer of the Indian Audit and Accounts Service. This system is called Performance-Audit. It acts as an online corrective mechanism for helping the local governments to put their systems in proper place. The Performance- Audit is conducted twice a year in all the local governments. Since the minimum grant-in-aid to a Grama Panchayat is Rs. 25 lakhs, the Accountant General also carries out grant-in-aid audit of all the local governments including the Village Panchayats. A Technical Audit Team consisting of senior Engineers mostly from outside Government, who are selected for their integrity, has been put in place at the State level. This Team looks into the complaints regarding execution of public works.

(7) *Social Audit*: A semi-structured social audit is conducted in Gram Sabhas and Ward Sabhas where the accounts of Village Panchayats, Municipalities and Corporations have to be presented and quarries have to be replied.

(8) *Awareness Building*: IEC campaigns explaining the right of citizen's *vis-à-vis* local governments have been conducted through the media of Press and TV. Special meetings of NGOs are also held to tell them every thing about citizen entitlements *vis-à-vis* local governments.

(9) *Filing of the Property Statements*: All elected members have to file their Property Statements immediately on election.

The cornerstone of Kerala's decentralisation has been people's participation. The processes have been designed to facilitate intervention by the interested citizen at all stages of the development process right from the generation of developmental ideas through project planning, project implementation, up to monitoring. Decentralisation has opened up opportunities for wide ranging reforms. Already, the right to information, the prescription of due process in giving of benefits, the outsourcing of technical services, the community management of assets and the simplification of procedures has taken place. More reforms in the form of independent regulatory institutions, improving management systems, both financial and administrative, and enhanced accountability mechanisms etc., are in the offing.

24

Working of Panchayat Raj Institutions at Grassroots Level : Experiences from the State of Madhya Pradesh

YATINDRA SINGH SISODIA

I

OVERVIEW

After independence, persistent efforts have been made to make rural local self-government viable and self-sustainable on the lines portrayed by Mahatma Gandhi. Unfortunately, the response of the state governments was of very different nature. And as a result, the pace of establishment of rural local political institutions was not very enthusiastic in the initial phase. The state governments showed very little interest to empower these institutions. The political leadership of some Indian states like Kerala, Karnataka, Maharashtra and West Bengal did come forward to establish Panchayats at local level. But on the whole, the pace of their development left much to be desired. The champions of local self-government, however, kept on arguing that the results of development planning did not reach the people concerned despite plethora of schemes and massive investments in rural sector. It was also realised that the infrastructure at the local level was in a very bad state and it was one of the obvious reasons for poor delivery system through local bureaucracy. People's participation was rarely seen and the development model was of that of the 'top-down approach'. Its accountability was nominal as the bureaucratic hierarchy looked at rural masses as mere recipients.

Almost after forty-five years, the Central Government realised that this delivery system was not effective and that without making people's participation through Panchayats, purposeful rural development was not possible. As a result, the 73rd Constitutional Amendment Act was passed in 1993. Its execution was made mandatory for all the Indian states and the Panchayats were provided a constitutional status. The Act has provided a uniform structure to self-governance for the sake of its effective functioning. It led to a fundamental restructuring of rural governance based on the philosophy of democratic decentralisation. Policy planners have come to realize that the new Panchayat Raj Institutions have the potential to usher in a new era of rural development in accordance with people's needs and priorities, (Behar & Kumar: 2002).

The 73rd Amendment Act could not be perceived as a response to pressure from the grassroots but an increasing recognition that the existing structure of government needed to be reformed. It was a political drive of the centre to see the PRIs as a solution to the governmental crises that India was experiencing (World Bank: 2000). These seek to use the concept of democratic decentralisation to accelerate socio-economic development and to usher in equity and social justice.

Contextually and theoretically too, the new Panchayat Raj System has been created as a model of self-governance (Sisodia: 2005). The objectives of decentralisation are to execute and implement schemes and programmes to meet the local needs, to mobilise people, to channelise their energies towards socio-economic reconstruction and to involve them in all the activities of the communities through the new institutions. Its objectives include reduction in the size of work of the higher level government and leaving the responsibility to the people to decide their destiny as per the new dispensation. Democratic Decentralisation is a much-debated issue in India and other countries with federal system of governance. Though there are various arguments for and against it, arguments in its favour far outweigh those against it because of the inherent potential of democratisation in the decentralised federal system through proper empowerment of people at the grassroots level.

The working of Panchayat Raj in India for a decade and a half shows that all the major states have completed at least one round of panchayat elections and in majority of cases there have been at least two rounds. Almost three million people including one million women and a sizeable number of SCs/STs took part in these elections. The sizeable presence of under privileged and poor as representatives through reservations in the grassroots political institutions is a landmark development in the rural politics of the country. This significant development has a special meaning because a decade earlier these groups were excluded from public life and political participation in most parts of rural India. This is also a matter of serious debate as to how this excluded group would be able to effectively tackle local power equation and set the agenda for development of its inclusion.

A perusal of state profiles would show that Panchayat Raj reforms have certainly taken place with vigour and zeal in some western and southern parts of the country, which are relatively sound from the point of view of economy, are vibrant socially, and have active civil societies. On the contrary, the northern states with the greatest degree of poverty and inequality and deep schisms of caste and low pace of governance resulted in weak Panchayats (Robinson: 2005).

In this mixed scenario of development, exemplary reforms have taken place in Kerala and Madhya Pradesh due to the strong political will of the political leadership of these states. In Kerala, the people's planning campaign led to a large level of popular mobilisation that was made possible by high level of literacy and professional support with a mass base social movement (Issac: 2000). In Madhya Pradesh, Chief Minister Digvijay Singh had introduced a series of reforms and amendments in Panchayat Raj to strengthen the grassroots institutions, specially the Gram Sabha. The example of West Bengal too is well known where the CPM government used the PRIs as a political support base in rural areas with a significant degree of success. The land reforms could take place in West Bengal mainly due to Panchayat Raj (Webster: 1993).

It is evident from the grassroots experiences that the State Acts have been amended from time to time to make PRIs genuine structures of grassroots democracy. Through a system of reservation, participation of the weaker sections has also been ensured. The three tiers of Panchayat Raj System have been significantly empowered to enable them to discharge their duties properly and to fulfil the expectations of the people. The Gram Sabhas have been bestowed with enormous power in the decision making process. But the evidences from the states suggest that the people's participation has remained low. The efforts to make the grassroots an institution viable have remained confined to a formality. Nevertheless a process of political socialization has begun within the society. The bureaucratic resistance is visible. Its stereotype mind-set also created hurdles in the beginning at the local level but the situation is changing slowly and gradually. The process of financial devolution, however, could not get momentum despite creation of State Finance Commissions to allocate funds to Panchayats. They are still dependent on state governments for funding. The untied funds are very limited and the resource generation at local level is also not very encouraging. A perusal of functioning of Panchayat Raj in a decade and a half shows a mix scenario of enough evidences of positive movements and several hurdles. Nevertheless, a hope for the best can be expected at this juncture.

II

BACKGROUND OF MADHYA PRADESH

The tribes of Madhya Pradesh have a long tradition of Panchayats, and their 'traditional' way of life was governed by these institutions. With modernisation, their strength has slowly diminished to some extent.

Efforts have been made to strengthen democratic decentralised rural governance by enacting laws. The Madhya Pradesh Panchayat Act, 1962, followed the recommendations of the Balvantray Mehta Study Team. A new Panchayat Raj Act was enacted in 1981, which was later amended in 1988 to provide reservations of seats for SCs, STs and women in the Panchayats. However, these institutions were given extremely restricted local functions and had no developmental responsibilities, which made them largely ineffective. Elections to these were not held regularly and they remained under the control of government appointed administrators. The Madhya Pradesh Panchayat Raj Act, 1990, did attempt to revitalise the Panchayat Raj Institutions. The key features of this Act were direct elections to these bodies, involvement of political parties, and the transfer of resources and developmental machinery to the Panchayats.

Later on, the Madhya Pradesh Panchayat Raj Act, 1993, was enacted to remove the lacunae in existing laws. This Act was drafted in conformity with the objectives, substance and directives of the 73rd Constitutional Amendment Act. The Act provides for a separate and independent audit organisation (under the control of the State Government) to monitor the audit of Panchayat accounts; a State Election Commission to supervise, direct and control the preparation of electoral rolls and to conduct elections to the Panchayats; and a State Finance Commission (SFC) to recommend to the State government the grant-in-aid as needed by the Panchayats. It was given Governor's assent on January 24th, 1994. The primary objective of the Madhya Pradesh Panchayati Raj Act (1993) is to empower the Panchayat Raj Institutions and to ensure their effective involvement in local administration and development activities. The idea is to make them more democratic through people's greater participation, and effective local self-governance, for ensuring of economic and social justice.

Amendments to the Madhya Pradesh Panchayat Raj Act, 1993

Several challenges have emerged to Panchayat Raj System during the last one and half decade of its operation in Madhya·Pradesh. Fortunately, a proactive State Government has responded to these needs and challenges. It analysed the strains on the system, identified the problem areas, and made a serious attempt to address these problem areas at all levels. It has changed and reissued its office orders, and also amended the Panchayat Act itself. This willingness and flexibility of the State Government to tackle bottlenecks has given strength to the Panchayat Raj System. It also reflects the political will to ensure the success of Panchayat Raj System in the State. The

Amendments in the Act have given the much-needed elasticity to the system and have contributed to their emergence as strong institutions of grassroots democracy.

An analysis of the Amendments clearly reflects the government's desire to institutionalise and empower the system. These deal with the teething problems of the system. Via the Amendments, the State Government has tried to overcome limitations that had cropped up during implementation of the Act. For example, when it was realised that women do not attend the Gram Sabha despite it being a crucial forum for public debate and decision-making on Panchayat issues, Madhya Pradesh Government amended Article 6 of the State Panchayat Act to make it mandatory to have one-third women members in the quorum. Another interesting example is the Amendment, which barred the Members of Parliament (MPs) or Members of the Legislative Assembly (MLAs) representing a completely urban constituency from the membership of the Zilla or Janpad Panchayat. This was done to protect the interests of rural areas in relation to urban areas.

A constant endeavour was to define the function of these institutions and devolve more administrative and financial powers made by the State Government on the Panchayats. Simultaneously, the Amendments tried to guarantee socio-economic change in favour of the marginalised. The State Government has tried to operationalise the Panchayats through these amendments in consistency with the ideal of 'power to people' and the concept of democratic decentralisation. The Amendments made in the Panchayat Act in 2001 have in fact paved the way for the introduction of Gram Swaraj in Madhya Pradesh.

III

EVIDENCES FROM THE FIELD

The Government of Madhya Pradesh was the first in India, to prepare its state legislation in accordance with 73rd Amendment Act and to conduct election in May-June 1994. It has been doing remarkable work for the strengthening of Panchayat Raj System since its inception. The elections for the second term of the Panchayats were held in January-February, 2000. After the completion of second term, the elections for the third term were held in January-February, 2005. As of now, the third generation of representatives is working in the Panchayats. The State has responded with innovativeness and remarkable commitment in making the system sustainable and successful. Its efforts to institutionalise the system are evident in the number of amendments that have been made to the State Panchayat Act as a dynamic response to the problems at the ground level. Madhya Pradesh did face several difficulties during the implementation of Panchayati Raj System but it overcame those. The experience of the State is extremely rich and provides vital insights into the process of institutionalising Panchayat Raj. On the one hand, the story is that of the bureaucratic resistance, functional problems, political and institutional challenges, financial inadequacy and mismatch of capacities and roles. On the other hand, it is a tale of a democratic and participative governance system at grassroots level. An attempt is being made in this paper to evaluate the ground reality and potentiality of the Panchayat Raj system in Madhya Pradesh. The issues of Gram Sabha, reservations, women representatives, working of Panchayats, Panchayats and bureaucracy, devolution of powers and finance are being dealt with under separate sub-headings in it.

People's Participation through Gram Sabha

The legislative empowerment of the Gram Sabha is a political development of utmost importance in India, because it marks the clearest break from the most dominant political orthodoxy of this century (Mander: 1999). This recent faith in it is based in the belief that the poor need to be directly involved in the process of formulation and implementation of decisions affecting their lives.

It is important to recognise that this faith is based on several important but untested assumptions. It is assumed, firstly, that even in a village society with deep schisms of caste, class and gender, an organic community still exists and that given appropriate legal and institutional space, it can act cogently and responsibly. The second assumption is that the collective decision of the Gram Sabha would be a more reliable vehicle for good governance than a relatively unencumbered bureaucracy or elected local representatives.

The experience of Panchayat Raj in Madhya Pradesh indicates that the State Act has been amended from time to time to make Gram Sabha a genuine structure of grassroots democracy. Original Act had a provision of one Gram Sabha meeting every year with a quorum of 10 per cent of members. By the very first amendment to the Act in 1994, the number of meetings was increased to three.

It is evident from the experience of Panchayat Raj in the State that participation of people at grassroots level was very low and it was almost a formal institution with no role in the assignment of various works related to rural development. Limited role of people in Gram Sabha has been a significant reason for the increased status of Sarpanches at Gram Panchayat level. This hegemonic scenario has led to the Sarpanch Raj. Therefore, the state government transferred nearly all of the powers previously exercised by Gram Panchayats to Gram Sabha through the introduction of Gram Swaraj on 26 January 2001. It has converted representative democracy at the grassroots into a direct democracy. More than 60 countries have experimented with some sort of democratic decentralisation over the last 15 years or so, that none has gone for direct democracy at the local level to the extent that Madhya Pradesh has now done (Manor: 2001).

The Gram Sabha has always been an integral part of the concept of a Gram Panchayat. Rajni Kothari visualises it as 'watchdog' coming between the politician-bureaucratic nexus (Kothari: 1998). It is unfortunate that both grassroots leadership and grassroots bureaucracy could not strengthen the Gram Sabha. It became dysfunctional due to the lack of leverage of local leaders to ensure meaningful participation in the Sabha and their incapability to persuade people to support local initiatives (Fernandes: 1999). It has been evident that meetings were mostly called without prior and adequate notice. Only a formality was observed merely; proxy meetings were held. At times even proceedings were written without the knowledge of those who had attended them. Even if held, these either proved to be abortive or unsuccessful because of thin attendance and no discussion on the issues. (Mander: 1999). It is certain that unless we have a vibrant Gram Sabha, we cannot have empowered and accountable Panchayats (Nambiar: 2001).

Legislation by itself is not adequate for correcting a wrong. The experience of the last one and a half decade has revealed a general indifference towards the functions of Gram Sabha and its meetings. Their eyes were still focused on the Gram Panchayat as the hub of all activity. Not only this, even Panchayat officials and the local elite had evinced little interest in the functioning of the Gram Sabha. But after the introduction of Gram Swaraj, all the powers were transferred to Gram Sabha instead of gram Panchayats. As many as eight committees were formed in Gram Sabha to look into different issues. A Gram Kosh was also constituted which would include both cash and kind. Conceptually the Gram Swaraj System was a form of direct democracy where the people were directly held accountable and responsible for all the local issues. It was the beginning of new experiment but the BJP government made an amendment after resuming power in 2004 and diluted the concept of Gram Swaraj before it could get momentum.

Gram Sabhas need to be made effective, active and creative so that the expected result could be accessible to the rural society. It is foremost responsibility of the Panchayat Raj representatives to convey to the people the real nature, functions and the real spirit of Gram Sabha. It can be a good platform for the solution of various day-to-day problems pertaining to the village society. This can also be used for the initiation of community work. Most of the basic rural problems, which hardly involve any cost, can be solved through the Gram Sabha that is the right forum to discuss all such issues. Its vibrancy and efficacy will remain dismal if it does not posses the capacity to perform assigned roles and responsibility. This question becomes more pertinent in a socio-cultural milieu where human resource development is low and the society is deeply fragmented and hierarchical. And, therefore it is urgently needed that marginalised sections of society, which have remained out from the process of decision-making, have to be taken in mainstream through sensitisation and capacity-building. The need is to address the issue of awareness generation among masses. Training camps, awareness campaigns and audio-visual media can be of critical importance for their sensitisation and capacity-building.

Representation of Marginalised Sections of Society

The state legislation has, as already mentioned, made provision for the reservations for the Scheduled Castes, Scheduled Tribes and Other Backward Castes. All these groups had negligible presence in the rural politics before this statutory provision. It is definitely a very important step through which very large political recruitment has become possible.

The Scheduled Castes have been provided reservation in proportion to their population. A basic difference between the SC and the ST is that while the latter reside in specific habitats, the former live along with the people of the general category. As a result, they face more difficulties because of social deprivations. Acute poverty, illiteracy and predominant position of rural elite have incapacitated them in discharging their duties effectively. Panchayats, which are 'institutions of self-governance', cannot function in a society that is ridden with castism, feudalism and poverty. Therefore, PRIs should be made effective instruments of social transformation through a vibrant democratic political process at the local level (Methew: 1996). The initial dissent and non-cooperative attitude towards SC leadership is gradually changing.

The state of Madhya Pradesh has the highest number of tribals in the entire country. They have also been given reservation in proportion to their population. When one examines the degree of their participation in the Panchayat Raj System, it emerges that much needs to be done to equip them for facing the new task. Many reasons such as : illiteracy, poverty, lack of awareness, socio-cultural deprivations, lack of experience and training etc can be pointed out for this situation.

The new Act, provides respectable space to the tribal people in the working of the Panchayat Raj System. But this legislation could not make the tribal communities the sole masters of their socio-political destinies in their homelands. The need was always felt that the institutional structures within the Scheduled Areas were to be in consonance with the tribal needs, ethos and tribal institutions with which these people were familiar for ages (Purohit: 2002). Accepting their felt needs the Union Government passed an amendment known as *Panchayat (Extension to the Scheduled Areas), 1996* and accordingly the State Government has also made an Amendment in the state legislation in 1997. A perusal of the catalogue of powers of scheduled area Panchayats convinces that they have been equipped with special powers for the preservation of tribal identities. The Gram Panchayat in scheduled areas shall work under the general superintendence, control and direction of the Gram Sabha.

The Panchayat Raj System in the Scheduled Areas of Madhya Pradesh has empowered Gram Sabhas with all such powers and duties to make them the real units of self-governance. As a result, there has been a growing concern for the speedy development of tribal areas. The State Government transferred nearly all of the powers previously exercised by Gram Panchayats to Gram Sabha. In theory, it has changed from a representative democracy to direct democracy at the grassroots. But despite this endeavour, there remains a clear cut gap between the macro level decisions and grassroots reality.

At the micro level, the Gram Sabha is a people's institution and has been made a statutory body through a Constitutional Amendment. Panchayat Raj System in scheduled areas has provided all powers and duties to it. The resource flow to Gram Sabha and its ever-increasing powers and authority have generated a lot of interest in people. It is expected that this interest is likely to be translated into a more broad based and participative leadership at grassroots level. The need is to address the issue of awareness generation among masses. Training camps, awareness campaigns and audio-visual media can be of critical importance for the sensitisation and capacity-building. However, a gradual process of change can be discerned. The tribal leadership is getting increasingly involved in understanding the system and coming to grips with it (Sisodia: 2002).

The OBCs hold a position different from that of the SCs and the STs. Even before reservation they had representation in the Panchayats as well as in other institutions. Their social position in the traditional social set up was also more respectable. The same can be said about their economic standing. As a result of these factors they have made use of the new Panchayat Raj System more effectively.

It is, therefore, essential that while the position of the OBCs needs further consolidation that of the SCs and the STs should be ameliorated a great deal. In this endeavour though, much more important is the attitudinal change on part of the administration and also of the society at large, the weaker sections need more training and experience in the exercise of their powers. Equally important are concrete measures to remove illiteracy and poverty from amongst them.

Only political recruitment of all the sections of society will help in attaining the desired goal. The basic idea behind the reservation was to provide an opportunity to the depressed classes to come forward and be a part of the total development process. In spite of all bottlenecks, the changes are taking place gradually. It happens so in a new system where representatives are not familiar with the working of the system. Slow but steady changes are visible. Taking lessons from the working of the Panchayats, the leadership is getting skilled. At the same time the other persons of the society are sharing several experiences with them. This process of decentralised governance will provide opportunity to rural people, particularly the persons of marginalised classes, to involve in development activities and several other works for the betterment of their life. The common man of the society will gradually become aware about day-to-day functioning and that way the coming generations will be well acquainted with the processes of development. This will certainly enthuse younger people to participate in the political process in the larger interests of the community.

Women's Participation in Panchayats

Women representation through 33 percent reservation of women by the 73rd Constitutional Amendment Act is a landmark decision. Women were being considered as a backward class because of their negligible representation in political process. As a result of this statutory provision, situation has dramatically changed. It is generally believed that the life of rural women is confined merely to kitchen and farms. This prolonged myth has changed. A large number of women have contested the Panchayat elections.

To ensure adequate and effective participation of women in the Panchayat Raj System, the Madhya Pradesh Panchayat Raj Act, 1993 reserves one-third of the seats for women in all the three tiers. Most of them have entered in the political process for the first time. However, some of women from the general and the OBC categories belong to the families which had traditional political base. Yet the working of women leadership is not very encouraging. The main reason for their poor performance is their overall backwardness. Other important bottleneck is the interference of male members of their families viz. of the husband, brother, father, son etc. However, in many cases such interference is now gradually declining. The reasons behind the involvement of male members are very clear: first, rural women do not have the required exposure; secondly, her lack of experience of working in Panchayats; thirdly, there is a non co-operative attitude of other Panchayat Raj representatives and government officials.

If an evaluation of their functioning is done, it becomes clear that with the passage of time the women leadership became more assertive and independent as well as aware of the systemic processes. However, it is necessary to do away with illiteracy, socio-economic deprivations and many other complexes to strengthen this segment. It is equally important to equip these women through sufficient training. There should also be a change in the attitude of their men folk and the administration. If women's empowerment has to be successful then the existing feudal patriarchal structure too has to be dismantled. Moreover, it requires a sustained campaign and vigorous efforts for creating awareness about their rights and duties (Datta: 1997).

It cannot, however, be denied that as a result of reservation for women, their participation in the political process has been ensured and they are now playing a constructive role in development and welfare activities. This will lead to positive changes in the entire social system. With the passage of time and by gaining the experience, it is believed women leadership will become more mature and effective.

Working of Panchayats

The Panchayat Raj institutions have been established as units of self-governance. There are many dimensions to the functions performed by them. The meetings have a pre-determined agenda. But discussion on new subjects can be taken up with the permission of the Chair. Personal issues, which are directly related to some members, are often debated at length. On many occasions, themes pertaining to rural development are overlooked due to involvement of vested interests. For the decisions by the Panchayats, the acceptance or approval of people's representatives or those in power is a must. This process of decision-making fails to fix correct priorities. Although elected on non-party basis, the functionaries are influenced in the decision-making process by political affiliations. It would be more meaningful if party politics brings about greater politicisation and participation rather than socio-political fragmentation. The influence of factors such as caste, class, community, religion too cannot be wholly denied as these do have a role to play. However, on few occasions, Panchayats have also played a cementing role.

They have been saddled with a plethora of activities, a lot of paper work has become necessary. While their records are properly maintained at the Janpad Panchayat and the Zilla Panchayat levels, the situation is not so rosy at the Gram Panchayat level due to inexperience of the Panchayat Raj representatives and lack of staff support. There is also an increasing need to inform the people about the meetings of Panchayats and their decisions and policies. The Panchayat functionaries are also not too keen to ensure transparency and to inform the people about their activities. Efforts should therefore be made to make the people more vigilant.

The Panchayat Raj Institutions have been given the responsibility of implementing different governmental schemes. For this, the Gram Sabhas select the beneficiaries and also examine the objectives of such schemes. They select people on economic basis so that the genuinely needy person get the benefits on a priority basis.

Though, the functioning of the PRIs, is improving, it still needs further streamlining. It has, however, to be understood that it is yet in infancy period. Things will definitely get better with more training, experience and increasing awareness about powers and duties. Their efficiency and effectiveness will surely infuse greater confidence among the people regarding their activities. Active participation of the members, co-operative response of the community and a spirit of selfless dedication to Panchayat work are necessary for the successful working of Panchayat Raj Institutions.

Panchayats and Bureaucracy

In the period prior to the implementation of the Madhya Pradesh Panchayat Raj Act, 1993, the control of bureaucracy over rural development was complete. However, now all the responsibilities relating to rural development have been handed over to the Panchayats. This has necessitated fundamental changes at the bureaucratic or technocratic level also.

There are however widespread feelings of fear, mistrust and insecurity among the Panchayat representatives regarding their staff. A greater understanding between the two sets of functionaries is needed to remove misperceptions and apprehensions regarding each other. The bureaucracy has to understand its position and responsibilities in a democratic system. A. system has to be developed where accountability informs the upper echelons of administration.

The Panchayats at all the three levels must be provided with a separate and autonomous cadre, which should be de-linked from the State Government. Responsibilities relating to recruitment, promotion, transfer etc. should be handled by the Panchayats themselves or through some relevant agency. Posting at local levels should be permitted on permanent basis. This would solve the problem of transfer and the official will have wide knowledge of his area. Misuse of power should be checked through a system of checks and balances. There is also a need of simplification of procedures so that usual and routine matters do not cause confusion, delay and deadlocks. A Panchayat Manual should be prepared as an authentic and ultimate source of eliminating all confusion or possible misunderstanding. Multiple and periodically recurring orientation programmes should be organised for both the groups.

Devolution of Powers

The Constitution of India vide Schedule 11 has laid down 29 subjects related to social justice and economic development. These have been devolved upon the Panchayats for planning and implementation. This Schedule finds a place in the Madhya Pradesh Panchayat Act as Schedule 4 and it is on its basis that important powers of all departments have been handed over to Panchayats. These departments are: social welfare, agriculture, mineral resources, food and civil supplies, sports and youth welfare, rural development, village industries, livestock, dairy and poultry development, revenue, public health and engineering, forest, school education, labour etc. However, most Panchayat representatives do not possess adequate knowledge about the functions and responsibilities entrusted to them by the various departments. As a result, their role in such departments is negligible. Such devolution, therefore, would be fruitful only when the representatives are made aware of their role and encouraged to perform the same.

The elected representatives have been provided with many administrative powers which relate to recruitment, supervision and control. However, many of them have no experience of such jobs and find it difficult to handle them judiciously. As a result, the importance of administrative officials and influential people has increased in the exercise of these powers. For proper use of these functions, the Panchayat representatives should be given proper training.

Members of Parliament and State legislators are *ex-officio* members of different tiers of the Panchayat Raj. They take part in the meetings. Though denied by the Act, in practice they exercise undue influence in the functioning of these bodies due to their political clout and access to the centres of power. Even the Panchayat representatives become subservient to them to seek favours from them. The MPs and MLAs have often shown

25

Punjab's Economy and Panchayati Raj Institutions : An Analysis

KESAR SINGH AND PARAMVIR SINGH

This paper scales to trace the evolution of Panchayati Raj Institutions, discuss their present status and present findings of an empirical study on their working in Punjab. The broad objectives behind this exercise are to find out as to how far the democratic decentralisation has led to good governance at grassroots level in the state, to identify the problems that have emerged and then to make suggestions for tackling those.

EVOLUTION OF PANCHAYATI RAJ IN PUNJAB

The Panchayats were first set-up formally in Punjab after the passage of the Punjab Village Panchayat Act (1912) after the Report of Royal Commission on Decentralisation (1907). The Punjab Village Panchayat Act, 1921 replaced the earlier legislation after the introduction of the Montague Chelmsford Scheme. Following the introduction of Provincial Autonomy through the Government of India Act (1935), the Village Panchayat Act, 1939 was enacted on the initiative of the then Development Minister in the Unionist Party Government, Chaudhary Chottu Ram. The other rural-level institution operating at that time was the District Board. There was a functional link between the Panchayats and the District Boards. But these were limited mostly to the functions of improvement and expansion of rural works and performance of some civic functions.

After independence, the Indian Constitution placed the Panchayats under Article 40 of Directive Principles of State Policy. In Punjab, Village locally. Various provisions are available to generate resources. This way alone the scheme of democratic decentralisation will bear fruits.

Decentralised Planning

Madhya Pradesh has been continuously devolving powers and authority on the Panchayats and has been initiating innovative measures to empower, strengthen and institutionalise the PRIs. In this process, Gram Swaraj is a new system of local self-governance at the village level, which is a move from indirect to direct democracy. It is based on the premise that people can assemble and sit collectively in a village, and decide the local issues. The new system intends to give power to the people and therefore all the powers previously exercised by Gram Panchayats are transferred to Gram Sabhas. The approach of decentralised planning is 'bottom up'. The planning starts from village itself. The new system has separate committees on village development, common resources, agriculture, health, village protection, infrastructure, education and social justice. Each committee is expected to meet periodically and prepare an action plan and discuss the issues related to the committee concerned. All the committee heads then meet in Village Development Committee to discuss all such matters. After scrutiny, the matter goes to Gram Sabha where all the adult villagers are authorised to participate. At village level, this long and systematic procedure of local planning can really make a significant move to yield the desired results.

If we look at the experience of Gram Swaraj, the local people are not yet well versed with the procedural aspects of Gram Swaraj : moreover the concept itself has been modified and diluted by an Amendment. The committee formation at local level has also not been a very enthusiastic and the meetings of Gram Sabha have again witnessed lack of quorum at times. These indications are not generalisations. There are examples where remarkable progress has been made in committee formation and initiation of local planning in Gram Sabha. These local plans are sent to Intermediate Panchayat (Janpad Panchayat) through Gram Panchayats. After scrutiny and compilation, it goes to Zila Panchayat. A consolidated plan for the district is prepared here and percolation of resource flow downward to Panchayats is done from here.

The decentralised planning is the need of the hour. The desired goals can only be achieved through it but it seems that the plans lack the vision for the multifaceted and balanced development at village level due to variety of reasons. It is therefore important to initiate special orientation and sensitisation training programme to give a better understanding of decentralised planning to the local people.

CONCLUSION

The establishment of Panchayat Raj System in Madhya Pradesh is in deference to the provision of the 73rd Constitution Amendment Act. The

State Act has been amended from time to time to make it suitable for making PRIs more effective as the genuine structures of grassroots democracy. Through a system of reservation, participation of the weaker sections has also been ensured. The three tiers have been empowered significantly to enable them to discharge their duties properly and to fulfil the expectations of the people. However, much still needs to be done. Even after Gram Swaraj, the Gram Sabhas are yet to perform their desired role in the Panchayat Raj System. Reservation has provided an opportunity to all marginalised classes to come out and play a significant role but the process of political socialization is slow among them. The enhanced Women representation in Panchayats is a matter of some satisfaction but their performance is poor as compared to the male representatives. The bureaucracy has to be made more responsive to the needs of the PRIs. Greater financial autonomy must be provided to the Panchayats. Better coordination has to be established among the three tiers of Panchayat. Greater clarity of roles and tier-wise division of functions are essential. Of no less importance is the optimal direct participation of people in the developmental process. To generate the principle of accountability, continual social auditing be prompted. The transparency in the form of Right to Information pertaining to administrative activities too need to be ensured. The Panchayats should be given the power to form organisations like neighbourhood groups to stimulate and direct people's participation in administration and development. Concrete efforts should also be made to reduce governmental interference in the day-to-day functioning of local self-government bodies and the process of their dissolution need to be made more politics proof. Such measures will go a long way in establishing the Panchayats as 'Village Republics'. The Panchayat Raj System has provided opportunities for wider political recruitment to all sections of the society, this should lead to achievement of the goals of social justice and economic development in the years to come.

References

Behar, Amitabh and Kumar, Yogesh (2002), "Decentralisation in Madhya Pradesh, India: from Panchayati Raj to Gram Swaraj (1995 to 2001)", *Working Paper, 170, ODI*, London, UK.

Datta, Prabhat (1997): "Political Empowerment of Rural Women in India", *Administrative Change*, 24 (2), January-June.

Fernandes, A. (1999): "Reconnecting the Sabha to Gram", Paper presented at the National Conference on Gram Sabha, National Institute of Rural Development, Hyderabad, July 28-29.

Issac, T.M. Thomas and Richard, W. Franke (2000): *Local Democracy and Development: People's Campaign for Decentralised Planning in Kerala*, Leftword, New Delhi.

Kothari, Rajni (1998): *State Against Democracy: In Search of Human Governance*, Ajanta Publications, Delhi.

Mander, Harsh (1999): "Towards Direct Democracy: The Legal Empowerment of Gram Sabha", *Kurukshetra*, Vol. 48, No. 1, October.

Manor, James (2001): "Madhya Pradesh Experiments with Direct Democracy", *Economic and Political Weekly*, March 3.

TABLE 3

District-wise Number of Scheduled Castes and Women Sarpanches in Punjab (1978-2003)

Region	District	Scheduled Castes					Women						Total
		1978	1983	1992	1998	2003	1978	1983	1992	1998	2003		
											GC	SC	Total
(1)	(2)	(3)	(4)	(5)	(6)	(7)	(8)	(9)	(10)	(11)	(12)	(13)	(14)
Majha	Gurdaspur	124	100	92	266	275	27	19	30	526	393	137	530
	Amritsar	44	32	32	278	276	26			417	314	143	457
Doaba	Kapurthala	59	49	67	111	116	— 11	1 6	7	183	118	56	174
	Jullundher	257	217	45	252	267	25	4	3	299	173	127	300
	Hoshiarpur	186	202	201	313	311	17	13	21	437	283	157	440
	Nawanshahr				112	119				147	88	59	147
Malwa	Rupnagar —	— 65	— 51	20	143	152—	— 18	— 4	4	274	207	76	283
	Ludhiana	46	41	49	206	206	12	6	3	289	188	103	291
	Ferozepur	21	16	25	166	152	12	6	11	406	289	71	360
	Faridkot	8	9	14	45	46	13	4	12	59	38	22	60
	Bathinda	16	7	7	62	70	9	7	4	103	64	30	94
	Sangrur	31	13	29	140	146		2	8	242	169	77	246
	Patiala	104	37	58	153	190 1	16	8	11	357	264	96	360
	Mansa			8	51	50			1	79	56	25	81
	Fatehgarh Sahib	—		24	90	89—	—		5	145	105	51	156
	Moga —	—			42	71—	—			63	72	35	107
	Muktsar —	—	—		69	62—	—	—		88	50	37	87
	Total	961	774	671	2499	2598	187	79	121	4114	2871	1302	4173

Source : Department of Panchayats and Rural Development, Punjab.

disinterestedness in successful functioning of the Panchayat Raj Institutions as in their perception this would limit their own area of influence. The feeling is growing that if direct elections were held to all the positions in the PRIs, the influence of the representatives would get augmented. It has also been suggested that the development fund available to MPs and MLAs should be spent in consultation with the Panchayat Raj functionaries. Separate development funds should be provided to the Panchayat representatives enabling them to spend it in accordance with the felt needs of the people. To streamline the division of functions between the three tiers, a suggestion has been made to establish State Commission to distribute the 29 subjects judiciously and also to include a 'local list' in the Constitution along with the Union, State and Concurrent lists.

Financial Status of Panchayats

Finance is the first and foremost necessity of any institution for its successful working. It is important to make Panchayat Raj Institutions financially sound and self-sufficient. Panchayats of Madhya Pradesh have two resources—funds from government and local tax collection. It is observed that majority of the Panchayats depend on funding from State Government but do not levy local taxes for political reasons. The State Government allocates the money for rural development to the three tiers. These bodies are also provided finances to implement government schemes.

The State Government has been sensitive to the need of financial efficacy of the Panchayat Raj institutions. These have been empowered by the Act to levy many new taxes, i.e. market fee, property tax, land tax, private toilet tax, etc. The Government also constituted two State Finance Commissions and many of their recommendations were accepted with regard to distribution of financial powers to the Panchayats. Yet the Panchayat Raj Institutions cannot be regarded as financially self-reliant. Their dependence on the State Government for grants is not conducive to their successful functioning. Not many Panchayats have utilised the powers given to them to levy local taxes. The functionaries have expressed the view that most of the people living in rural areas are poor and it would be improper to levy more taxes on them. Moreover, such new taxes would make them politically unpopular among the people. As such, the taxes should be levied only on those who are able to pay. The rural leadership should also realise the significance of tax collection, as these constitute the major source of their income. They have to establish examples of devoted and transparent work so that people do not mistrust them when new taxes are levied. Greater participation of the people in the whole process should be ensured.

Despite all these efforts, one would not be in a position to say that the Panchayats are financially self-sufficient. Dependence of Panchayats on State Government for funds is not good for the health of the new system. The leadership will have to come forward to meet the financial needs

Panchayats were democratised and re-empowered through a new act, the Punjab Gram Panchayat Act, 1952. It provided for the constitution of Village Panchayats on a mandatory basis through universal adult franchise. The Punjab Government decided to introduce the Panchayati Raj System in 1961 by enacting the Panchayat Samitis and Zila Parishads Act, 1961 and by amending the Punjab Gram Panchayat Act, 1952. The District Boards were also abolished for this purpose. The three-tier system of Panchayati Raj, comprising of Gram Panchayats at the village level, Panchayat Samiti at the block level and Zila Parishads at the district level, became operative from 1962. The Panchayat Samitis and Zila Parishads functioned as representative bodies up to 1970 and again from 1975 to 1978. In the intervening period from 1970-1975, these bodies had been dissolved. After the eighties, these two-tiers remained under the management of government officials till 1994. Elections to the Gram Panchayats (first tier) were held almost regularly (1962, 1968, 1973, 1978, 1983, 1992, 1998 and 2003) with the exception of 1988 due to the turbulent situation in the state. Meanwhile, various committees were constituted to suggest improvements in the working of PRIs in the state. The important one was the Badal Committee, which recommended indirect election of the Sarpanch of Gram Panchayat. The election to Gram Panchayats in 1978 was held as per this recommendation. With the passing of the 73rd Constitutional Amendment Act (1992), the State Government enacted the Punjab Panchayati Raj Act, 1994, which came into force on 21 April 1994. New rules were framed under the provisions of this new Act and the first elections to 138 Panchayat Samitis and 14 Zila Parishads were held in 1994. The next elections of these bodies were held in 2003, and presently these institutions have 2485 and 283 elected members respectively. The Gram Panchayat elections were held in 1998 and 2003. Presently, the number of Gram Panchayats in Punjab is 12443. They are having 88170 Panches and Sarpanches. The information of the number of Gram Panchayats in the state, since its reorganization, on November 1, 1966, is as Table 1.

TABLE 1

District-wise Number of Gram Panchayats in the State of Punjab (1968-2003)

Region	*District*	*1968*	*1973*	*1978*	*1983*	*1992*	*1998*	*2003*
Majha	Gurdaspur	870	1056	1246	1335	1451	1589	1592
	Amritsar	1009	1045	1080	1088	1164	1268	1287
Doaba	Kapurthala	236	340	427	449	490	533	535
	Jullundher	833	878	1055	1084	1113	886	886
	Hoshiarpur	835	1035	1294	1350	1432	1314	1317
	Nawanshahr	—	—	—	—	—	440	445
Malwa	Rupnagar	611	629	716	757	805	856	852
	Ludhiana	805	824	877	884	840	871	876

Ferozepur	658	756	907	931	1036	1202	1089
Faridkot	536	542	552	552	581	180	181
Bathinda	481	510	516	516	278	303	306
Sangrur	574	657	683	685	703	727	735
Patiala	970	1059	1258	1318	1035	1063	1079
Mansa	—	—	—	—	241	243	242
Fatehgarh Sahib	—	—	—	—	428	438	430
Moga	—	—	—	—	—	191	326
Muktsar	—	—	—	—	—	265	265
Total	8418	9331	10611	10949	11597	12369	12443

Source : Department of Panchayats and Rural Development, Punjab.
* The Panchayats of newly carved districts of Barnala are included in Sangrur district, of Taran Taran in Amritsar district and of Ajit Nagar in Rupnagar and Patiala Districts.

The number of the elected members of Gram Panchayats has been tabulated in Table 2.

Table 2
District-wise Number of Panches and Sarpanches in Punjab (1968-2003)

Region	*District*	*1968*	*1973*	*1978*	*1983*	*1992*	*1998*	*2003*
Majha	Gurdaspur	4942	5963	7746	7683	10748	10677	10734
	Amritsar	6638	6985	8234	7176	8951	9328	9397
Doaba	Kapurthala	1431	2092	2918	3440	3032	3554	3570
	Jullundher	5159	5988	7602	7049	8211	6229	6260
	Hoshiarpur	5106	5576	7191	7224	10696	8705	8700
	Nawanshahr	—	—	—	—	—	3103	3132
Malwa	Rupnagar	3195	3415	4948	5978	6380	5676	5564
	Ludhiana	4676	4780	6327	5167	6428	6540	6504
	Ferozepur	4371	5082	5848	6250	6342	8341	7553
	Faridkot	3531	3748	4417	4339	4806	1418	1428
	Bathinda	3055	3380	3893	4392	2407	2589	2667
	Sangrur	3807	3833	5226	5239	4932	6067	5818
	Patiala	5728	6424	9060	9078	7366	7001	7206
	Mansa	—	—	—	—	2005	2013	2016
	Fatehgarh Sahib	—	—	—	—	2807	2754	2814
	Moga	—	—	—	—	—	1690	2626
	Muktsar	—	—	—	—	—	2157	2181
	Total	51689	57266	73410	73015	85111	87842	88170

Source : Department of Panchayats and Rural Development, Punjab.

Methew, George and Ramesh C. Nayak (1996): "Panchayat at Work: What it means for Oppressed?", *ISS Occasional Paper Series-19,* Institute of Social Sciences, New Delhi.

Nambiar, Malini (2001): "Making the Gram Sabha Work", *Economic and Political Weekly,* Mumbai, August 18.

Purohit, B.R. (2002): "Panchayat Raj System in Scheduled Areas of Madhya Pradesh" in eds. Palanithurai, G., *Dynamics of New Panchayati Raj System in India,* Vol. I., Concept Publishing Company, New Delhi.

Robinson, Mark (2005): "A Decade of Panchayat Raj Reforms: The Challenge of Democratic Decentralisation in India" in L.C. Jain (ed.), *Decentralisation and Local Governance,* Orient Longman, New Delhi.

Sisodia, Yatindra Singh (2005): A Decade of Panchayat Raj System in Madhya Pradesh in Yatindra Singh Sisodia (ed.), *Functioning of Panchayat Raj System,* Rawat Publications, Jaipur.

Sisodia, Yatindra Singh (2002): "Decentralised Governance in Madhya Pradesh: Experiences of the Gram Sabha in Scheduled Areas", *Economic and Political Weekly,* Mumbai, October 5.

Webster, Neil (1992): "Panchayat Raj in West Bengal: Participation for the People or the Party?", *Development and Change,* Vol. 23, No. 4.

World Bank (2000): *Overview of Rural Decentralisation in India,* Volume III, p. 24.

After the implementation of new Panchayati Raj System, in consonance with the 73rd Amendment, drastic changes have occurred in their structure. The number of scheduled castes and women Sarpanches in these has increased as given in the Table 3.

PRESENT STATUS OF PRIs

Since 1994, as already mentioned, all the three tiers of PRIs have been working as per the provisions of the Punjab Panchayati Raj Act, 1994. The current status of PRIs has been tabulated below:

The nomenclature used for the three-tier Panchayat Raj system in the state is:

Level	*Name used as*	*Total number*
District Council	Zila Parishad	17
Block Council	Panchayat Samiti	141
Village Council	Gram Panchayat	12443

Source : Department of Panchayats and Rural Development.

Three newly created districts namely Taran Tarn, Barnala and Ajit Nagar have no separate Zila Parishads.

The number and the percentage of elected representatives in all the three tiers are as following:

Office	*Total Number*	*General Castes*	*General Castes (Women)*	*Scheduled Castes*	*Scheduled Castes Women*	*Other Backward Classes*
			Gram Panchayats (12443)			
Sarpanches	12443	5672 (45.50)	2871 (23.10)	2598 (20.90)	1302 (10.50)	—
Panches	75689	30068 (39.70)	18790 (24.80)	15628 (20.60)	7912 (10.50)	3291 (4.30)
			Panchayat Samitis (140)			
Chairperson	140	60 (44.30)	32 (22.81)	26 (18.60)	20 (14.30)	—
Vice-Chairpersons	140	56 (40.00)	30 (21.40)	28 (20.00)	26 (18.60)	—
Members	2483	1101 (44.30)	546 (22.00)	526 (21.20)	268 (10.80)	42 (1.70)
			Zila Parishads (17)			
Chairpersons	17	7 (41.20)	3 (17.60)	4 (23.50)	3 (17.60)	—
Vice-Chairpersons	17	8 (47.10)	3 (17.60)	3 (17.60)	3 (17.60)	—
Members	281	126 (44.90)	62 (22.10)	60 (21.30)	29 (10.30)	4 (1.47)

Source : Department of Panchayats and Rural Development.

The following seven subjects/departments have been devolved to the PRIs in Punjab:

- Social Security & Women and Child Development
- Scheduled Castes and Backward Classes
- Water Supply and Sanitation
- Rural Development and Panchayats
- Health and Family Welfare
- School Education
- Veterinary Services

➢ The State Government has set-up a fund for the disbursement of social security pensions to the concerned beneficiaries. The Gram Sabha has been empowered to identify and select the beneficiaries. The disbursement of pensions was being done through the Gram Panchayats, but the procedure has been changed recently and the pensions are now being disbursed through cheques. Direct link of the Gram Panchayats has been established with Anganwaries for their better functioning.

➢ The scheme for distribution of scholarship and free books to the Scheduled Castes students is also being operated by PRIs in co-ordination with Education Department.

➢ Out of total 3200 rural water supply schemes, 876 single village schemes and their 1294 regular and 656 muster roll employees have been transferred to Gram Panchayats.

➢ The Department of Rural Development and Panchayats works in co-ordination with and the cooperation of Panchayat bodies.

➢ The control of Rural Subsidiary Health Centres has been given to Zila Parishads and requisite funds have also been given to manage the centres. 1186 Rural Dispensaries have been transferred to the Panchayat bodies. To run these 1158 Service Providers had been recruited till September, 2007 and there is also provision of medicines for them. The Panchayat Secretaries have been authorised to register births and deaths and to issue certificates

➢ The management of Primary Education has been transferred to Zila Parishad. A total of 5752 Primary Schools with sanctioned posts of 13034 ETT teachers have been transferred to the panchayat bodies. Till Sept. 2007, 11465 posts of ETT teachers had been filled up. The supplementary nutrition and scholarships as well as distribution of books to Scheduled Castes children in the primary schools is also being operated by the Panchayat bodies.

➢ The Zila Parishads have been empowered and given requisite funds to manage Rural Veterinary Dispensaries. This includes provision of veterinary services through Veterinary Service Providers and provision of medicines. Till Sept. 2007, 581 Rural Veterinary Dispensaries had been transferred to Panchayat bodies and 382 Service Providers had been recruited.

The Service Providers, in both health and veterinary services, are paid Rs. 30,000 per month as lump sum and Rs. 7,500 per month for medicines.

- A draft of Activity Mapping has been prepared for all the 29 subjects/departments and has been circulated to various departments for their responses.
- The Government has enhanced the financial powers of panchayat bodies for granting administrative approval for Gram Panchayat (up to 10 lacs), Panchayat Samiti (up to Rs. 20 lacs) and for Zila Parishad (more than 20 lacs)
- Although the DRDA remains a separate identity, it has been made accountable, to some extent, to the Panchayat bodies.
- The employees of transferred departments have been made accountable, to some extent, to the Panchayat bodies. The Panchayat Secretaries have been made answerable to the Panchayats.
- The Meetings of Gram Sabha have been made compulsory. If these are not held, then Sarpanch can be suspended. His reinstatement will be done only by the Director, Panchayats.
- The devolution of finances to Panchayats is as under:

Level of Panchayat	*Obligatory resources*		*Discretionary resources*	
	Tax revenue	*Non-tax revenue*	*Tax revenue*	*Non-tax revenue*
(1)	*(2)*	*(3)*	*(4)*	*(5)*
Gram Panchayat	(a) tax on lands and buildings (b) tax on professions, trades, and employment other than agriculture (c) admission to any entertainment (d) surcharge on stamp duty by state govt. for gram Panchayat	(a) sale proceeds of dung etc. (b) income from village fisheries (c) income from common land (d) proportion of land revenue by state govt.	(a) fee on registration of vehicles (b) special tax on adult males for community works	(a) fee for sanitary arrangement (b) water rate (c) lighting rate (d) conservancy rate
Panchayat Samiti	local rate @ 25 paise per Rs. of land revenue	rent from property managed by samiti	(a) tolls on persons, vehicles, animals etc. for using roads, bridges and ferries under samiti control	(a) water rate (b) lighting rate

(Contd.)

(1)	*(2)*	*(3)*	*(4)*	*(5)*
			(b) fee for registration of vehicles other than Motor Acts 1986 (c) fee for license for market or any other road cess and public works cess.	
Zila Parishad	any tax or duty or fee which is not levied by any Panchayat with permission from state government	(a) contribution and grant by central/ state governments including part of land revenue (b) penalties and fines (c) gifts and contributions (d) all receipts in respect of schools/hospital buildings, institution, works (e) contribution and grants by Panchayat Samiti		

- ❖ The State Government has so for constituted Three Finance Commissions. But, their recommendations have been implemented half-heartedly.
- ❖ The constitution of the Districts Planning Committees had been approved by the state cabinet in October 2005. However, they have not been formed so far.
- ❖ The sequence of reservation for women in Panchayat bodies is as under:
  - ➢ First the reservations are made for the Scheduled Castes, then for SCs women.
  - ➢ After the reservations for SCs and SCs women, the reservation is done for the OBCs and OBC women on the same lines.
  - ➢ Finally, the reservations are done for women out of the unreserved seats.

No efforts have been made for harmonisation of other laws with Panchayati Raj Act. The Sections of the following Acts/Laws require harmonisation with the Panchayat Act:

- ❖ Punjab Cattle Fairs (Regulation) Act, 1967
- ❖ Punjab Livestock Improvement Act, 1953

- Punjab Cinemas (Regulation) Act, 1952
- Punjab Livestock and Birds Diseases Control Act, 1948
- Punjab Agriculture Produce Markets Act, 1961
- Punjab Minor Canal Act, 1905
- Punjab Fisheries Act, 1914
- The East Punjab Holding (Consolidation and Prevention of Fragmentation) Act, 1948
- The elections to all the three tiers have been held simultaneously since 1994 under the over-all supervision of State Election Commission. But, there is no model code of conduct for Panchayat election. The election expenses are monitored by State Election Commission
- There is no provision for Social Audit in the law
- E-government of Panchayats is at incipient stage, only a few of them have computers, generally funded by the NRIs
- The State Institute of Rural Development (SIRD) Nabha (Patiala) is the nodal agency to impart training to the elected representatives and the officials of the Panchayat bodies.

THE STUDY AREA

The CRRID was commissioned in 2005 by the Ministry of Panchayati Raj, Government of India, to study the extent of equity in the benefits of the central schemes to various sections of the rural population of Punjab. It selected 300 villages from all the 17 districts by combining stratification and random sampling method.

The survey was conducted with the help of two modules; (i) Village Module, which provided information on general socio-economic characteristics in the village, as well as detailed expenditure and income accounts of Panchayat's and (ii) school survey questionnaire that provided information on schooling enrolments in private and government schools to assess the effect of the growing privatisation of social services in the delivery of social services on the involvement of Village Panchayats.

The data on socio-economic characteristics of the village show that their average population size was 1421, with population ranging from 38 to 6314. On an average, the Scheduled Castes constitute 35 percent of the total village population. However, it comprises of over 50 percent population in 25 percent of the villages. In another 25 percent villages, they are less than 20 percent in the overall population.

Approximately two-thirds of the villages have a separate Schedule Castes locality, called a *vehra*. Typically these were located close to the main village. The data indicated that only a few households of them own land. On average, 30 percent of the households living in these were below the poverty line. They possess no more than 1 percent of the total land in all the surveyed villages.

The average village land was 1031 acres. It ranges from 20 to 8400 acres. The size of Common Property Resources varies across villages. On an average every village has 22 acres of *shamlat land*. Other types of Common Property Resources include fishing ponds and shops from which the Panchayat derives rental income. Only 12 percent of them have access to fishing ponds. But few (7 percent) are deriving income from shops on Panchayat land.

On an average about half of the households in a given village own no land. Only 1.5 percent of them have more than 10 hectares of land. Self-employment in agriculture provides the major source of income for about half of the households (47 percent). After agricultural, casual agricultural work generates the most of their income, with 21 percent of households in this category. The growing importance of non-agricultural work is seen in the relatively high percentage of people who reported that their major source of income is casual non-agricultural employment (16 percent). However, only 6 percent of them reported non-agricultural self-employment as their major source of income, and only 8 percent earn their income primarily from a salaried job. The percentage of households with a Non-Resident Indian (NRI) members in sampled villages is 7 percent.

STATUS OF SERVICE DELIVERY

The most common pension is the old age pension. On an average, 51 people per village receive it. When taken as a percentage of village population, on average 4 percent are receiving the old age pension. Among the other types of pensions, on an average 4 people per village are receiving disability pension, 8 widow/widower pension and 2 destitute pension. The percentage of those receiving disability pensions is less than one percent of a village. The same is true of widow/widower and destitute person's pension.

Most villages have access to a Government Health Sub-Centre as these are within 5 km of them. The government medical facilities are far more readily available than private facilities. Only 1/3rd of the villages have private facilities available within a 5 km. radius. However, 75 percent of villages have reported some form of private health facilities within 10 km. Government health facilities charge substantially less than the private ones. For example, the Consultancy Fee in a Community Health Centre (CHC) is only Rs. 1.5, in contrast to Rs. 54 in a private hospital. Similarly, the cost of a delivery in a CHC is Rs. 1,593 against Rs. 4,311 in a private hospital. Despite this difference in accessibility and cost, the use of private health facilities is pervasive. As many as 69 percent of households have reported using these for common illnesses and for emergency care. These are also commonly used for the delivery of a child. However, very few households use them for routine checkups, or pre/post natal care.

In about 57 percent of the surveyed villages, the ground water is safe, and in about 60 percent of these its quantity is sufficient. 75 percent of them have 24 hours supply of electricity, and in 60 percent of the villages the community raised funds to get 24 hours the same. Of the communities which raised money for electricity, 85 percent have raised these funds in the last 10 years.

Over the past five years, there has been little change in the main source of drinking water in the surveyed villages. Most of these still have private hand pumps and tube wells as their main source of drinking water. The recent phenomenon is of submersible pumps. Borewells-based waterworks have become more common in recent years. The major shift in the main source of drinking water has been from private hand pumps and tubewells to borewell-based waterworks. As many as 37 villages made this shift during the five years.

Over 65 percent of them have waterworks projects in their villages. Of these, over half of the waterworks programs began functioning in the last 10 years. In addition, most of these have multiple village projects (80 percent of projects) and the water is available not only for the main village but also for the Schedule Caste *Vehra* (80 percent of projects). Only three villages have water works from Swajaldhara projects.

PANCHAYAT BODIES AND LOCAL LEVEL DEMOCRACY

Most of the villages have a Single Panchayat serving the village. Four of them have Multiple Panchayats serving a single village, while 9 shared a Panchayat with a neighbouring village.

Data were collected on the gender and caste characteristics of the Sarpanches elected during the past three elections that were held in 2003, 1998 and 1993. In 1993, the system of reservation of the position of Sarpanch for women and members of scheduled castes was not in place. In our sample of 300 villages, over 250 reported election of males from general castes as Sarpanches. This number fell dramatically, both in the 1998 and 2003 elections.

But 25 percent of the Sarpanches have less than primary level education. Only 15 percent have higher than 10th grade education. Most of them are self-employed. The occupation of most of Women Sarpanches is domestic work. Very few of the Sarpanches are engaged in casual labour or are having salaried positions.

While the characteristics of the Sarpanches have changed as a consequence of the system of reservation, there has been little change in the number of candidates contesting the election for Sarpanch. Data reveal that most villages had two candidates for the office of Sarpanch in each of the three elections. Moreover, on an average the winner on the election received 60 percent while the runners up got around 30 percent of the votes. This trend has remained unchanged over time.

Information had also been collected on the number of the meetings of Gram Panchayat and Gram Sabhas to measure the degree of local democracy. These data suggest that the Panchayats are holding regular meetings, with villages reporting an average of 12 meetings per year. Gram

Sabha meetings also appear to be regularly held, with villages reporting an average of two Gram Sabha meetings per year. However, participation in these meetings is limited, as only 28 percent had participated in these.

PANCHAYAT INCOME AND EXPENDITURE

Data were also collected on the income of Panchayats for the years 2004-05 and 2005-06. These reveal the complete lack of local taxation. The only tax being collected, the house tax, generate less than 1/100th of the total income of Panchayats in 2004-05 and 2005-06. In contrast, the income from *shamlat land* is considerable. Indeed, averaging across the villages in our sample, income from this source constitutes the single most important source of income for the Panchayats, accounting for 26 percent of income in 2004-05 and 34 percent of it in 2005-06.

Other significant sources of income are the SGRY grants (21 percent of income in 2004-05 and 17 percent in 2005-06), state government grants and transfers (16 percent and 22 percent in each of the two years), and grants from the Member of Parliament Local Area Development Scheme (MPLADS) which generated 21 percent of average Panchayat income in 2004-05 and 15 percent in 2005-06

Panchayat Income, 2004-05 and 2005-06, in Surveyed Gram Panchayats

Income source	*2004-05*		*2005-06*	
	Mean	*Std. Dev.*	*Mean*	*Std. Dev.*
House tax	110.07 (0.00)	767.55	119.81 (0.00)	899.79
Shamlat land	60,579.25 (25.61)	138,991.70	64,496.98 (33.96)	151.555.3
Other rental income from own property	4,512.17 (1.91)	20,181.22	4,774.34 (2.51)	22,140.02
SGRY (Total)	50,521.87 (21.36)	63,615.00	33,092.51 (17.42)	46,496.43
Of which, SGRY direct to Panchayat	13,094.48 (5.53)	24,023.29	8,613.05 (4.53)	21,258.74
Other Central Govt. grants	10,746.10 (4.54)	55,607.64	5,498.88 (2.90)	32,155.88
MPLADF	50,606.78 (21.39)	246,217.70	28,366.10 (14.94)	69,928.84
State Govt. grants	36,868.47 (15.58)	145,422.40	42,444.07 (22.35)	117,266.90
Total Income	236,578.00 (100.00)	358,416.20	189,923.00 (100.00)	220,636.10
Sample size	295		295	

Note : Figures in brackets are percentages to total income. All amounts are in Rupees.
Source : Field Survey.

The data reveal that the funds on which the Panchayat has full discretion is primarily the income from *shamlat land*. They have no choice in the funds for the centrally sponsored schemes like IAY. Similarly, funds from the MPLADF and central government grants are 'tied', as it is made available for a pre-specified purpose. While the Panchayats do have control over some proportion of SGRY funds, this is restricted to those received directly by them as opposed to those that are passed on to the Panchayats from the district and block level bodies. The latter are specified by the higher level governments. The amount of 'unrestricted' SGRY funds made available directly to the Panchayats for use according to their own preferences amounted to approximately 5 percent of total village income.

Data on Panchayat expenditures for 2004-05 and 2005-06 were also collected. These provide information on total Panchayat expenditures and, separately, on the investment in the Schedule Caste *Vehras* in the villages which are having these. In other villages, because of the lack of residential separation between schedule castes and other caste households, it was not possible to collect data on the investments in schedule caste localities.

The data reveal that the most important item of the total expenditure on Schedule Castes *Vehras*, is that on sanitation projects. Their share was as high as 48 percent in 2004-05, and 51 percent in 2005-06. Sanitation projects constitute an even larger share of expenditure in these, accounting for 66 percent of it in 2004-05 and 53 percent in 2005-06. This is not surprising in view of the emphasis being given by the State Government to sanitation projects. There is a stress on environmental improvement of these with emphasis on sanitation. Funds are being given to Village Panchayats only for the investment on the sanitation in the Scheduled Caste habitations.

The other important expenditure includes local roads (14 percent of total expenditures in 2004-05, and 16 percent in 2005-06), and schools (10 percent and 8 percent of expenditures in the two years respectively). In comparison with expenditure on sanitation projects, there is relatively less expenditure on roads for the Schedule Castes *Vehras*. Only a small component of it is being spent for schooling, mainly in the form of subsidies to their members.

To assess how much of total expenditure was incurred on the Schedule Castes *Vehras*, attention was focused on the Panchayats in which such *Vehras* exist. These appear to be relatively more prosperous in income. Therefore, these could incur an average expenditure of Rs. 1,79,155.9 and Rs. 2,28,330.3 in 2004-05 and 2005-06 respectively on various projects. Out of it the expenditure on these amounts to 44 percent and 31 in the two years. This is proportionate to their 35 percent share in the population of these Panchayats. It is not possible to say whether the Central Government mandate requires a stipulated level of investment in these which completely restrict investment to such localities and bind the allocative decisions of Panchayats, because these mandates apply only to some part of their total income. For example, the percentage expenditure on the Schedule Castes localities does not match the central government mandate that 50 percent of

Panchayat Expenditure in 2004-05 and 2005-06 in the Surveyed Gram Panchayats

Income source	*2004-05*		*2005-06*	
	Total	*In SC Vehra*	*Total*	*In SC Vehra*
Electricity projects	2,321.57 (20240.39) 1.48%	—	1,814.05 (10.735.5) 0.92%	—
Irrigation	4,471.19 (18317.82) 2.85%	—	3135.59 (15311.85) 1.59%	134.53 (2008.95) 0.22%
Drinking water	4944.89 (18958.19) 3.15%	2,145.29 (7938.73) 3.11%	8,914.58 (54617.18) 4.51%	5,402.24 (34015.46) 8.73%
Sanitation projects	75,971.90 (149596.50) 48.39%	45,514.33 (143439.90) 66.04%	101,372.60 (400660.10) 51.28%	32,511.26 (53725.46) 52.53%
Local roads	21,297.63 (77257.56) 13.56%	3,117.94 (14283.42) 4.52%	31,562.46 (119878.10) 15.97%	7,673.77 (31347.75) 12.40%
Schools & Schooling items	15,152.54 (47522.65) 9.65%	721.97 (6064.51) 1.05%	15,233.66 (46258.74) 7.71%	753.36 (6540.74) 1.22%
Health centres	2,671.19 (40882.99) 1.70%	—	1,545.09 (11459.63) 0.78%	—
Street lighting	1,953.73 (14665.90) 1.24%	713 (5619.96) 1.03%	575.25 (6579.92) 0.29%	165.92 (1460.23) 0.27%
Panchayat building	10,685,76 (36262.94) 9.34%	—	13,762.27 (34659.68) 6.96%	—
Other projects	17,540.43 (40101.31) 11.17%	16,708.52 (49816.75) -24.24	19,778.87 (47685.30) 10.00%	15,252.91 (36779.79) 24.64%
Total expenditure	157,010.40 (215521.50) 100.00%	68,921.06 (153239.40) 100.00%	197,694.40 (450527.50) 100.00%	61,894.00 (83020.80) 100.00%
Sample size	295	223	295	223

Note : Figures in brackets are standard deviations. Percentages reported are percentages to total expenditure in the respective column. All amounts are in Rupees.

Source : Field survey.

SGRY funds provided directly to the Panchayats are spent on the Scheduled Castes. However, as noted above the SGRY funds constitute only about 20 percent of total Panchayat income.

Not surprisingly, almost all the Panchayats (87 percent) reported investments on sanitation projects. Other important projects in which they spent money are schools, roads and drinking water. Even though the amount of expenditure on drinking water projects is small (approximately 3 to 5 percent of total expenditure), 31 percent of Panchayats reported such investments. The same is true for investments on electricity projects and irrigation, both of which amounted only to 2-3 percent of total expenditures. As many as 17 percent of Panchayats reported incurring of expenditures on electricity projects, and 12 percent on irrigation, which almost exclusively benefits households of the other castes. One-third (35 percent) of them reported investments on Panchayat buildings.

Most of the candidates in the elections of the Panchayat Samiti and Zila Parishad, it was found, come from relatively well-off families. Almost all the leading agriculturist families had their members in the fray. Besides this, many ministers and legislators had put up their close/blood-relations as candidates. Several members of Panchayat Samiti and Zila Parishad belong to the leading families of their respective areas. Some of them have become Chairpersons and Vice-Chairpersons of these bodies. Many of the Schedule Caste and women members also come from relatively well-off families.

Accountability in the Panchayats needs frequent interaction and communication between the community and the elected representatives. At the Panchayat level, the villagers interact among themselves informally and communicate more frequently in a face to face manner. There are several ways in which this takes place in rural communities, starting from informal gatherings in community halls, meeting in village central place; *sath*, in the agricultural fields, near the village ponds and religious places to formal meetings of Gram Sabhas. Therefore, the degree of accountability at least, in principle, should be well established in such a context. However, the empirical observations suggest otherwise. In contrast to the general principle, the informal and face to face interactions have not resulted in strengthening the accountability of elected representatives.

The interactions among the villages are mostly non-political in nature. In the course of *sath*, in the agricultural fields, community halls and other such informal places, men are more concerned about rain, market prices, daily wage rates, agricultural produce, harvesting, incurable diseases and about their personal matters than politics. The women's informal gatherings focus on family issues. But it is not always that political issues get ignored and are not talked about in the village public space. In the discussions, including the political issues, the villagers do assert their interests and rights. Therefore, the education and training of Gram Sabha members is a must for making the community more assertive for its rights and responsibilities.

PROBLEMS AND SOLUTIONS

(i) Problems

Data analysis of the empirical survey, undertaken to understand the present status of PRIs in Punjab, shows that the elected representatives of

PRIs as well as members of Gram Sabha are not satisfied with their present status due to the following reasons:

- Non-functional standing committees,
- More responsibilities, less powers,
- Interference of politicians and bureaucrats,
- Resource crunch,
- Conflictual relationships between the officials and the Chairpersons of PRIs at all the three tiers,
- Negligible role in transferred departments,
- Non-accountability of staff to elected members of Samitis,
- Insufficient honorarium,
- Encroachment of PRIs properties by influential elites under the patronage of politicians and police,
- Source income of PRIs is being squeezed due to non-cooperative behaviour of state,
- Representatives of PRIs have little administrative powers over the developmental activities,
- Instead of the elected members, the officials are being taken into confidence in the implementation of planning strategies,
- Employees of the transferred departments do not show respect/ regard to the elected members,
- Illiteracy or insufficient education among the elected members is a major hurdle. Even the educated members have very little knowledge about the accounts and technical and legal aspects of the management in the PRIs,
- Little control over the technical wing at all levels,
- Devolution of powers is only on paper. It has, as a matter of fact, adversely affected the working of transferred departments. The employees of these departments have become more lazy and non-responsive as neither the department's heads nor the PRIs have got powers of control on them in real terms,
- Women and Schedule Caste members are generally neglected in Panchayat bodies,
- Factional politics is creating hurdles in the smooth working of PRIs,
- Line departments are working parallel to Panchayat bodies, and
- Lack of capacity-building on a sustainable/regular basis.

(ii) Solutions

The representatives of PRIs suggested the following remedies to overcome the problems:

- Powers should be given as per the letter and spirit of 73rd Amendment,
- Common Property Resources of all the three tiers of PRIs should be protected,

- Role clarity in the working of seven departments transferred to the PRIs,
- Make PRIs active partners for the proper maintenance of natural resources, i.e. ground water, fertility of land, forestation, etc.,
- Make PRIs effective partners in the development of social sectors i.e. promotion of health facilities and better education,
- Although the PRIs are consulted in chalking out strategies in the fields of social security, nutritional food, rural health, rural education, yet the need of the hour is to empower them by taking people-friendly decisions in these areas. It can be possible only if funds, functions and functionaries are transferred to Panchayat bodies in the real sense,
- Neither the politicians nor the bureaucracy but only the Panchayat bodies should be taken into confidence while taking decisions for employment generation in rural areas,
- Ensure some minimum honorarium to the members of all the three tiers of PRIs,
- Lay more stress on grass roots level planning, based on multilevel decentralised planning system,
- Make the technical wing of Panchayat Department more accountable to the members of PRIs,
- Ensure an appropriate strategy for distribution of grants-both tied and untied,
- Use information technology, i.e. computerisation of the records of PRIs as the main tool for maintaining the accounts of Panchayat bodies,
- Develop a healthy atmosphere in the PRIs by promoting better cooperation and coordination among the elected members of PRIs and block and district level officials,
- Do not take the recommendations of State Finance Commissions lightly,
- Educate and activate representatives of PRIs, focusing on the Women and Scheduled Castes, through capacity-building activities,
- Arrange inter-district, inter-state and inter-country tour programmes for the members of PRIs to equip them with knowledge and information about the best practices adopted by the local self-governments in those states or countries,
- Adopt progressive political approaches to check factional politics,
- Constitute District Planning Committees, and
- Activate statutory committees of all the three tiers.

References

Report of the Expert Group on Planning at the Grassroots level" : An Action Programme for the 11th Five Year Plan, 2006, Ministry of Panchayati Raj, Government of India, New Delhi.

Report of 10th Five Year Plan Working Group, Govt. of India, New Delhi.

Singh, Sukhpal (2007), "Rural Poverty, Local Democratic Institutions and Sustainable Development of India" in book "Local Governance in India—Ideas, Challenges and Strategies", (edited by T.M. Joseph), Concept Publishing Company, New Delhi.

Challiah, Raja, J. and K.R. Sharmugan (2007), "Strategy for Poverty Reduction and Narrowing Regional Disparities", *EPW*, August 25-31.

Oommen, M.A. (2005), "Twelfth Finance Commission and Local Bodies", *EPW*, May 7-14.

Naryana, D. (2005), "*Local Governance without Capacity Building: Ten Years of Panchayati Raj*", *EPW*, June 18-25.

Kumar, Anil, Vaddiraju and Shagun Mehrotra (2004), "Making Panchayats Accountable", *EPW*, Sept., 4-11, pp. 4139-41.

Rai, Manoj *et. al.* (2001), "Gram Sabha: The People's Council, State of Panchayats: A Participatory Perspective", PRIA and Samskriti, New Delhi, pp. 77-104.

Palanithurai (2005), G., "*Panchayats: Relevance and Potential*", in "Panchayat Raj Reforms in India: Power to the People at the Grassroots", edited by D. Sundar Ram, Publisher Acedemy of Grassroots Studies and Research in India, Tirupati.

Nath, K. Chandra, and S. Mishra (1996), "Women and Grassroots Politics: Assertion of the Political Powerless, A Report," Centre for Social Research, New Delhi.

Nirmala, Buch (2000), "Women's Experience in New Panchayats: the Emerging Leadership of Rural Women", *Occasional Paper No. 35*, Centre for Development Studies, Delhi.

Statistical Abstracts of Punjab, Govt. of Punjab, Chandigarh.

Eleventh Five Year Plan (2007-12), and Annual Plan (2007-12), Department of Planning, Govt. of Punjab, Chandigarh.

1st Punjab State Finance Commission Report (2002), Govt. of Punjab, Chandigarh.

2nd *Punjab State Finance Commission Report* (2002), Govt. of Punjab, Chandigarh.

3rd Punjab Finance Commission Report (2007), Govt. of Punjab, Chandigarh.

Twelfth Central Finance Commission Report, Govt. of India, New Delhi.

Annual Plan 2006-07, Department of Punjab, Economic Adviser to Govt. of Punjab, Chandigarh.

Economic Survey of Punjab (2006-07), Economic Adviser to Govt. of Punjab, Chandigarh.

Punjab State Development Report (2003), Planning Commission, New Delhi.

Punjab Panchayati Raj Act, 1994, (2nd edition, 1998), Chawla Publications, Chandigarh.

CRRID (2007), "A Report on Fiscal Decentralization and Resource Mobilization by the Panchayats for Social Sector Development in Rural Punjab: An analysis of Efficiency and Equity Effects," submitted to the Ministry of Panchayati Raj, New Delhi.

Ministry of Panchayati Raj, Govt. of India (2006), "The State of the Panchayats—A Mid Term Review and Appraisal", Vols. I and II, New Delhi.

26

Major Trends in the Panchayati Raj System of Himachal Pradesh

MRIDULA SHARDA

This brief paper is a modest attempt to discuss the major trends that have emerged in the Panchayati Raj System of Himachal Pradesh after the 73rd Amendment to the Indian Constitution accorded a constitutional status to the scheme of democratic decentralisation in 1992. It may be mentioned at the outset that these trends have been influenced by peculiar topographical, demographical, social, cultural, economic and political features of this hill state located in the north-western India.

The State Government has devolved powers, functions and responsibilities relating to 15 departments covering 27 subjects out of 29 mentioned in the 11th Schedule of the Constitution to the PRIs on 31st July, 1996 to strengthen the democracy at the grassroots level and to make them viable institutions of self-governance. Besides, it has been delegating powers to the PRIs specially to the Gram Sabha and the Gram Panchayat from time to time through administrative orders. These have been assigned the functions of micro-level planning, monitoring of various works, selection of beneficiaries and have also been given more taxation powers.

But the performance of the PRIs in Himachal Pradesh has not been very encouraging over the years. Although, it is mandatory on the part of Gram Panchayats to perform statutory functions, a study conducted by State Finance Commission has revealed that few of them have been performing these. Main statutory functions performed by the Gram Panchayats are the maintenance of paths and construction of toilets and drains. But only 41.5% out of 2910 Panchayats have performed these functions. The main reason for this lack of performance has been the shortage of funds and staff at their disposal.

The information on the devolved functions too depicts a dismal picture. The data from 2000 to 2005 reveal that an insignificant number of Gram Panchayats have been performing these functions. They are mainly confined to the construction of school buildings and other works, the funds for which have been given to them by the State Government.

But despite all this, people in the State are optimistic regarding functional aspects of the PRIs. They consider these as the base of the democratic edifice. They also regard them as the basic organs for rural development. They feel that the government would not be able to achieve the goal of the rural development without their active involvement. But the empirical evidence is contrary to it.

The District Panchayat Officers continue to act in a biased manner. In some cases, they have even suspended the Pradhans of the Gram Panchayats to appease the MLAs of ruling party. It happened in two cases when the Congress was the ruling party in the State. There has been little change in this context after the BJP came to power in 2007. Even the Deputy Commissioners, who have been given a key role in the decentralised rural governance of the state, do not take the needed interest in development activities. In case of technocrats, it has been observed that developmental funds are not used by them in a genuine manner. As a result, corruption level has been increasing day-by-day. As a matter of fact, the bureaucrats, technocrats as well as the elected representatives have all been involved in corrupt practices.

Besides, the other retrograde trends that have emerged after the 73rd Amendment are the criminal incidents during elections, increased groupism in various Panchayati Raj bodies and misutilisation of powers by their leaders.

It is encouraging that the District Planning Committee, with Pradhan of the Zila Parishad as its Chairperson, has been constituted in the state. It has been assigned the function of preparing the plans for the district as a whole on the basis of the plans submitted by the Panchayats, Panchayat Samiti, Zila Parishad and the Urban Local bodies. But the discouraging practice is that the District Planning Committees do not hold regular meetings before submitting plan proposals to the higher authorities. Moreover, there is poor coordination between rural and urban local bodies in them. As a result, the idea of decentralised planning has virtually become a failure in the State. The plan proposals under the micro-planning are initiated by the Panchayats but these proposals fail to provide the needed inputs for planning because of the lack of capacity in them.

Three State Finance Commissions have been appointed by Himachal Government. They did prepare and submit their reports but the State Governments did not take effective steps to implement these. Besides, the local bodies too have not shown any interest in adopting the measures to improve the financial position.

Another retrograde trend that has come to sharp focus is that PRI leaders are generally dominated by the bureaucrats, who are more experienced, more educated and belong to higher strata of society as compared to PRI leaders. Besides, the State Government has been given extensive powers of control over the PRIs under the Himachal Pradesh Panchayati Raj Act, 1994. These include the powers to dissolve the PRIs, to cancel the resolutions passed by them, to remove non-official members and to end deputation of government servants posted in these. Besides, it has been given the powers of inspection and access to Panchayat records. It can also hold inquiries in the affairs of Panchayats to ensure coordination and check misuse of powers. These powers have been, as has been mentioned earlier, sometimes misused.

Being the potential centres of people's power, the Panchayats have created an apprehension in the minds of bureaucracy and the political leaders at the state level that their powers will be gradually usurped by the institutions of decentralised rural governance. Hence they are not willing to share power.

An analysis of the working of Panchayati Raj System in Himachal Pradesh also shows the following trends:

- The PRIs have not as yet been able to become the third-tier of the Indian polity.
- In practice, they are still the agencies of the Central and State Governments to implement their programmes and schemes.
- The decentralisation and devolution in the fields of finances, functions and functionaries continues to be unsystematic and slow
- Ignorance and apathy of the masses are the basic causes of poor performance of the system.
- The negative attitude of the state bureaucracy has remained the major cause of failure of the system. It has not become compatible with this people-oriented system.
- Traditional institutions of caste is another factor which has been creating hindrances in the evolution of successful system of Panchayati Raj.
- Social fabric based on the male dominance has remained a hurdle in the way of gender equality. Despite their one-third reservations, the women representatives have failed to acquire their independent identity as decision-makers. It is mere proxy representation of the males of their families.
- Level of corruption has increased. In some of the cases, development works that have been completed on papers, do not exist in fact in some of the remote areas of Himachal Pradesh.
- Poor coordination among the three tiers has been one of the major reasons for their poor performance.
- Undue interference from local MLAs, MPs has also been

responsible for increased factionalism in the PRIs as well as in the villages.

- In theory, there has been emphasis on democratic decentralisation since 1994. But in practice, the entire system is still centralised.

Although, the working of 'New Panchayati Raj' has not been very impressive during the last fifteen years, a number of steps are being taken by the state governments to make the system effective. But something more is needed. In this context, the following suggestions may be considered by the State Government:

- Centralised planning and centre-sponsored schemes should be replaced by a decentralised system which prevails in the states like Kerala.
- The State Government should act as the facilitator and it should give a free hand to the local bodies to design their plans according to the local needs.
- The PRIs should be empowered to recruit their own staff and encouraged to finance their projects by raising their own resources.
- The MPs, MLAs and the representatives of the urban and rural local bodies should pool their funds. They should join hands to formulate plans and implement these effectively. This model will give real shape to the good governance. It shall increase transparency, accountability, effectiveness and participation to a great extent. The MP's constituency should be made the unit for un-decentralised micro-planning. All the rural and urban bodies of the area should submit plan proposals and these should be discussed at this level by a Committee of experts and the representative of various areas. The Committee should formulate the plan and it should be approved by the representatives. Representatives should inform their mother bodies. Then these plans should be implemented by local bodies. They should be given a free hand in implementation also. This model of decentralized system would lead to real democratic decentralisation.
- e-Governance should be encouraged. It would bring government to the door steps of the masses. It will also bring transparency, enhance accountability and check corruption. It shall also be helpful in proper monitoring, supervision and evaluation. In addition to the elementary education, government should also make knowledge of IT compulsory for the promotion of e-Governance. Since all the centre-sponsored schemes can not be suitable for Himachal Pradesh due to its specific topographic and

socio-economic structure, the state should be empowered to make suitable changes in these. For illustration, NREGA may be very successful scheme in the state like Bihar and Orissa but it does not suit Himachal Pradesh where people earn two to three hundred rupees as daily wagers.

- Report of the Third State Finance Commission indicates that the PRIs have not been interested in raising their own resource. Only the Panchayats, try to do so to some extent. The Panchayat Samitis and Zila Parishad do not levy any tax. The non-tax income from their sources is meager. Therefore, these bodies should be encouraged to raise their own resources through incentive grants.
- There should be proper coordination among the MPs and the MLAs and the representatives from rural-urban local bodes. Some mechanism needs to be developed for this purpose.
- Economic independence is basic to make the women representation effective. Local bodies should plan such projects where the women folk can work and earn in the free time. They should be given freedom to work at any time from morning till evening. But they should not be forced to work for more than five hours.
- Vocational training, according to the local needs should be imparted even to the illiterate women. They should be motivated to work in groups. Their products should be sent to markets by the Panchayats.
- Effective steps should also be taken to make the Gram Sabha effective by giving it more powers. The Panchayat should work according to the proposals made by it. It should also be made compulsory for the Panchayats to report all its decisions to Gram Sabha.
- Government as well as the NGO should take effective steps to make masses aware about the functioning of PRIs because no system can be successful without it. A drive should be launched at a large scale, otherwise no efforts of government can make the democratic decentralised rural governance system successful.

Before closing, it is pertinent to mention that the Government of Himachal Pradesh has started the process of drafting the Document on Activity Mapping in collaboration with the German Technical Mission. It has also enhanced the reservations for women in the Panchayati Raj Institutions at various levels from 33% to 50%. Both these steps may be able to strengthen the process of good governance through democratic decentralisation in Himachal Pradesh in the times to come. The stress on social development that has been made by all the governments of the state, that have been in power since its formation is likely to stand in good stead in this context.

References

Rattan Ghosh and Alok Pramanaik, *Panchayati Raj System in India*, New Delhi: Kanishka Publishers, 1999.

Census of India, 2001, H.P., Provisional Population Totals, Directorate Census Operations, Himachal Pradesh.

Jagmohan Balokhra, *The Wonderland Himachal Pradesh*, New Delhi: H.G. Publications, 1985.

Himachal Pradesh Panchayati Raj Act, 1994.

V.S. Mahjan (ed.), *Agriculture, Rural Development and Panchayati Raj: Regional Level Strategies and Policies*, Vol. II, New Delhi: Deep & Deep Publications, 1999.

O.C. Sud, *Administrative Problems of Rural Development in India*, New Delhi: Kanishka Publishers, 1992.

Ms. Sumedha Sharma, "Impact of Socio-Economic Modernisation on Political Behaviour: A Case Study of Dangri Panchayat, District Solan, H.P.", An unpublished M.Phil. Dissertation, Department of Political Science, H.P. University, Shimla, 1986.

Ram Krishan Sharma, "Changing Role of Caste in the Decision Making of Panchayats: A Case Study of Juni Panchayat, Tehsil Sunni, Shimla", Unpublished M.Phil. Dissertation, Department of Political Science, H.P. University, Shimla, 1985.

Mridula Sharda, "Organisation and Working of Panchayat Samiti, Una", Unpublished M.Phil. Dissertation Submitted to Department of Public Administration, H.P. University, Shimla, 1990.

The Report of the Third Finance Commission, 2005-06, Government of Himachal Pradesh, Shimla.

27

Structural and Functional Dimensions of Panchayati Raj in Haryana

VIMLESH RATHORE AND PARMOD CHAND

This paper is a modest attempt to describe and analyse the structure and working of the scheme of democratic decentralisation, popularly known as the Panchayati Raj in Haryana—a north western state of the Indian Union located on the threshold of the National Capital Territory of Delhi.

This seventeenth state of the Indian Union which came into existence on November 1, 1966 as a result of the linguistic reorganisation of Punjab has been able to make rapid economic development after the attainment of statehood despite the fact that it was a backward region of Punjab prior to its formation on November 1, 1966. But despite rapid economic development, Haryana lags far behind most of the states of the Indian Union in democratic decentralisation.

The state had inherited a pattern of Panchayati Raj based on the model of democratic decentralisation suggested by Balvantrai Mehta Study Team (1957) from Punjab at the time of its creation. It had a three-tier structure of Panchayati Raj with the Gram Sabha (General Body of the Voters) and the Gram Panchayat (its Executive Committee) at the village level; Panchayat Samiti at the block level, and the Zila Parishad at the district level.

The Gram Panchayat had been given civic, developmental and petty judicial functions. The Panchayat Samiti had been given the role of planning and its implementation. The Zila Parishad was made advisory, supervisory and coordinating body.

But the three-tier structure of the Panchayati Raj was made a two-tier structure in 1973 by abolishing the Zila Parishad. Besides, the Panchayati Raj

Institutions had been further weakened in the State due to gradual erosion in their powers, depletion in their resources owing to reduction of government grants and the creation of the District Rural Development Agency for the implementation of the rural development programmes of the Government of India.

However, the enactment of the 73rd Amendment Act (1993) not only constitutionalised the Panchayati Raj Institutions but also listed 29 items in the Eleventh Schedule, the power on which was to be devolved by the state legislatures on the Panchayati Raj Institutions.[1]

Besides, the Act provided for the State Finance Commission to ensure adequate resources for the Panchayati Raj Institutions and the State Election Commission to ensure direct, free and regular Panchayati Raj elections after every five year term. Moreover, reservation of one-third membership and offices has been made for the women at all the levels. The reservations have also been made for the Scheduled Castes/Tribes in accordance with their proportion of the population. It has also enabled the states to provide the reservation to the Backward Classes in the Panchayati Raj Institutions.

The Panchayati Raj Institutions were to become institutions of Self-Government under the 73rd Amendment Act. These were to perform the role of making and implementing plans of economic development and social justice. Besides, they could also implement the programmes of the rural development of the Government of India and the State Government and exercise such powers as were given to them by the state legislatures.

Haryana enacted the Haryana Panchayati Raj Act, 1994, for implementing the 73rd Amendment Act. The elections to the Panchayati Raj Institutions were held in 1994, 2000, and 2005. In other words, the structure of Panchayati Raj created by the Haryana Panchayati Raj Act, 1994 has been working for the last 15 years.

However, the pattern of its structure and working has assumed a peculiar character due to the specificities of the historical, social, cultural, economic administrative and political environment of the state. This paper seeks to discuss the same.

SURVEY OF THE EXISTING LITERATURE

For giving our study the needed perspective and for getting a roadmap for the description and analysis of the structure and working of Panchayati Raj in Haryana, we have reviewed the following studies on this theme:

Mahipal (1996)[2] has critically analysed the Haryana Panchayati Raj Act, 1994. He has criticized it on account of the fact that the Act has given power to the state government to revoke any resolution of the PRIs on the ground that it is against the public interest. He has concluded that instead of decentralisation of powers to the PRIs, the Act has centralized the powers in the hands of state government.

Surat Singh (1996)[3] has criticized the Haryana Panchayati Raj Act, 1994 on the ground that there are serious defects in the new legislation.

According to him, the Act has not made a clear-cut distribution of powers among the institutions at the three levels. Besides, the provision of no-confidence motion against the Chairman of the Panchayat Samiti and President of the Zila Parishad has made their position rather unstable.

In his second study, Surat Singh (1998)[4] has observed that the PRIs in Haryana have not been able to work in accordance with the spirit of 73rd Amendment Act. He has pointed out that the schedule caste and women members of these bodies have not been able to perform their duties properly on account of lack of political consciousness. He has suggested that they should be given required training. Besides, he has also suggested that provision should be made in the Haryana Panchayati Raj Act, 1994 for punishing those males who attend meetings in place of the women members. Lastly, he has pointed out that Zila Parishad has emerged as the most ineffective body among the PRIs.

In his third write-up, Surat Singh (2004)[5] has made an empirical study of six Gram Sabhas of Kurukshetra and Karnal districts. He has found that their meetings are not being attended by adequate number of members. He has also made concrete suggestions for making the meetings of the Gram Sabha meaningful.

In one of his studies, Ranbir Singh (1995)[6] has observed that the Haryana Panchayati Raj Act 1994 broadly resembles the 73rd Amendment Act in its form. It has established a three-tier system of PRIs with the Gram Panchayat at the village level, Panchayat Samiti at the block level and the Zila Parishad at the district level. But, the Act has violated the sprit of 73rd Amendment by establishing tight control of the state government over these bodies.

In another study, Ranbir Singh (2000)[7] has analysed the working of PRIs in Haryana. He has pointed out that the elections of the PRIs were not contested on party basis. However, the party cadres took keen interest in the elections of the Sarpanches of Gram Panchayats, the Chairmen of Panchayat Samitis and the Presidents of the Zila Parishads.

In yet another study, Ranbir Singh (2008)[8] has argued that the Haryana Panchayati Raj Act, 1994 has failed to empower the PRIs. Even the Notification of 1995 and the Instructions of 2000-2001 could not devolve function, functionaries and funds on these. He has expressed the hope that the Document on Activity Mapping (2006) may bring about some improvement in this context. According to him, recommendations of the State Finance Commissions have not been fully implemented and that there has been no real transfer of powers to these institutions.

Amit Jha (2004)[9] has found that devolution of functions, funds and functionaries has been an important feature of the PRIs during the period 1995-2002. He has, however, argued that the role of Gram Sabha and PRIs in planning needs to be enhanced by giving them untied grants on the Kerala pattern and through capacity-building.

K.K. Mor (2004)[10] has analysed the management of common property resources by the Gram Panchayats in Haryana. He has argued that this should be included in the agenda of Gram Sabha meetings by the Gram Panchayats for making it more effective.

Raj Singh and Chander Bhan (2004)[11] have examined PRIs in Haryana from a politico-legal perspective. According to them, the transfer of funds, functions and functionaries to these Institutions is inadequate in this state. They have argued that the role of the PRIs has been undermined not only by the Village Development Committees (VDCs) but also by the powers given to the bureaucracy in the Haryana Panchayati Raj Act, 1994.

D.P. Singh Mor (2004)[12] in his study on the PRIs in Haryana, based on perspective of the discipline of Social Work, highlighted the issues of gender discrimination, caste inequalities and election sponsorship, non-involvement of NGOs, negative role of Khap Panchayats and the emergence of Village Development Committees (VDCs) as parallel bodies. These, according to him, have been the major hurdles in the way of the strengthening of the PRIs.

S.P. Sinha (2004)[13] has found that the VDCs have not weakened the PRIs. According to him, these 'work in unison with the community at large'. These keep a constant watch on development works and perform the role of social audit. The VDCs, according to him, are not rivals but partners in the process of development at grassroots.

S.S. Malik (2004)[14] has described the structure and functions of the PRIs from the perspective of the discipline of Public Administrative. He has expressed the view that the elected representatives are unable to perform their role on account of their ignorance about the rules and regulations of the government.

An overview of the above review, however, makes it clear that despite these valuable contributions, there remains a need for a more comprehensive study on the structure and working of the PRIs in Haryana. This paper is an attempt in that direction.

THE OBJECTIVES OF THE STUDY

1. To discuss the features of the structure of Panchayati Raj Institutions in Haryana.
2. To describe the powers that have been devolved by the Notification of 1995.
3. To trace the extension in these powers by the Instructions of 2000-01.
4. To discuss the impact of the Document on Activity-Mapping (2006) on the devolution of functions, functionaries and funds on the PRIs.
5. To make suggestions for the strengthening of the PRIs in Haryana.

METHODOLOGY

This study is based on descriptive-*cum*-analytical approach. It is also based on a historical/evolutionary/development perspective in the sense that it seeks to discuss the evolution of Panchayati Raj in Haryana from 1994 to 2007. Archival method has been used for data collection in this study instead of using the survey research techniques due to the constraints of time and resources.

The data used in this study are mainly secondary in character as these have been collected from the unpublished reports, books and research articles published in the journals. However, it has been cross-checked through the primary data gathered from the in-depth discussions with the leading experts on the PRIs in Haryana. Moreover, the researchers have also made use of participatory observation by taking advantage of their role as a Resource Person and as a Trainer respectively in the training programmes organized by the Haryana Institute of Rural Development, Nilokheri for the Capacity-building of the elected representatives of PRIs in 2003-04 and 2006-07.

FINDINGS

1. The Haryana Panchayati Raj Act (1994) has made the Gram Sabha as the General Body of the Gram Panchayat and has given it an important role. It has made the Gram Panchayat responsible to the Gram Sabha. But the working of this institution shows that either the meetings of Sabha are not held or these are very poorly attended because of the apathy of the people and the attitude of the Sarpanches.
2. The members of the Gram Panchayats, Panchayat Samitis and the Zila Parishads are directly elected. The Sarpanch of the Gram Panchayat is also elected directly. However, the Chairperson of the Panchayat Samiti and the President of the Zila Parishads are indirectly elected.
3. One-third membership and offices have been reserved for women at all the three levels. Provision has also been made for the reservations for the Scheduled Castes in proportion to their population. But the Backward Classes have been given only token representation.
4. The women have been able to get adequate representation but empowerment continues to elude them. The male members of the families (the husband and the sons) act on their behalf. This is on account of the fact that Haryana has a male dominated, traditional and conservative society in the rural areas despite the rapid economic development that it has made after its formation on November 1, 1966. Like women, the Scheduled Castes have been able to get adequate representation due to reservations. But they too do not have the powers in the PRIs because the rural society of Haryana remains semi-feudal. It continues to be dominated by the landowning castes.

5. The provision of vote of no-confidence against the Chairpersons of the Panchayati Samitis and Presidents of Zila Parishads has made their position rather unstable. However, the position of the Sarpanch has been stabilised by making her/his removal rather difficult.
6. The Gram Panchayat and Panchayat Samiti have been given a long list of duties but the Zila Parishad has been made merely an advisory, coordinating and supervising body. Moreover, the duties of the Gram Panchayats and Panchayat Samitis have not been differentiated.
7. The Gram Panchayats, Panchayat Samitis and Zila Parishads have been given powers of raising financial resources. But these have been reluctant to exercise these powers. While the Gram Panchayats are able to have some resources of their own through the auction or lease of Village Common Land, the Panchayat Samitis and the Zila Parishads do not have much income.
8. The Gram Sachiv, the Block Development and Panchayat Officer and the Additional Deputy Commissioner have been made the Executive Officers at the Gram Panchayat, Panchayat Samiti and the Zila Parishad levels respectively but their Chairpersons have not been given any control over them.
9. The provision has been made for the setting up of the Committees at all the three levels. But these have remained defunct not only in the Gram Panchayats and Panchayat Samitis but also in the Zila Parishads.
10. The District Planning Committees have been constituted. But these continue to exist only on paper. Actually the District Plan is prepared by the District Administration and the District Planning Committee which is headed by the Deputy Commissioner merely ratifies it.
11. The State Finance Commission has been created but their reports have been implemented only partially.
12. There are Panchayats (Gram Panchayats, Panchayat Samitis and Zila Parishads) at the village, block and the district levels) in Haryana but these have no Raj as they have virtually no powers. These are under the tight control of the political leadership and the bureaucracy because strong control has been provided to the Government and the District Administration over the Panchayati Raj Institutions under the Act.
13. The Notification of 1995 for the devolution of powers pertaining to 16 departments on the PRIs remained only on the paper. Even the extension in these powers by the Instructions of 2000-01 failed to make any difference. The PRI got neither functions nor

functionaries not funds despite the Notification of 1995 and the Instructions of 2000-01 due to lack of political will and hostility of bureaucracy.

14. The Document on Activity-Mapping (2006) is a distinct improvement on the Notification of 1995 and the Instructions of 2000-01. It has certainly given some functions, functionaries and funds to the PRIs pertaining to ten departments. However, it too remains unimplemented and the empowerment continues to be denied to the elected representatives of the PRIs due to the lack of political will and the continuation of the old mindset of the bureaucracy.

CONCLUSION

The above findings lead to the logical conclusion that the institutional framework of the Haryana Panchayati Raj follows the letter of the 73rd Constitutional Amendment (1993) but grossly violates its spirit. The scrutiny of the structure and working of the Panchayati Raj Institutions shows that Haryana continues to have a centralised decentralisation instead of democratic decentralisation.

This dismal situation has to be ascribed to the lack of political will for devolution of functions, funds and functionaries to the PRIs. It is pertinent to mention here that Haryana has got a highly centralized and personalised political system. The hostility of bureaucracy and technocracy too has been a major barrier in this context. Besides, the lack of capacity-building of the elected representatives is also responsible for this situation. The elected representatives too have never put pressure on the Haryana Government for devolution of powers. The weakness of civil society could also be blamed for it.

SUGGESTIONS

Accordingly, the following suggestions are being made in this paper to strengthen the PRIs for the genuine democratic decentralisation through the empowerment of the PRIs:

1. The Haryana Panchayati Raj Act (1994) needs to be amended. There must be a clear-cut differentiation of the functions between Gram Panchayats and the Panchayat Samitis. The Zila Parishad too should be given some powers.
2. The tight system of control of the Government over the PRIs be replaced by the control of semi-judicial and independent authorities like Ombudsman at the district level.
3. Special capacity-building programmes should be organized for women and the Scheduled Castes representatives of the PRIs.

4. Pressure be built by the civil society on the political leadership and the bureaucracy to change their mindset
5. Functional literacy programmes be carried out for the illiterate representatives of PRIs by the National Literacy Mission as a part of its programme of Continuing Education.
6. Land reforms be introduced for bringing about a change in the neo-feudal economic structure of Haryana.
7. Efforts should also be made for changing the culture of rural Haryana. The NGOs, the Media and the Academia will have to join hands in this endeavour.

Notes and References

1. For details, refer to Dalia Goswami, "Evolution of Panchayati Raj in Haryana", M.Phil Dissertation (unpublished), Directorate of Correspondence Courses, Kurukshetra University, 1996.
2. Mahipal, Centralised Decentralisation, "Haryana Panchayati Raj Act, 1994", *Economic & Political Weekly*, July 16, 1996.
3. Surat Singh, "Haryana, New Panchayati Raj Legislation: A Critical Review", *Journal of Rural Development*, Vol. 14, No. 1, 1995.
4. Surat Singh, "Empowerment of Women Representatives in Panchayati Raj, A Profile from Haryana", *Kurukshetra*, Vol. 52, No. 19, 2004.
5. Surat Singh, "Working of Gram Sabha, The Haryana Experience" in Surat Singh (ed.), *Decentralised Governance in India : Myth or Reality*, Deep & Deep Publications, Delhi, 2004, pp. 359-67.
6. Ranbir Singh, "Haryana, in George Mathew (ed.), "*Status of Panchayati Raj in the States of India*", *1994*, Concept Publishing Company, New Delhi, 1995.
7. Ranbir Singh, "Haryana" in George Mathew (ed.), "*Status of Panchayati Raj in the States of and Union Territories of India*", *2000*, Concept Publishing Company, New Delhi, 2000.
8. Ranbir Singh, "Reforming Panchayati Raj Institutions in Haryana", *Panchayati Raj Update*, June, 2008.
9. Amit Jha, "Devolution of Powers and Functions to the Panchayati Raj Institutions in Haryana". Surat Singh (ed.), *op. cit*, pp. 351-58.
10. K.K. Mor, "Panchayats and Management of Common Property Resources in Haryana", *Ibid.*, pp. 368-74.
11. Raj Singh and Chander Bhan, "Strengthening PRIs in Haryana—A Political-Legal Perspective", *Ibid.*, pp. 375-81.
12. D.P. Singh Mor, "Strengthening Panchayats in Haryana—Challenges to be Met", *Ibid.*, pp. 382-86.
13. S.P. Sinha. "Development at Micro Level, The Role of Village Development Committees in Haryana", *Ibid.*, pp. 404-10.
14. S.S. Malik, "Panchayati Raj System in Haryana : An Evaluation", *Ibid*, pp. 388-96.

PART V

Democratic Decentralisation and Women Empowerment

28

Genesis and Development of Women Empowerment in India

JAGROOP KAUR

This brief paper is a modest attempt to discuss evolution of empowerment of women in India through a study of the impact of the scheme of democratic decentralisation suggested by Balvantray Mehta Study Team (1957) which was institutionalised in the form of Panchayati Raj and constitutionalised by the 73rd Constitutional Amendment Act (1992).

It has been divided into the following parts:

1. Status of women empowerment before the introduction of the scheme of democratic decentralisation in 1959.
2. The impact of its introduction on it.
3. The status of women empowerment after the 73rd Amendment.
4. Conclusions and suggestions.

I

The makers of Indian Constitution had resolved to empower the women, who had a subordinate status during the colonial period on account of historical reasons and cultural factors, in view of the significant role that they had played in the freedom struggle after their mobilisation by Mahatma Gandhi in the Civil Disobedience Movement in 1931. Another factor that made the Constitution-makers to make provisions for the empowerment of women was that most of them had been able to imbibe the values of liberal democracy which advocates it.

The empowerment of the women was implicit in the Preamble of the Indian Constitution in the promise to secure justice, social, economic and political; equality of status and opportunity; and assuring dignity of the individual.

It was to achieve the above objectives that the provision was made in the Chapter on Fundamental Rights which included the Right to Equality—including equality before law (Article 14), prohibition of discrimination on grounds of religion, race, caste, sex or place of work (Article 17) and equality of opportunity in matter of public employment (Article 16).

The empowerment of women was also promised in the Chapter on Directive Principles of State Policy. It was inherent in Article 38 which provides:

(i) The State shall strive to promote the welfare of the people by securing and protecting, as effectively as it may, a social order in which justice, social, economic and political, shall inform all the institutions of the national life.

(ii) The State shall in particular strive to minimize inequalities in income and endeavour to eliminate inequalities in status, facilities and opportunities, not only amongst individuals but also among groups of people residing in different areas or engaged in different vocations.

Article-39 was more specific in this context. It provides that the State shall in particular direct its policy towards securing the following principles:

(a) that the citizens, men and women equally, have the right to an adequate means of livelihood;

(b) that the ownership and control of the material resources of the community are so distributed as best to subserve the common good;

(c) that the operation of the economic system does not result in the concentration of wealth and means of production to the common detriment;

(d) that there is equal pay for equal work for both men and women;

(e) that the health and strength of workers, men and women, and the tender age of children are not abused and that citizen are not forced by economic necessity to enter avocations unsuited to their age or strength;

(f) that children are given opportunities and facilities to develop in a healthy manner and in conditions of freedom and dignity and that childhood and youth are protected against exploitation and against moral and material abandonment.

But, in spite of the above mandate of the Constitution, the women remained un-empowered at all the levels. Although, the women had been enfranchised and had also been empowered to contest for Lok Sabha and Vidhan Sabha elections, their representation in these bodies never reached even upto 10% despite the fact that they constitute almost 50% of India's population. This happened because they were not given reservations in the elections. The position was no better in the Gram Panchayats that had been set-up in various states after the 1952 general elections. Here too, they had been given right to vote and the right to contest elections, but their representation was almost negligible. Very few women had come forward to contest elections to the Gram Panchayats and hardly any one of them could be elected as Sarpanches in the Gram Panchayats. However, some of them were co-opted as Panches because various acts had provided that if women candidates contest election, the candidate getting higher votes among them was to be declared as elected to the Gram Panchayats. But, if no women contested Panchayat election, one woman was to be co-opted by the members of Gram Panchayats. This gave women bare nominal representation in these institutions of grassroots governance. (H.D. Malviya, *Village Panchayats in India*, Economic and Political Department, All India Congress Committee, New Delhi, 1956).

II

The situation remained more or less unchanged even after the introduction of the scheme of democratic decentralisation, as already mentioned, on the recommendation of Balvantray Mehta Study Team (1957). The Study Team had been appointed by the Committee on Plan Projects of the Planning Commission with the following terms of reference:

1. To find out the reasons for the failure of the Community Development Programme.
2. To suggest the ways and means to streamline its functioning.
3. To find out whether the existing institutions of rural local self-government such as the Gram Panchayats, District Boards, Rural Boards and School Boards, could be used for making the implementation of Community Development Programme effective.
4. To suggest an alternate system of rural local-self-government in case the above institutions are found to be inadequate.

The Study Team concluded that the Community Development Programme had failed because it was being implemented by bureaucracy and hence it could not enlist mass support or generate popular enthusiasm for itself. Therefore, the team suggested a scheme of democratic decentralisation in which the Gram Panchayats were to be set-up at village level, Panchayat Samiti at the block level and the Zila Parishad at the district level. These were to be democratically elected and organically linked. While the Panchayat Samiti was to undertake the task of planning, the Gram

Panchayat was to do its implementation. The Zila Parishad was supposed to act as a coordinating, supervising and advising body. (*Report of the Team for the Study of Community Projects and the National Extension Service*, Government of India, Delhi, 1959).

This scheme was given the name of Panchayati Raj at the time of its inauguration on October 2, 1959 by Pandit Jawaharlal Nehru, the then Prime Minister of India, at Nagaur, Rajasthan. Although the Panchayati Raj was set-up in almost all the states, no provision was made for the reservation for women in the Gram Panchayats, Panchayat Samitis and Zila Parishads. The only exceptions were Karnataka and Andhra Pradesh. The Karnataka Act provided for reservation of two seats for women at both the Village and Taluka levels. The Andhra Pradesh Act provided for the reservation of one seat for women in the Gram Panchayat if the total strength of Panchayat was seven or less and two seats if the total seats were nine or more. Similarly, two women were to be included in the Zila Panchayat constituted under the State Panchayat Act. The Panchayati Raj Acts of other states did provide for a system of cooption of women in Gram Panchayats, Panchayat Samitis and Zila Parishads which enabled women to get merely notional representation but no real representation. (G. Ram Reddy, *Pattern of Panchayati Raj in India*, Macmillan Company of India Ltd., New Delhi, 1978). It was this dismal state of affairs that made Professors Iqbal Narain and V.M. Sirsikar, who were studying the issue of women's political participation for the Committee on the Status of Women in India, Towards Equality (1974), to observe that there is a wide gap between symbolism and actuality. They rightly concluded that the political rights have failed to bring about the desired changes in the empowerment of women.

However, a highly laudable initiative was taken in Karnataka in 1983. The Karnataka Zila Panchayat, Taluka Panchayat Samitis, Mandal Panchayats and Nyaya Panchayats Act of 1983 provided for the reservation of 25% seats for women in both the Zila Panchayats and Mandal Panchayats. It was indeed a bold step in the direction of empowerment of women in the Panchayati Raj Institutions. Perhaps, it was this path-breaking step that inspired Rajiv Gandhi, the then Prime Minister of India to advocate the cause of reservations for women for making the Panchayat Raj Institutions inclusive in character.

The 64th Constitutional Amendment Bill presented by him in Lok Sabha in 1989 stated that 30% seats be reserved for women in the Panchayats at all the levels. The Bill also made provision for the reservation of one out of the two seats reserved for the scheduled castes and scheduled tribes for women. However, it left it to the state legislatures to decide whether the office of Chairperson has to be reserved for them or not. But this Amendment Bill failed to get two-third support in Rajya Sabha and hence could not become an Act. However, despite this, Orissa, Maharashtra and Kerala made provision of 30% reservation for women in the membership of the Panchayats at various levels.

Thus, we find that women could not be empowered in the Panchayati Raj Institutions even after the introduction of the scheme of democratic decentralisation, popularly known as the Panchayati Raj. The only exceptions were the states of Karnataka, Orissa, Maharashtra and Kerala. Even in these states, the women had been empowered more than three decades after the introduction of Panchayati Raj. (Nirmala Buch, "Panchayats and Women" in George Mathew (ed.), *Status of Panchayati Raj in the States and Union Territories of India, 2000*, Concept Publishing House and Institute of Social Sciences, New Delhi, 2000).

III

The enactment of 73rd Constitutional Amendment Act (1992) which inserted in the Constitution Part-IX and the 11th Schedule, could be legitimately regarded as a great landmark in the process of the empowerment of women. It made the following provisions in Article 243-D:

1. Not less than one-third (including the number of seats reserved for women belonging to the scheduled caste and the scheduled tribes) of the total number of seats to be filled by direct election in every Panchayat shall be reserved for women.
2. Not less than one-third of the total number of offices of Chairpersons of the Panchayats at each level shall be reserved for women.

It had the desired effect. This is evident from the fact that the women now have 975116 out of 26564476 seats in Gram Panchayats, 58094 out of 156609 in Panchayat Samitis and 5779 out of 156987 in Zila Parishads. Thus the women have been able to get more than 33% share of representation in the Panchayati Raj Institutions at various levels. They also occupy more than one-third offices of Chairpersons at the three levels (*The State of Panchayats, A Mid-Term Review and Appraisal*, 22 November, 2006, Vol. III, Ministry of Panchayati Raj, GOI, Krishi Bhawan, New Delhi).

However, the above figures should not push us to conclude that the empowerment of women in the Panchayati Raj Institutions has become a reality. There has, indeed, taken place a quantum jump in their representation. However, the goal of empowerment has remained, largely, elusive so for. The power is exercised by the male members of their families in case of the most of the women Chairpersons, Vice-Chairpersons and Members at various levels. There are very few exceptions. Only those women office bearers/members have been able to become really empowered who are educated and articulate and enjoy political patronage of the powerful political leaders at the state level.

The above hypothesis has been fully substantiated by the following studies on the impact of the 73rd Amendment on the empowerment of women:

E.K. Shanta, (*Political Participation of Women in Panchayati Raj*, Institute of Social Sciences, New Delhi, 1999) has found on the basis of her field study of Haryana, Kerala and Tamilnadu that there has been greater empowerment of women in terms of political participation in Kerala than in Tamilnadu and Haryana. However, the situation is relatively better in Tamilnadu than Haryana. According to her, the greater empowerment of women in Kerala has to be ascribed to the higher level of female literacy and to the impact of social reform movements. On the other hand, the situation is not encouraging in Haryana because female literacy is low and social reform movements are conspicuous by their absence. In Tamilnadu, the status in above respect is higher than that of Haryana but lower than that of Kerala because female literacy there is higher than Haryana but lower than Kerala. And social reform movements have been stronger than Haryana but weaker than Kerala.

Prabhjot Kaur (The Impact of 73rd Amendment on Women's Political Empowerment: A Study of Punjab, in Surat Singh (ed.), *Decentralised Governance in India: Myth and Reality*, Deep & Deep Publications, Pvt. Ltd., 2004) has found that majority of women representatives in Punjab, particularly Jats, belong to the families of Ex-Sarpanches or Panches. This has strengthened the grip of the existing rural elite. She also observed that as a result of socio-cultural factors, the real power remains in the hands of men-folk.

Arun Chaturvedi ("Working of Panchayati Raj in Rajasthan: A Review", in *Ibid.*) has found that the performance of women members in the PRIs has been a mixed bag with many success stories as well as problem areas. The social bias against women continues and the women representatives have the feeling that they were being harassed by officials because they are women.

S.S. Sree Kumar ("Women Empowerment through Panchayati Raj Institutions: A Study", *the Grassroots Governance Journal*, Vol. IV, No. 1, June 2006) has found that with the passing of the 73rd Amendment Act, almost all the states in India have enacted statutes to establish the new pattern of Panchayati Raj System. These institutions work as pillars for citizen participation in development administration in rural India. Advent of the new set-up at the local level has increased people's participation especially that of the women at the grassroots level. However, empowerment in the real sense would be attained only when women are actively induced in the larger struggle for social change.

Jagendra Kumar Das ("Women in the Panchayati Raj Institutions: An Empirical Study in Kamrup District of Assam", *Ibid.*) has found on the basis of empirical data that majority of the women incumbents, according to their own perception, have been fully taking part in the decision-making process in the PRIs. They are very much interested in rendering their services to the rural people. Men do not suppress the women and allow them to play the necessary role in grassroots movement. The women leaders have been successful in working for the rural poor women by organising them in Self-Help Groups.

IV

Thus, it may be concluded that despite the constitutional provisions, women remained unempowered not only in National and State Legislatures but also in the Panchayats before the introduction of the scheme of democratic decentralisation. Even that made little difference except in states like Karnataka, Orissa, Maharashtra, and Kerala. The 73rd Amendment has brought about a quantitative change of great magnitude. However, the qualitative change is still to be brought about. The long-term solution for the empowerment of women is dependent on a radical change in the social, cultural, economic and political environment of rural society which has been acting as a barrier in the way of the genuine empowerment of women in the Panchayati Raj Institutions in spite of an astronomical increase in their representation as a result of the above mentioned Amendment. The short-term remedy lies in their capacity-building by organising foundation and refresher courses for the elected women representatives of the Panchayati Raj Institutions. Besides, functional literacy courses need to be organised for illiterate among them by the National Literacy Mission as a part of its Continuing Education Programme. Moreover, it will be useful to organise special training programmes for them because they are reluctant to participate in an active manner in the presence of their male counterparts. Lastly, networking among women representatives should be encouraged and their associations and federations should be created at various levels for attaining the goal of women empowerment.

29

Women Empowerment, the National Perspective

S.K. SINGH

The 73rd Amendment to the Indian Constitution sought to empower the women in the Panchayati Raj Institutions. It inserted Article 243D which provided them one-third reservation at all the levels of Panchayati Raj Institutions. This also included the one-third of the seats to be reserved for the scheduled castes and the scheduled tribes in proportion to their population at various levels.

This paper attempts to discuss the impact of these provisions on the empowerment of women, who are also included in the deprived sections, marginalised sections and the weaker sections. It has been divided into four parts. The first demystifies the concept of empowerment, the second describes the findings of the study of Ministry of Panchayati Raj, Government of India, the *State of Panchayats a Mid Term Review and Appraisal* (2006); the third gives the findings of the *Study on Elected Women Representatives in Panchayati Raj Institutions* (2008) and the last makes the concluding observations.

I

Empowerment is a complex phenomenon and it entails radical social transformation for common/ordinary citizen. People in all walks of life often have difficult choices to make. But for some of them, the range of options is more restricted than the others. In rural areas, women have limited choices available to them. They are socio-economically an underprivileged section. They have limited employment opportunities and little voice in decision-making on the distribution of locally available resources. They suffer from inequality in terms of the power to change their lives. The scheduled caste women are even more disempowered than other women. Some of the reasons for the disempowerment have been illustrated below.

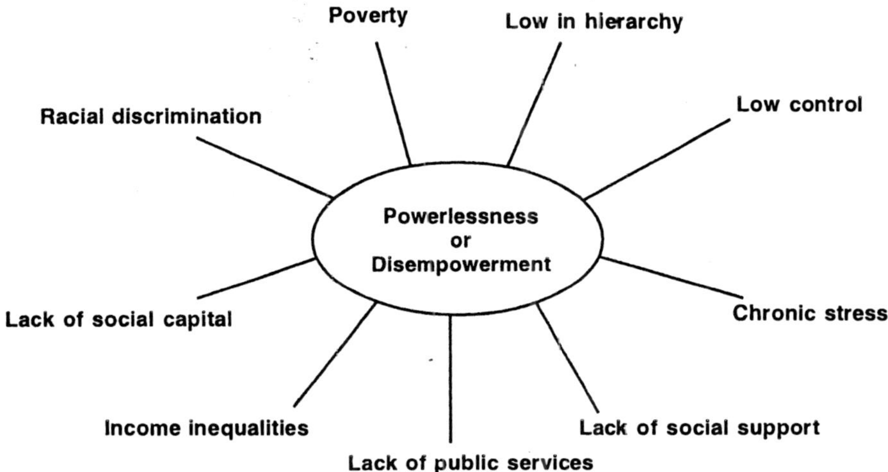

To overcome this grim scenario, *empowerment* has become a familiar term with the international development agencies, governments and the civil society. Empowerment objectives appear with increasing frequency in the policy documents issued by governments, especially on the strategies dealing with poverty reduction.

Now, let us see how empowerment has been defined by different scholars and various orgnisations:

> "Empowerment is a multi-dimensional social process that helps people gain control over their own lives. It is a process that fosters power (that is, the capacity to implement) in people, for use in their own lives, their communities, and in their society, by acting on issues that they define as important." (Nanette Page and Cheryl E. Czuba, 1999).

According to this definition, three components are basic to the understanding of empowerment. The empowerment is multi-dimensional as it occurs in sociological, psychological, economic, and political processes. It also occurs at various levels, such as individual, group, and community. Empowerment, by definition, is also a social process, since it occurs in relationship to others. This is a process that is similar to a path or journey that one covers as she/he works through it. Other aspects of empowerment may vary according to the specific context and people involved, but these remain constant. In addition, one important implication of this definition of empowerment is that the individual and community are fundamentally inter-connected.

According to World Bank, "Empowerment is the process of increasing the capacity of individuals or groups to make choices and to transform those choices into desired actions and outcomes."

Central to this process are the actions which build both individual and collective assets, and improve the efficiency and fairness of the organisational and institutional contexts which govern the use of these assets. Here the assets are psychological, informational, organisational, material, social, financial and human. These assets predict an individual's or group's ability to make purposeful choices—that is that they are able to envisage and purposefully chose the options.

An individual may be able to choose options, but the effective realization of those choices will largely depend upon the opportunity structure or the institutional context within which the individual or group lives and works. The opportunity structure comprises those institutions that govern people's behaviour and that influence the success or failure of the choices that they make. Institutions can be formal or informal. Formal institutions include the sets of rules, laws, and regulatory frameworks that govern the operation of political processes, public services, private organisations, and markets. Informal institutions include the 'unofficial' rules that structure incentives and govern relationships within organisations such as bureaucracies, firms, or industries, as well as the informal cultural practices, value systems, and norms of behaviour that operate in the households or among the social groups or communities.

In other words, empowerment invokes human rights, basic needs, economic security, capacity-building, skill formation and conditions to lead a dignified social existence. It also refers to power, authority and legitimacy. The empowerment is creating popular knowledge and questioning the monopoly of the dominant paradigm. It is the only effective answer to oppression, exploitation, injustice and other maladies prevailing in the society. There are various types of empowerment—legal, economic, political, cultural, human, social, etc.

Since empowerment is context-driven, so specifically for this paper, we will consider empowerment as assured representation of the 'women' in elected rural local institutions in order to assure their participation.

II

According to the first study that has been referred to in the introduction of the paper, there took place a quantum jump in the representation of the women in the Panchayati Raj Institutions as a result of the 73rd Constitutional Amendment Act (1992).

They had only nominal representation prior to the above mentioned Act. But now they have been able to get 36.75% representation. It was 3.09%

higher than that provided under the Amendment. It proved this apprehension wrong that the one-third seats reserved for women shall not be filled up because they shall not come forward for contesting the elections. It was all the more encouraging to note that this phenomenon of women empowerment was visible at all the three levels. They got 36.75% representation in the village panchayats, 36.79% share in the intermediate panchayats and 36.98% presence in the Zila Panchayats.

The radical transformation of the Panchayati Raj Institutions through reservations has not only made these inclusive but has also deepened and broadened the democracy. It has ended the hegemony of the males of the high castes in the Panchayati Raj Institutions. It has also made Panchayati Raj Institutions fit for performing the role of inclusive development because the women representatives could ensure that they are able to get their due share in the process of rural development.

III

The second study highlighted the positive impact of the enhanced representation of women on their empowerment. It brought to the sharp focus the perceived benefits that accrued to the women because of their entry into the system of Panchayati Raj. The study reported that about 79% of women representatives informed about their enhanced self-esteem and 67% of women expressed that their respect within the household has gone up. A sizeable 82% perceived improvement in the respect commanded from the members of the village community. The recognition across various caste groups in the villages was reported to be 91%. They did not face any opposition from their male counterparts after being elected to panchayats. Regarding personal effectiveness of the elected women representatives, the study found a significant improvement and perceived self-confidence in 81% of them and enhanced ability of decision-making in 74%. This enquiry of the Ministry of Panchayati Raj also probed into the instances of gender discrimination in panchayats. About 61% women representatives said that they never faced such discrimination and were not ignored because they were women. However, the proportion of Ward Members facing such discrimination was higher as compared to Pradhans of the Intermediate Panchayats. It was also found that the women representatives got a better recognition from other panchayat members for their efforts. Similarly, a high proportion of them reported getting more recognition as compared to their male counterparts.

The study also examined the level of acceptance of women representatives and the degree of their voice in the Gram Panchayat meetings. A sizeable proportion (95%) claimed that they could freely raise issues during the Gram Sabha meetings and a negligible proportion felt that their views were not considered in the Panchayat or in Gram Sabha meetings.

According to this document, the thrust of the local government system and particularly of the reservations for women was to encourage their participation in the system. It found that about 74% of them reported that the attendance of the women in Gram Sabha has increased and the frequency of their raising issues has also gone up. Similarly, a high proportion of them (75%) reported an increase in the political awareness of ordinary women of the villages.

Another encouraging finding was that the elected women representatives have begun to play an important role in providing civic amenities like street lights, drinking water, etc., during their tenure. About 72% of them mentioned about their involvement in providing basic services to the people. But among them a higher proportion was that of Pradhans instead of the Ward Members. It also reported that the entry of women has made a positive impact on the working of panchayat functionaries. The above findings make us optimistic about the empowerment of women through Panchayati Raj Institutions.

CONCLUSION

The above discussion leads us to the conclusion that women have been given adequate representation in the Panchayat system. This is indeed, a very impressive achievement. The silver lining of the reservations is that they are getting elected from the unreserved seats also. This is testified by the fact that women have much more representation than the reserved quota. This has also refuted the lurking suspicion that women will never be able to step out of their household to fight elections for the seats that have been reserved for them in the Panchayats at all the three levels. Despite this positive achievement, there is a dire need for their capacity-building so that their entry into the local governance system becomes more effective and meaningful. The capacity-building efforts have to be prioritised. Once they are capacitated, we may get the expected results and it will further deepen democracy in the country. The political space provided to them can bridge gender disparities. Notwithstanding the fact that gender power equations in the village have not undergone a dramatic change, we expect a new paradigm in which the grassroots unit of governance will bring overall development in the rural area. This is how the democratic system will get strengthened as a result of the reservations for the women that have been made under the 73rd Amendment to the Indian Constitution. They have been able to come to the centre of the rural power-structure after remaining on the periphery since long. This will also promote good governance at the grassroot level. It will not only lead to inclusive governance but inclusive development. But this will also need changes in the nature of social structure, culture and mindset of the rural society. Let us hope that the emerging women leaders shall be able to act as catalytic agents for bringing about these changes in due course of time.

References

Nanette Page and Cheryl, E., Czuba, Empowerment: What Is It? *Journal of Extension*, Volume 37, Number 5, 1999.

Ruth Alsop, Mette Frost Bertelsen, Jeremy Hollan, Empowerment in Practice—*From Analysis to Implementation*, The World Bank Publication, 2006.

http://worldbank.org/S9B3DNEZ00

The State of Panchayats—A Mid-Term Review and Appraisal, Ministry of Panchayati Raj, Government of India, 2006.

Study on Elected Women Representatives in Panchayati Raj Institutions, Ministry of Panchayati Raj, Government of India, New Delhi, 2008.

30

Women Empowerment in the Panchayati Raj Institutions of Uttarakhand after the 73rd Constitutional Amendment Act

NEHA KIRTI PRASAD AND M. PADALIA

The present paper makes an attempt to find out the extent of empowerment of the women of Uttarakhand, which has come to existence on November 9, 2000, through the Panchayati Raj Elections held in 2008-09 after the provision enhancing it as stipulated by 73rd Constitutional Amendment. It also seeks to identify the hurdles in the path of their empowerment, and to make possible suggestion for their effective empowerment in the Panchayati Raj Institutions. This empirical study is based on the participative observations of the electoral process.

I

It is confined to the elections for the post of Pradhans of the Gram Panchayats and the members of the Kashetra and the Zila Panchayats in all the districts of Uttarakhand except Hardwar where these elections had been held earlier.

WOMEN'S SHARE IN THE POSTS OF PRADHANS OF THE GRAM PANCHAYATS

The Pardhanship of the Gram Panchayat has emerged as the most powerful elected position in the three-tier structure of the Panchayati Raj Institutions of Uttarakhand. More than 50 percent (3646 out of 7239) posts have been captured by women. These figures include 750 Scheduled Caste, 121 Scheduled Tribe and 334 Other Backward Class women. The highest number of posts have been captured by them in Pithoragarh and the lowest in Udham Singh Nagar in Almora. The share of the Scheduled Caste women is also highest in Almora but lowest in Udham Singh Nagar. For the category of the Scheduled Tribes, it is minimum in Dehradun and none in Tehri-Garhwal and Rudra Prayag districts. As far as the Other Backward Class women are concerned, it is highest in Uttarakashi and lowest in Rudrapur. These inter-district variations in their share are due to difference in the demographic structures of those districts.

TABLE 1

Women's Share in the Posts of Pradhans of the Gram Panchayats

Sl. No.	*Name of the District*	*Total Panchayats*	*Sc .eduled Caste Women*	*Scheduled Tribes Women*	*Other Backward Class Women*	*General Women*	*Total*
1.	Almora	1146	132	1	20	422	575
2.	Udham Singh Nagar	309	24	2	46	65	137
3.	Champawat	290	26	1	9	111	147
4.	Nainital	460	60	1	11	160	232
5.	Pithoragarh	669	87	12	27	213	339
6.	Bageshwar	397	53	2	9	136	200
7.	Uttarakashi	454	57	4	84	84	229
8.	Chamoli	601	57	9	11	223	300
9.	Tehri Garhwal	979	74	0	57	360	491
10.	Dehradun	403	43	68	39	54	204
11.	Pauri Garhwal	1208	107	1	15	487	610
12.	Rudra Prayag	323	30	0	6	126	162
	Total	7239	750	121	334	2441	3646

WOMEN'S SHARE IN MEMBERS OF THE KSHETRIYA PANCHAYATS

Among the members of Kshetriya Parishads, again more than 50 percent seats (1553 out of 73075) are represented by women. The share for the Scheduled Caste, Scheduled Tribe and the Other Backward Class Women is 326, 60 and 106 respectively. The inter-district comparison shows that it is the highest in Pauri Garhwal and lowest in Bageshwar. In case of the Scheduled Tribes, it is highest in Dehradun but altogether missing in

Almora, Champawat, Tehri-Garhwal and Rudra Prayag. As regards, the Scheduled Tribe women, it is highest in Dehradun but is conspicuous by its absence in Almora, Champawat, Tehri-Garhwal and Rudra Prayag districts. As far as Other Backward Class among them are concerned, it is maximum in Udham Singh Nagar and minimum in Rudra Prayag. These variations are on account of differences in their demography.

TABLE 2
Women's Share in Members of the Kshetriya Panchayats

Sl. No.	*Name of the District*	*Total Wards*	*Scheduled Caste Women*	*Scheduled Tribes Women*	*Other Backward Class Women*	*General Women*	*Total*
1.	Almora	405	48	0	10	146	204
2.	Udham Singh Nagar	273	21	17	20	79	137
3.	Champawat	130	12	0	4	50	66
4.	Nainital	257	34	1	7	88	130
5.	Pithoragarh	299	39	5	11	96	151
6.	Bageshwar	120	16	1	4	39	60
7.	Uttarakashi	204	26	2	12	63	103
8.	Chamoli	249	27	3	7	91	128
9.	Tehri Garhwal	350	27	0	9	139	175
10.	Dehradun	240	24	31	14	51	120
11.	Pauri Garhwal	432	41	0	5	172	218
12.	Rudra Prayag	116	11	0	3	47	61
	Total	3075	326	60	106	1061	1553

WOMEN'S SHARE IN MEMBERS OF THE ZILA PARISHADS

Like the Gram Panchayats and in Kshetriya Panchayats, more than 50 percent seats (192 out of 371) have been captured by women. These include 41 seats represented by the Scheduled Castes, 6 by the Scheduled Tribes and 17 by the Backward Classes. Their share is maximum in Pauri-Garhwal and minimum in Champawat. For the Scheduled Caste women, it is highest in Pithoragarh and lowest in Udham Singh Nagar, Champawat and Rudra Prayag. The representation of Scheduled Tribes among them is highest in Dehradun but none in Almora, Champawat, Nainital, Bageshwar, Uttarakashi, Champawat, Tehri-Garhwal, Pauri-Garhwal and Rudra Prayag districts. So far as the Other Backward Class women are concerned, it is the highest in Tehri-Garhwal and lowest in Almora, Champawat, Nainital, Bageshwar, Chamoli and Rudra Prayag districts. These variations have to be ascribed to differences in the demographic structures of those districts.

TABLE 3
Women's Share in Members of the Zila Parishads

Sl. No.	Name of the District	Total Wards	Scheduled Caste Women	Scheduled Tribes Women	Other Backward Class Women	General Women	Total
1.	Almora	48	6	0	1	17	24
2.	Udham Singh Nagar	32	2	2	2	10	16
3.	Champawat	15	2	0	1	5	8
4.	Nainital	26	3	0	1	9	13
5.	Pithoragarh	35	5	1	1	12	19
6.	Bageshwar	19	3	0	1	6	10
7.	Uttarkashi	23	3	0	2	7	12
8.	Chamoli	27	4	0	1	9	14
9.	Tehri Garhwal	45	4	0	3	16	23
10.	Dehradun	33	3	3	2	9	17
11.	Pauri Garhwal	49	4	0	1	20	25
12.	Rudra Prayag	19	2	0	1	8	11
	Total	371	41	6	17	128	192

II

But now arises the question. Whether the 50 percent reservations in the seats which enabled them to win more than half of the total seats has really helped the empowerment of women of Uttarakhand? The answer to this question is a bit surprising. The fact of the matter is that it has actually empowered the male members of their families. It would be more appropriate to say that it was in reality "EMPOWERING MEN THROUGH WOMEN".

This appears paradoxical, because the women have been playing an important role in the economy of Uttarakhand for the past several generations. This is well reflected by the fact that the worker participation rate of women in the state is significantly higher as compared to other states of the country and also above than the national average. Moreover, it has been constantly increasing over the years. They had also played a historic role in the Chipko Movement for the protection of environment and in the movement for the formation of the separate state of Uttarakhand. But these Panchayati Raj elections have nullified all their accomplishments on account of the following reasons:

1. Due to the quest for power, capable women activists in different organisations became rivals to each other. This left the field free for the incompetent women.

2. Earlier, the political parties did no interference in Panchayati Raj elections but in these it was the other way round. They openly nominated their candidates. The MLA's and the ministers openly supported their candidates by deploying themselves in the respective regions.
3. Money was offered to the rival candidates to persuade them to step down. It too proved damaging for women empowerment.
4. The male members of the family took the initiative in assisting the women in contesting these elections. They even canvassed for them in their own names. In the posters and banners, along with the women contestant, the photograph of their husbands, fathers and brothers could also be seen. Consequently males kept their dominance and women's independent identity got eclipsed. Be that as it may, women representation has made a great leap in the state, thanks to the 50 percent reservations. But, to be really empowered, many of obstacles will have to be removed. The Uttarakhand Panchayati Raj elections 2008-09 clearly prove that women have still to go a long way for getting out of proxy syndrome.

III

The illiterate women Panchayati Raj representatives will have to be made literate through courses on functional literacy as a part of the Programme of Continuing Education of the Computer Literacy Mission. The State Government should take concrete steps for promoting female education in the state. The State Government should come out with a blue print of training policy in which there should be provision for continuous training of women Panchayati Raj representatives. Separate and special capacity-building programmes should also be organised for them. Their networking too should be ensured by forming their associations and federations at various levels. The NGO's and social organisations should come forward to take this responsibility of developing leadership qualities in them.

Since poverty and unemployment also prevents the rural women from participating in decision-making process at the grassroots level, their economic position also needs to be improved by providing them vocational training for undertaking various self-earning ventures. The employment generation programmes such as the SGSY should also be implemented for the formation of their Self Help Groups. These can lead to their economic empowerment.

Besides, a continuous communication is required to be maintained between the State Government and the Panchayat Raj Institutions through media. Moreover, the National level Seminars and Workshops on the working of the Panchayats should also be organized. The issues of the participation and role of women as decision-makers should be highlighted in these. The old myths such as male superiority, hesitation of women to work in public life, economic dependence on men, etc. should be broken through sustained and systematic extension work by the teachers of the university, colleges and schools.

It may be safely concluded that mere enhancement of representation through the reservations for women in Panchayat Raj Institutions is not a sufficient condition for their effective empowerment. Unless and until it is supplemented by the measures which help in removing the socio-economic barriers inhabiting them, the women cannot be empowered in the true sense of the word.

References

Singh, Katar, *Rural Development: Principles, Policies and Management*, Sage Publication, Delhi, 1999.

Mathew, George, *Panchayati Raj from Legislation to Movement*, Concept Publishing House, New Delhi, 2006.

Singh, Katar, *Rural Development: Principles, Policies and Management*, Sage Publication, Delhi, 1999.

Maheshwari, Shriram, Avasthi, Amreshwar, *Public Administration*, Lakshmi Narain Agarwal, Agra, 2004.

Agrawal, T.K., *Public Administration*, Lakshmi Narain Agarwal, Agra, 2004.

Mahanta, Upasana, "The Political Empowerment of Women through Panchayati Raj Institutions : A Critical Assessment of India's Experiment with Affirmative Action", Paper Prepared for the Third International Congress of the Asian Political and International Studied Association (APISA) on 23rd-25th November 2007, New Delhi.

Singh, J.L., *Women and Panchayat Raj*; Sunrise Publications, Delhi; 2005.

Prasad, Narendra, *Women and Development*, APH Publishing Corporation, New Delhi, 2007.

The Indian Journal of Public Administration, January-March 2008.

Mehta, G.S., *Development of Uttarakhand Issues and Perspectives*, APH Publishing Corporation, New Delhi, 1999.

http/ncw.nic.in/pdfreporsts/Gender %20 Profile-Uttarancha .pdf.

Panchayat Raj Update, February 2008.

Mehta, G.S., *Development of Uttarakhand Issues and Perspectives*, APH Publishing Corporation, New Delhi, 1999.

Giri, V. Mohini, *Deprived Devis: Women's Unequal Status in Society*, Gyan Books, 2006.

Singh, J.L., *Women and Panchayat Raj*, Sunrise Publications, Delhi, 2005.

Yojana, October 2008.

31

Empowerment of Women in the PRIs of Haryana

REKHA CHAUDHARY

This brief paper is a modest attempt to describe and analyse the impact of 73rd Amendment Act (1993), which constitutionalised the scheme of democratic decentralisation, on the empowerment of women in Panchayati Raj Institutions in Haryana. However, instead of covering all the three levels, it has been decided by us to cover only the Gram Panchayats because the Panchayati Raj System in the state has become Panchayat centric. It is pertinent to mention in the above context that the Haryana Panchayati Raj Act (1994) has assigned to the Gram Panchayats almost all the 29 subjects listed in the 11th Schedule for the devolution by the state legislatures on the PRIs for enabling them to become institutions of self-government for performing the role of economic development and social justice. Although, the Panchayat Samiti too has been legally given almost all those functions, in fact, these are being exercised not by the Samiti but the Gram Panchayats alone. The Zila Parishad has been made merely an advisory, guiding and coordinating body and has not been given any executive powers.

The paper has been divided into four parts:

1. The first discusses the representation of women in the PRIs before the 73rd Constitutional Amendment.
2. The second describes an analyses of the changes in it after it.
3. The third presents the findings of an empirical study of Rohtak and Mewat districts of Haryana.
4. The fourth gives the conclusions and suggestions.

I

The Gram Panchayats were established in Haryana region, then a part of pre-partitioned Punjab, by the Punjab Village Panchayat Act, 1912. The Act was enacted for implementing the recommendations of the Royal Commission on Decentralisation (1907) which had suggested the creation of Village Panchayats for the performance of the civic functions through their own resources. It may be stated here that the women did not have even the voting rights in the elections to the Gram Panchayats under this Act. The situation remained un-changed even under the Punjab Village Panchayats Act, 1921 which had been enacted after the introduction of Dyarchy that had been introduced under the Government of India Act, 1919. It may be recailed that the Act had been made for giving effect to the recommendations of the Montague Chelmsford Reforms that aimed at the gradual establishment of responsible government in the provinces and wanted that the beginning be made from the local self-government institutions. Even the Punjab Village Panchayats Act, 1939 which had been made after the introduction of the Provincial Autonomy under the Government of India Act, 1935, too failed to bring about any change in the above context. This Act had been framed for the abolition of Dyrachy and for extending responsible government at the provincial level in view of the recommendations of the Statutory Commission and the outcome of the Round Table Conferences. Thus the women remained outside the Gram Panchayats during the colonial period.

The Punjab Gram Panchayat Act, 1952 that had been made to implement Article 40 of the Directive Principles of the State Policy incorporated in the Constitution of India and sought to make them institutions of local self-government, however, did give voting rights to the women as well as gave them the right to contest elections. But it did not make reservations for women. Consequently, they remained almost completely unrepresented in the Gram Panchayats of Haryana region.

The introduction of the Panchayat Raj for implementing the recommendations of Balvantray Mehta Study Team (1957) did bring about a marginal change in this context. The Amendment in the Punjab Gram Panchayat Act, 1952 that has been made in 1961 did make provision for the co-option of women in the Gram Panchayats in case of their failure to get elected. This enabled of the women to get 5,948 out of 40,746 (14.59%) membership in the Gram Panchayats despite the fact that they constituted almost half of the population of the State. This relatively low representation of the women was on account of their reluctance to contest elections owing to the predominantly traditional, conservative and male dominated character of the rural society of Haryana.

II

But, there took place a quantum jump in the representation in the representation of women in the Gram Panchayats after the implementation of the 73rd Amendment to the Indian Constitution by the Haryana Panchayati Raj Act, 1994. As a result, one-third seats were reserved for the women at all the levels of the Panchayati Raj Institutions. Consequently, the representation of women increased in Gram Panchayats to 19,922 out of 60,117 (33.13%) in the first elections to the Panchayati Raj Institutions held in 1994. In terms of the figures, the representation of women increased more than three-fold—from about six thousands to about twenty thousands. All those pessimists who feared that the women shall not contest elections and the seats reserved for them shall remain un-filled were proved wrong. They did come forward to contest elections in large numbers. But they did not contest elections on their own. We cannot overlook this fact. The males who had been occupying positions in the Gram Panchayats before the 73rd Amendment, now decided that these be filled up by the women members of their families in the wards reserved for the ladies.

Women Sarpanches and Panches in Gram Panchayats

Year	*No. of Women*	*Total Numbers*	*Percentage*
1992	5948	40746	14.59
1995	19922	60117	33.13
2000	20024	60692	32.99
2005	24407	66588	36.65

Source : Compiled from *The Statistical Abstracts of Haryana*, 1992-93, 1995-96 and 2005-06.

There was however, a very marginal decline in their representation in the 2000 elections. Although their number increased from 1992 to 2002 but their percentage declined to 32.99. However, it was too insignificant and hence merits no explanation. But, the representation of women increased to 36.65% in 2005 elections which was 3% higher than the prescribed reservations. This shows that some women were elected as Sarpanches and Panches even from the non-reserved seats. This is certainly very encouraging if we keep in view the non-egalitarian nature of Haryana's rural society.

III

The author conducted a field study of Rohtak and Mewat districts in 2007 for finding out the ground realities regarding the empowerment of women in the Panchayati Raj Institutions of Haryana. While Rohtak, a Hindu Jat dominated district, was selected for this purpose because it is politically the most developed district of the State. Whereas, the choice of Mewat, a Muslim Meo dominated district, was made as it is politically the most backward district of Haryana. We selected two out of the five blocks of Rohtak and two out of the five blocks of Mewat through stratified sampling method. From each block, two Gram Panchayats, one having a General Caste Woman Sarpanch and the other having a Scheduled Caste Woman Sarpanch were selected by random sampling method. The sample of our study included the following Women Sarpanches from Rohtak and Mewat districts:

District Rohtak

General Women Sarpanches

1. Sunita w/o Sh. Kumar, Gram Panchayat Kahanaur, Block Kalanaur, Community—Hindu, Caste—Khatri.
2. Kailash Devi s/o Jagannath, Gram Panchayat-Bansi, Block—Lakhanmajra, Community—Hindu, Caste—Jat.
3. Sushila Devi w/o Pawan Kumar, Gram Panchayat—Kishangarh, Block Meham, Community—Hindu, Caste—Jat.
4. Dhanpati w/o Shriram, Gram Panchayat-Jassia, Block—Rohtak, Community—Hindu, Caste—Jat.
5. Kasturi w/o Mahender Singh, Gram Panchayat—Gandhre, Block—Sampla, Community—Hindu, Caste—Jat.

Scheduled Caste Women Sarpanches

1. Bimla w/o Azad, Gram Panchayat—Kabulpur, Block Rohtak, Community—Hindu, Caste—Chamar.
2. Parmeshwari w/o Banwari, Gram Panchayat—Gari Ballab, Block—Kalanaur, Community-Hindu, Caste—Balmiki.
3. Phulli w/o Manphool, Gram Panchayat—Kheri Meham, Block Meham, Community—Hindu, Caste—Chamar.
4. Tarawati w/o Sh. Ved Parkash, Gram Panchayat—Morkheri, Block Sampla, Community—Hindu, Caste—Balmiki.
5. Anju w/o Sh. Dharambir, Gram Panchayat—Guggaheri Block—Lakhanmajra, Community—Hindu, Caste—Chamar.

District Mewat

General Women Sarpanches

1. Juhiri w/o Islamuddin, Gram Panchayat—Ghata Shamshabad, Block—Firozpur Jhirka, Community—Muslim, Caste—Meo.
2. Ashia w/o Noora, Gram Panchayat Jakhokar, Block—Punhana, Community—Muslim, Caste—Meo.
3. Usmani w/o Unwas, Gram Panchayat Bukara, Block—Tauru, Community—Muslim, Caste—Meo.

4. Menuna w/o Ajmat, Gram Panchayat—Basai, Block—Nuh, Community—Muslim, Caste—Meo.
5. Hasanki w/o Budha, Gram Panchayat—Mohalka, Block—Nagina, Community—Muslim, Caste—Meo.

Scheduled Caste Women Sarpanches

1. Resham Devi w/o Lakipal, Gram Panchayat Bisar Akbarpur, Block—Tauru, Community—Hindu Caste—Balmiki.
2. Kisni w/o Dalu, Garm Panchayat—Hasanpur Bilonda, Block—Firozpur Jhirka, Community—Hindu, Caste—Balmiki.
3. Santra Devi w/o Amir Chand, Gram Panchayat—Akara, Block—Nuh, Community—Hindu, Caste—Chamar.
4. Asarfi w/o Sampat, Gram Panchayat—Marora, Block—Nagina, Community—Hindu, Caste—Chamar.
5. Missi w/o Mangla, Gram Panchayat—Jalika, Block—Punhana, Community—Hindu, Caste—Chamar.

The participatory observation method was used by the author for finding out the role performance by them for judging the extent of their empowerment.

On the basis of the above exercise, she arrived at the following conclusions:

1. It is mostly the husbands of the women Sarpanches who attended the meetings of the Gram Panchayats on their behalf. As a matter of fact, people addressed their husbands as Sarpanch Sahibs instead of giving this honour to the Women Sarpanches.
2. In most of the Gram Panchayats, the decisions were taken on their behalf by the Gram Sachivs and their husbands.
3. The proceedings of the meetings of the Gram Panchayats were recorded by the Gram Sachivs in consultation with their husbands without holding the meetings. These were later on got signed or thumb impressioned from the Women Sarpanches and the Panches supporting her (in fact their husbands).
4. Few Women Sarpanches visited the office of the Block Development Panchayat Officer (BDPO) themselves. Instead, their husbands performed this role on their behalf.
5. Even the few Women Sarpanches who themselves went to that office were invariably accompanied by their husbands who would not let them go alone.
6. Very few of them went all alone to the office of the BDPO in connection with works pertaining to the Gram Panchayats.
7. Even in the training programmes organised by various agencies for their capacity-building, some of the Women Sarpanches were

reluctant to participate. Instead, their husbands attended these.

8. Even in those cases in which they themselves attended these programmes, they were always accompanied by their husbands.
9. During the course of her field work, the researcher found that most of the Women Sarpanches were reluctant to answer her questions.
10. In some other cases, their husbands tried to answer these on their behalf and did not let the Women Sarpanches to answer the same.
11. No perceptible inter-district variations could be found in the above context despite the fact that there are significant differences in the demographic, social, cultural, economic and political environments of the two districts.
12. No significant intra-district differences could be noticed in various blocks despite some variations in their demographic structures.
13. No significant differences could be noticed in the two communities regarding the role performance by the Women Sarpanches of these.
14. There was, however, a small difference in the above context in those belonging to the General Category and those belonging to the Scheduled Castes.
15. The educated Women Sarpanches did act on their own to some extent. However, their number was very small.
16. Very few illiterate but politically aware Women Sarpanches also acted on their own. But their number too was very small.

IV

The above discussion and analysis leads us to the conclusion that the reservations for women under the 73rd Amendment Act have brought about a qualitative change in their share in the Panchayati Raj Institutions. It is encouraging to note that some of the women have been elected even from those seats which have not been reserved for them. But, it is depressing to find that most of them have not been empowered as yet. One of the reasons is the lack of education, awareness and confidence in them. But, more important than this is the mindset of the male members of their families on account of the patriarchal character and conservative culture of the rural society of Haryana.

Therefore, there is an urgent need for the capacity-building of the women representatives of the PRIs by organising special training programmes for them including the programmes on functional literacy. Besides, the education of girls needs to be encouraged in the state. Moreover, the Sakshar Mahila Samoohs will have to be activated for guiding the women representatives. Furthermore, the mindset of their husbands and the male functionaries of the Development and Panchayat Department will also have to be changed by organising special orientation programmes for them. Lastly, concerted and systematic efforts will have to be made by the Government of Haryana, the teachers in the universities, colleges and schools, the NGOs and the media to bring about a cultural change in the rural Haryana. The Women Study and Research Centre of Kurukshetra University and the Women Cells in the colleges of Haryana too can undertake this responsibility. The units of the NSC and NCC can also be used for this purpose. The Haryana Institute of Rural Development and State Community Development Training Centre, both of which are located at Nilokheri (Karnal) will have to act as the nodal agencies in this context. Otherwise, the objective of the women empowerment shall remain unachieved.

Index